HISPANIC CULTURE AND CHARACTER OF THE SEPHARDIC JEWS

HISPANIC CULTURE AND CHARACTER OF THE SEPHARDIC JEWS

by

Mair José Benardete

Second, corrected edition
edited and augmented
by Marc D. Angel

SEPHER-HERMON PRESS, INC.
for
The Foundation for the Advancement of
Sephardic Studies and Culture, Inc.
and
Sephardic House
at Congregation Shearith Israel
New York, 1982

HISPANIC CULTURE AND CHARACTER
OF THE SEPHARDIC JEWS
2nd, corrected edition
Published by
Sepher-Hermon Press, Inc.
Copyright © 1982
The Foundation for the Advancement
of Sephardic Studies and Culture, Inc.
and
Sephardic House
at Cong. Shearith Israel

LCC No. 79-92737
ISBN 0-87203-100-4

Library of Congress Cataloging in Publication Data

Benardete, Maír José, 1895-
    Hispanic culture and character of the Sephardic
Jews.

    Bibliography: p.
    Includes index.
    1. Sephardim.   I. Angel, Marc.   II. Title.
DS134.B4   1981   909'.04924   79-92737
ISBN 0-87203-100-4   AACR2

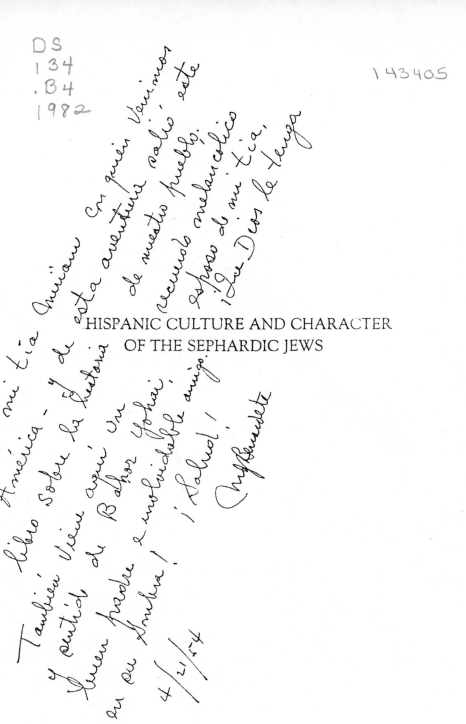

HISPANIC CULTURE AND CHARACTER
OF THE SEPHARDIC JEWS

*Fascimile of the author's inscription in copy of the first
edition of his book presented to his aunt, Mrs. Mary Yohai.*

FOREWORD

Professor Maír José Benardete has had a profound influence on Sephardic studies. His book, *Hispanic Culture And Character Of The Sephardic Jews*—first published by the Hispanic Institute in the United States in 1953—has filled a major void in Jewish historiography. Benardete has attempted to describe the Sephardic historical and cultural experience following the expulsion from Spain in 1492. His book follows the Sephardic exiles to the Ottoman Empire, to the ex-Marrano settlements in Europe, and to the United States. As the book's title indicates, Benardete is interested in demonstrating how the Jews' experience in Spain shaped and influenced their destiny in the lands of their exile.

This book is nothing less than a cultural monument. First, it provides a "synthetic history", bringing together diverse sources in a thoughtful and original way. But the book's significance transcends its contents. It gains a special significance because of its author. Professor Benardete was himself born in Çanakkale (Dardanelles), Turkey. He was raised within a natural and vital Sephardic milieu. His family name—originally Benadrete—carries with it memories of the family's Iberic background. After coming to the United States at an early age, Benardete studied diligently in American schools and advanced academically. He was the first Turkish-born Sephardic Jew to become accredited as a public school teacher in the United States. During the period of his studies at Columbia University and of his teaching at Brooklyn College, Benardete devoted much effort and talent to generating interest in Sephardic life. He attempted to enlighten his own co-religionists by teaching them, by writing in the Judeo-Spanish newspapers, by lecturing. He created cultural relationships with scholars and students in Spain, as well as with hispanists in New York. He served as a spokesman of Sephardic culture, the culture of which he himself was part.

Benardete's book is not only filled with information and scholarly insights. It is a nostalgic work. It describes the searchings and yearnings of an intellectual Sephardic Jew who wants to understand his own being. This work, then, is interesting both for its objective and subjective meanings.

In preparing this volume, many of the typographical errors which had crept into the first edition have been eliminated, and we acknowledge the cooperation of Mr. Henry V. Besso in this task. This edition also includes an index as well as an updated bibliography.

We wish to thank a number of individuals who have been helpful in seeing this project through to completion: Mr. Louis N. Levy, President of The Foundation For The Advancement of Sephardic Studies and Culture; Mr. Samuel Gross, of the Sepher-Hermon Press; the members of Sephardic House, a national cultural organization based at the Spanish and Portuguese Synagogue in New York City; and of course, Professor and Mrs. Maír José Benardete.

We express a special word of thanks to the children of **Robert** and **Mary Yohai** who have generously contributed towards the publication of this book. As relatives of Professor Benardete as well as appreciative students of Sephardic culture, the Yohai family deserves the sincere gratitude of all of us.

Marc D. Angel,
August, 1981

CONTENTS

HISPANIC CULTURE AND CHARACTER OF THE SEPHARDIC JEWS

I

Introduction

The History of this Book

It has been profoundly observed that the exact sciences can dispense with their history;[1] that is, the more abstract they are the more readily can they get along without presenting their origins for an understanding of their methodology and their principles. Mathematics and physics, the sovereigns in the realm of the abstract, are not ushered in by the fanfare and cymbals of history. Their august presence suffices to impress the subjects who come before them. If on the whole this view is correct for the exact sciences, it does not necessarily follow that the other ramifications of the tree of knowledge must be considered less worthy because they require other procedures for their envisagement. Professor Etienne Gilson made the defense of the other sciences on the basis of the Aristotelian premise that each thing must be grasped in the light of its own essence.[2] The promiscuous application of laboratory and mathematical techniques to some subject matters has not been as fruitful as, in the early days of scientificism, it was confidently expected to be. Positivism, an excrescence of the laboratory method, played havoc with linguistics and the arts, by levelling the aesthetic subject matters like the exact sciences.[3] There might be some sort of vicarious aesthetic fruition in the various steps undertaken for getting at the truth in physics and mathematics, but in so far as the materials utilized are only means and not ends, mathematics and physics, devoid of the sensuous as they are, bear no resemblance to the arts. The exact sciences differing as they do from the arts, the methods to be used ought to be different. If Professor Gilson's criticism means anything, then in the fields of literature and the other arts we must discover the methods best suiting our aims: an understanding of their being and an application and enjoyment of their structurized unity. Economics was considered a dismal science, but nothing is so depressing as the perusal of a history of Spanish literature written in accordance with the rules dictated by Positivism. In brief, it is our conviction that the approach to the social sciences and the arts must be made with some deference to the techniques of the exact sciences, borrowing from them discipline and goals, and then, having learned what we need, to proceed with other methodology.

For my own sake, if not for anybody else's comfort, I believe it necessary to present my credo before presenting the development of my theme. In 1923, through the encouragement of Professor Federico de Onís, I offered as my thesis for the Master's Degree at Columbia University, a preliminary study of the Spanish ballads which have survived among the Spanish Jews of Levantine origin living in New York. I knew that not all that could be said about the Spanish ballads harvested in the slums of the East Side and Harlem had been said by me, and furthermore that not all the ballads that could be collected among the various small nuclei of Sephardic Jews hailing from cities like Monastir, Castoría, Salónica, Adrianople, Constantinople, Gallípoli, Dardanelles, Smyrna, the Island of Rhodes, etc., had been collected by me. Exigencies relating to one's own intellectual development and to the demands of my teaching position made me unduly postpone the development of the thesis started in 1923. Intermittently in the past twenty-odd years, I have gone on collecting more and more specimens and considering ways and means for incorporating them into a book. When I came to the need of giving the antecedents of the interest shown by scholars in the collecting and conserving of Spanish ballads I became painfully aware of how superficially these ballads had been studied. Some eminent men collected ballads in Turkey from among the Sephardic Jews. They were well versed in Oriental languages and in French but had no knowledge of Spanish literature. How in the world could anyone attempt to understand the Spanish ballads, their structure, their themes, their ancestry, their literary flavor, who did not know the Romancero? Men like Danón and Galante[4] belong to this category. Spanish Jews and scholars of no mean worth were prepared in schools excluding the study of Spanish history and civilization. On the other hand, eminent savants like Menéndez y Pelayo had to depend upon the garnerings of men like Galante and Danón to get the crude materials of their folklore explorations in order to establish relationships between these Hispano-Levantine importations and the Peninsular pristine prototypes. But men like Menéndez y Pelayo were too busy to stop to consider all the implications involved in the Hispano-Jewish folklore traditions. When a man like Don Ramón Menéndez Pidal had the fortune to receive from a Moroccan Jew, José Benoliel, over one hundred and fifty romances, displaying an extraordinary purity of language and ballad pattern, the fortunes of the Judeo-Spanish Romancero were considerably enhanced. First, because Señor Menéndez Pidal, having made the Middle Ages his exclusive study, naturally broached the subject from the field of the epic poem of Spanish literature, which in turn gave rise to the luxurious growths of Spanish balladry. Second, he was superbly prepared to study the Hispano-Levantine ballads in connection with the entire range of the Romancero. Unlike his predecessors, he combined to a very high degree the explorations of field work in the hamlets and villages of Spain in pursuit of the survivals of *romances* with the elaborations and analyses of his private study. But again the treatment of the ballads found among the Jews of Morocco, Greece, Yugoslavia, Rumania, Turkey, the Mediterranean islands such as Rhodes, fell short of thoroughness and inclusiveness. It would be absurd to expect Don Ramón Menéndez Pidal to devote too much time to a rivulet forming part of an Amazonic fluvial system, which for centuries had been meandering very far from its source. For the needs of Hispanic culture, the preparation of Spain's greatest scholar of today is more than sufficient to link the Hispano-Levantine and the Hispano-Moroccan ballads with their originals. But can we say that the ballads of the Spanish Jews have only an Hispanic interest? The fact that they were sung for over four centuries away from the mother land would suggest that in due time they came to have a function all their own in the small Mediterranean theocracies of the exiles of 1492.

Neither the Spanish-Jewish scholars nor the eminent Peninsular savants have so far treated in a thorough fashion the *romances* of Judeo-Spanish origin like the Spanish ballads I have collected among the Sephardic Jews who in recent times emigrated from the Levantine countries to the United States. The scholars of the Near East did not know Spanish literature and the erudite Peninsular hidalgos had no intimate personal experiences with the life of the Spanish Jews. Besides lacking personal experiences they did not have the time to fathom all the relationships sheaved around the ballads. If these two sets of scholars have failed so far, how was I, so poorly prepared, very far from being their match in knowledge and training, to succeed in presenting an acceptable picture of these fascinating ballads!

Thoughts like these discouraged me more than I can tell. The collecting of the ballads in a city like New York was not an easy task. There was an urgent need to hurry with the work of conserving these precious heirlooms from the last century of the Middle Ages because the new environment was most hostile to their continued existence. In 1922, the Judeo-Spanish immigrants of Levantine origin were fairly accessible. In their early settlement in New York, they huddled in the East Side and in Harlem. Through friends and acquaintances it was not impossible to visit their homes and by persuasion and entreaty make them dictate to me the venerable *romances* they knew. As time flowed on, the Sephardic immigrants had learned enough and prospered sufficiently to wish to move to more congenial surroundings. Now they live in two or three distinct sections of Brooklyn, and are scattered on various blocks in the Bronx, ramifying also into the other boroughs. Their dispersion has made contact with them more and more difficult. The absence of new contingents of immigrants has tended to Americanize the crop of the first decade of this century most rapidly, to their benefit and to the detriment of my pursuit.

There still remained the necessity of studying the *romances* of the Spanish Jews in relation to their pattern of life. In other words, the literary sociology of these folklore themes and tunes demanded treatment. Happily, scattered materials are available here and there, especially in the writings of Sephardic Jews who in the past fifty years have been made aware of the Philo-Sephardic movement in Spain. The remark about sustained enthusiasm is applicable in the case of those Spanish Jews who, upon discovering the sympathetic attitude of cultured Spaniards in their meagre treasures from their Peninsular past, unashamed, displayed interest and love in those folk elements which they had been taught, in their superficial education, to despise. Men like Ángel Pulido, Emilio Castelar, Hartzenbusch, Galdós, Menéndez y Pelayo, Menéndez Pidal, Cansinos Assens, Manual Ortega, Federico de Onís and Giménez Caballero, encouraged directly and obliquely the Sephardic Jews to maintain their traditions and reverentially love and study them.

Obviously the place of the ballad in the lives of the Spanish Jews must be treated for a clear idea of the persistence of the *romances* in an atmosphere most uncongenial to their preservation. For the re-creation of the background of these ballads, the lyrical outbursts, redolent of nostalgic undertones in the ballads they heard at weddings and parties, in the hushed hours of the night, beside baby's cradle, or at the feet of the dead, do not suffice. In the flush of their interest and enthusiasm the Spanish Jews and their sympathizers overlooked the communal environment in which these ballads were sung. Quite true, these ballads, in accordance with the positivistic approach, have a substantive existence and can be subjected to a scientific analysis. Why not study them linguistically? All kinds of permutations and distortions are observable in the vocabulary; foreign intrusions abound, strange and non-Hispanic ideas and sentiments may very likely have been incorporated into the originals. Are these problems not enough? Why go in search of noon-time at fourteen o'clock, as the French put it? I bore in mind the fact that scholars who knew better have established another procedure for treating the ballads and other folk elements. Have they not linked available items of one region with similar and analogous items of lands far and near? The linguistic study and the tracing of origins cannot be scorned. Most particularly we must not fail to show the interconnectedness between the ballads found among the Spanish Jews and the ballads surviving in printed form from the fifteenth century and even later through the sixteenth and seventeenth centuries. These ballads after all are Spanish; their adoption and conservation among the Spanish Jews must be merely fortuitous. When the Moor was being defeated at Granada, when the Castilians had fought the Portuguese over the question of who had a right to the throne, the step-sister of Henry IV or his illegitimate daughter La Beltraneja, the Spanish ballads were heard in the market place, in the seigniorial mansions, and on the battlefields. When in Spain, the Jews could not have helped learning the most popular songs of the day: the Catholic Sovereigns, the Court, the aristocrats, everybody sang them. The Jews could no more avoid singing the ballads than they could avoid speaking Spanish. But once away from Spain there was no reason for them to sing these ballads at Orán, Tangier, Tetuan, Larache, or in the Venetian ghetto, or in the so-called Sephardic republic of Salonica, or again in the mystic city of Safed. Apparently the Jews kept these inconsequential folk songs alive independently of their new surroundings. The ballads of the Spanish Jews are not

Hebraic, not Jewish; their form and essence are Spanish. Once the ballads were transferred from their natural soil there was no reason for the Spanish Jews to continue fertilizing them, and thus prevent them from dying. The ballads had no utilitarian value for them; neither, so it seemed at first blush, had they any integral function to contribute to the perpetuation of their religion, on whose behalf they had left their milennial moorings. Granting all these arguments that seem to damage our position, we still maintain that the Spanish ballad in the new environment did come to play an important role in the lives of the Spanish Jews. How otherwise explain their preservation for over four hundred years? Since this preservation is a fact, we are forced to have a very precise idea of the history of these Jews in order to understand the functions of these secular songs in the Hispano-Levantine communities. In short, the Sephardic ballads must be related to the communities where they were sheltered from destructive internal and external forces.

Just about the time these thoughts were taking shape in my mind and were directing the line of approach I decided to follow, I became dimly aware, in 1937, of the importance of the research carried on by Arabic scholars in Spain around the moot question as to the origin of the European lyric. Our ever-dependable Don Ramón delivered in that year, in Havana, a lecture on the *zejel,* under the modest title of *Poesía Árabe y Poesía Europea.* Enthusiasm possessed me and I began to guess that the great Sephardic poets of Arabic Spain must have had a very intimate connection with the writing of *zejels.* Don Ramón, who in that year came to Columbia University as a visiting professor, was very much surprised when I called his attention to my "hunch" concerning the role the *zejels* must have played in the history of Hebraico-Hispano poetry. A brief footnote in his more scholarly version of *Poesía Árabe y Poesía Europea,* which he published the following year in *Bulletin Hispanique,* acknowledged most generously my having given him the transcription in Latin characters, of a *muwassaha* or *zejel* by Solomon Ibn Gabirol. Since 1937 I became more and more interested in the numerous studies on the Andalusian lyric. The conclusion to which I was led irresistibly was most obvious to me. Besides the *romances* we had to reckon henceforth with another Peninsular poetic creation—the *muwassaha.* The *muwassaha* has been in the Sephardic tradition in Hebrew and in Judeo-Spanish for almost a thousand years. It was a delightful experience to have found numerous *muwassahas* in the Sephardic books of prayer.

The very presence of the *muwassaha* in the Sephardic tradition made me reconsider the whole problem of the *romance*. No longer was it permissible to see it as merely a bit of folklore enlivening the humdrum existence of my ancestors. A culture is an organic whole. What seems extraneous and disconnected on closer analysis shows itself to be integrally and functionally related to the whole cultural pattern. Then we see that two forms of poetry originating in Spain, the *mussawaha* and the Spanish ballad or *romance* entered the ever-living tradition of Spanish Jewry. The *muwassaha* was Hispano-Arabic in origin and the *romance*, on the whole, was purely of Hispano-Romanic derivation. Both of these forms were adopted and conserved by the Peninsular Jews. Differing considerably in one fundamental respect from the Muslims who in the XVI century became outwardly Catholics, the *exiled Jews*, notwithstanding the fact that they were not the beneficiaries of the marvelous Castilian literature that renovated its syntax and vocabulary in the Golden Age of that literature, have lived from the inspiration emanating from the *muwassahas* in Hebrew and Spanish during several centuries after their expulsion. Both *muwassahas* and *romances* were also the patrimony of the *moriscos*.[5] The latter made a futile effort to keep alive their Spanish on African soil. But the Jews in the Diaspora without any apparent intent have kept alive to this very day their Spanish dialects and *koiné*. Wherein are we to find the *raison d'être* for this strange phenomenon?

The Spanish of the morisco *muwassaha* and *romance* was as up-to-date as the Spanish of the *Comedia* and the Gongoristic poetry then in vogue. Proximity to the golden evolution of the Spanish language and propinquity to the Spanish mainland did not prevent the disappearance of the Spanish language and folklore from among the moriscos.

There may be many reasons for the disappearance in one case and the conservation on the other of the Spanish language and the folk literature cast in that language. It seems that what gives us the clue to this phenomenon is to be found in the character of the Jewish ethos. Mostly of Berber ancestry, the moriscos entered Islam without any cultural inheritance of their own. In the case of the Jews we know that they never lost their grip on their milennial tradition. What concerns us here is the alert responsiveness to the novelty of *muwassaha* and *romance* on the part of the Jews and their capacity to accept the new songs and in time use them as models for new compositions in those forms. At this juncture we will state categorically one fundamental sociological principle that appears to have always characterized the Jews: *Hermeticism to all influences that in the long run would disrupt the quintessence of Judaism; and porousness to all new forms and ideas that possibly could modernize and revitalize the venerable tradition.* This double-edged mechanism of living Judaism explains why the *sefardíes* were capable of incorporating the *muwassaha* into the corpus of their modes of being.

Hermeticism and porousness or permeability, then, give us the answer to our question. Once the Jews began to move on the road and by-paths of History, nothing could have happened to them without finding a place in their ever-expanding treasure-box of spiritual experience. The explanation of this principle does not ignore the times when genuinely Judaic innovations of a revolutionary import have been left by the roadside, precisely because the hermetic side of the polarity was relentless in excluding them.

Whereas before, all of us working in the field of the Judeo-Spanish ballad ignored the *muwassaha* because no one knew up to very recently what this seminal song of Spain really was like, now that we have a clear idea of its origins, influence and significance in the history of European culture, no one can discuss in the future the Hispanic song among the Sephardic Jews without including it in the study of their culture.

The *muwassaha,* was both an artistic creation fathered by known authors and—in its Spanish versions—a folk product without any recognized paternity. We said above that it was the seminal song of Spain. Originating in Arabic the *muwassaha,* like springtime pollen, fertilized the poetic genius of all the peoples of Western Europe. The Sephardic Jews were most receptive to its pollenization.

The New Discovery

In 1948 S.M. Stern, a scholar from the Hebrew University in Jerusalem, published in *Al-Andalus* an article innocuously entitled, *Les vers finaux en espagnol dans les muwassaha hispano-hebraiques. Une contribution à l'histoire du muwassaha et à l'étude du vieux dialecte espagnol mozarabe.*[6] A year later Francisco Cantera re-examined Stern's contribution with the view in mind to make suggestions and corrections to what has since come to be considered a major event in the historical and philological field dealing with Arabic culture as fast as its influence on European civilization is concerned. Cantera's emendations did not have any sensational title either: *Versos españoles en las muwassahas hispano-hebreas.*[7] Dámaso Alonso saw in Stern's and Cantera's complementary study an extraordinary clarification of the question on which scholars and critics had been working for more than a century—what a *muwassaha* was, what were its origins, and what was its influence in the formation of lyric poetry in Western Europe. With disarming simplicity Dámaso Alonso likewise did not conceal his excitement when he headed his article, *Cancioncillas 'de amigo' mozárabes.*[8] A Hebraico-Arabic scholar, a specialist in Sephardic Hebrew literature and a literary critic, in less than a year's time, made us fully aware of the complexity and far-reaching implications of the *muwassaha* problem; and now we begin to systematize our notions on the European lyric gathered from our assiduous readings in the works of Julián Ribera, A.R. Nykl and Menéndez Pidal dealing with this theme.[9] But although we cannot here enter into the study of the *muwassaha,* and the significance it has had among the Sephardic Jews for almost a thousand years, let us none the less summarize the contributions of the three scholars.

A blind poet from Cabra in the province of Córdoba, named Mocaddem (ninth century), hit upon a new form of Arabic poetry. It was strophic in composition; a form that had not been known in classic Arabic poetry. This new type of poetry received, characteristically enough, the name of *muwassaha,* evoking in us, by the way, the arabesque soul of the Orient. Four Muslim savants—Ibn Bassam, born in Santarem, Portugal, in the eleventh century, Ibn Sanä-l-Mulk, an Egyptian anthologist and critic of the twelfth century, Ibn Khaldun, the Spengler and Toynbee of the Arabic world, born in Tunis in the fourteenth century and Al Makkari, author of *The Mohammedan Dynasties in Spain* (written in the seventeenth century)—are the chief sources for the structure and importance of the *muwassaha.* Julián Ribera, A.R. Nykl and Menéndez Pidal became convinced that the *muwassaha* was a genuinely original cultural product of Al-Andalus. What had intrigued them most were two phases of the problem: 1) its possible influence in the gestation and birth of the Provençal lyric and the lyric of the rest of Europe, and 2) its mosaic or bilingual character.

A.R. Nykl's edition of *El Cancionero de Aben Guzmán* (Madrid,

1933), showed all of us who did not know Arabic what a *zejel* or *muwassaha* was really like. *Zejel* number Ten in the above work had this for its second stanza:

> Yā mutarnani *Šil(i)bāto*
> *Tu 'n* hazin *tu 'n bēnato*
> *Tarā al-yauma wāštāto*
> *Lam taduq fīh geir luqueymah.*[10]

The italicized words, Šil(i)bāto, tu, bēnato and waštāto, struck Nykl and all who have had to deal with the subject, as being not Arabic but words of Latin origin as they made their appearance in the Mozarabic dialect of Spain. Menendez Pidal reconstructed the stanza, basing himself on Ribera's and Nykl's indications, as follows:

> Oh, mi locuelo *Salvado*
> *tú* estás triste, *tú penado*
> verás el día *gastado*
> sin probar mas que un poquito.

There could not be any doubt in anybody's mind that the Bohemian poet of twelfth century Córdoba, Aben Guzmán, mottled his Arabic poems with Spanish expressions. Up to 1948 we could not see further through the opaque screen of the history of this very old Andalusian lyric. Martin Hauptmann, Ribera and Nykl had read carefully Ibn Sana-l-Mulk's treatise on the *muwassaha* but somehow they could not make clear to us the presence of a Romanic dialect within an Arabic poem. Unfortunately the word *Markaz* was translated as *refrain* or *estribillo,* when really it is the name given to the last stanza of the *muwassaha. Markaz* and *harja* are synonymous. Henceforth we will use the word *harja.*[11]

Stern's significant discovery really lies in his having understood what the *harja* was. The Egyptian critic has said that a *muwassaha* could end in a strophe written in a Romanic dialect. But all Stern's efforts up to the time he was writing his epoch-making study to find a *muwassaha* written in Arabic with its colorful tail in Spanish were in vain. *To the delighted surprise of all of us interested in this subject Stern found no less than twenty muwassahas in Hebrew with Mozarabic Spanish in their last stanza.* We, no more than Dámaso Alonso, can suppress our joy over this memorable discovery. We will point out now three legitimate inferences of great import: First we have in *muwassahas* of

Judah Halevi's, samples of the oldest literary Spanish known to us; second, now for once we have the brief songs (cancioncillas) of Mozarabic Spain—and the fact that such songs existed in the eleventh century destroys the centuries-old notion that Spain's pristine poetry was epic; and third, as far as Sephardic Jews and their culture are concerned, we now know that they were at least trilingual, *and what is still more significant is the fact that from the eleventh century on Spanish and Hebrew struck a partnership that was to last for centuries.*

We shall try to communicate our jubilation at this juncture by singling out the *harja* number Nine as Stern and Cantera have interpreted it. The transition or penultimate stanza usually introduced a conventional literary type, person, being, animal or even a material object which interrupted the poetic flow of the *muwassaha* that was the poet's conception, and this "literaturized" mouthpiece was made to word metaphorically the intent of the poem. This *muwassaha* was a panegyric on a friend of Jahuda Halevi's, named Abraham.[12] The next to the last strophe reads:

> My heart is torn to shreds
> On my seeing a thirsty fawn
> —The tears on her fresh and pure cheeks
> she raised heavenward;
> When she was told:
> —Now it is a long time since your beloved friend
> has been ill,
> She bitterly exclaimed:

Of course this poem was in Hebrew up to the *harja,* which in turn was in Spanish. The fawn's words were, then:

> Vayse meu Corachón de mib
> ¿Ya Rab si se me tornarad?
> ¡Tan mal meu doler li-l-habib?
> enfermo yed ¿cuando sanarad?[13]

Dámaso Alonso, whose *Poesía Española: Antología de Poesía de la Edad Media y Poesía de Tipo Tradicional* had demonstrated to many of us that he possessed a fine sensitivity in the appreciation of purity in lyrical poetry, overflows with almost youthful enthusiasm upon coming on this *harja:*

Y otra vez nos recorre un escalofrío. ¡Qué voz tan pura! De un hondón de siglos llega a nuestra embotada sensibilidad de hombres de estos angustiosos mediados de siglo XX. Una voz fresca y desgarradora. Nítida, exacta, como si brotara ahora a la garganta en flor y de labios que transparentaban la sangre moza. ¡Eterna doncella enamorada, eterno grito, repetido siempre y siempre nuevo! Etas *jargas,* ésta y otras. . .nos mueven no sólo por su viejísimo léxico y morfología en comparacíon de los cuales el *Poema del Cid* parece de ayer y aun moderno parece el *Au'o de los Reyes Magos* (atribuido a la segunda mitad del siglo XII). Nos mueven no sólo por ser una bocana horadante hacia una oscuridad profunda (orígenes de la lírica europea), sino aun más por su desnuda, sencilla, trémula e impregnante belleza. Y nos viene a la memoria en seguida una bella desnudez igual: la de la que hasta hoy considerábamos primitiva lírica trádicional de Castilla. . .

To show that this *harja* has affinities with the airy poems of Spanish literary history, Dámaso Alonso gives several samples. Here is an anonymous one:

> Vaisos, amores
> de aqueste lugar.
> ¡Tristes de mis ojos
> y cuando os verán!

And the quatrain by Gil Vicente, which we quote forthwith, reminds us that the *harja* number Nine and Gil Vicente's poem are somehow very closely related:

> *Vanse* mis amores, madre,
> luengas tierras van morar
> y no los puedo olvidar.
> ¿Quien *me* los hará tornar?. . .

The Need for a Synthetic Account
of Hispano-Levantine History

In the study of the exact sciences the focal point, temporally speaking, is the present. Ideas, principles, equations, formulae, are eternal, timeless. Time does not bite into their substance. Being incorporeal they are not subject to the processes of growth and decay. But the products of human culture, such as customs, gestures, art, are intimately woven in the strands of time. They cannot be studied in timelessness, they have a habitation. No study of them is possible unless the past is introduced. This granted, we cannot approach the study of these ballads and lyrical poems without exploring the history of the Judeo-Spanish communities after the Peninsular Diaspora.

Who are these Spanish Jews after all? Can much be said about them after their dispersion throughout the continents, the new and the old? Were they so homogeneous that no distinctions can be made? The perplexing and acute problem of the history of the Spanish Jew now intrudes into the study of their ballads and *muwassahas*. (And of course no one as yet has written anything on the recent discovery, the Hispano-Arabic song among the Spanish Jews.) All those who collected and wrote on these ballads, irrespective of their motives, have recognized the need of saying something on the history of the people who preserved these ballads. Perfunctory accounts to satisfy the curiosity of readers with no other than ceremonial value and more significant résumés of Judeo-Spanish history in the Diaspora were offered by critics and scholars. In the latter case, for example, we must include the notes on the Spanish Jews of Ramón Menéndez Pidal when presenting fragments of the *romances* collected in Morocco and elsewhere, in order to correct the egregious error committed by Abraham Danón in naively believing the *romances* found among his people were all of the fifteenth century.[14] Don Marcelino Menéndez y Pelayo had been the first to indicate the continuous contact between the Spanish Jews and the Peninsula for more than two centuries after the expulsion. Menéndez Pidal very justifiably showed types of contact between Spain and Portugal and the Sephardic communities; such as Marranic infiltrations in the sixteenth century through Portugal, Flanders, France, Italy and Turkey; and also through constant and sometimes casual contacts between Catholic Spaniards in Morocco, Aleppo, Constantinople and Spanish Jews. In the *Lozana Andaluza,* in the *Viaje de Turquía,* in the *Historia Pontifical* of Gonzalo de Illescas, in the annals of the Inquisition, are references to these communications and contacts. Señor Menéndez Pidal has not yet said the last word on the Judeo-Spanish *romancero*. He has shown the absolute need of exploring the historical antecedents. The inclusion of ballads of Spanish Renaissance composition among those found in Morocco and even in the Levant argues favorably for the thesis that Spain did not completely ignore the existence of the *Sefardíes* and similarly the *Sefardíes* did not forget Spain.

History then is an invaluable adjunct for the study of Spanish ballads among the Jews of the Peninsular Diaspora. But where is there a history book discussing the subject? Up to very recent times no one took the trouble to write an acceptable history of the Jews since their dispersion. Now we must pause in order to clarify some misunderstandings. In the next chapter we shall treat in greater detail that which we shall only hint at here.

The Jews who left Spain at various times can be classified as medieval Jews and Renaissance Jews. Those Jews who remained behind after the expulsion of 1492, as Neo-Christians, came under influences of religion and culture denied naturally to their brethren in exile. Tremendous forces of *Weltpolitik* and cultural currents transformed Spain in the sixteenth century. Manners, language, professions, business pursuits, family life, all received the impact of a new world in the making. When eventually thousands left Spain and Portugal in groups, these Neo-Christians, or Marranos, in many cases reverted to the ancient covenant of Abraham. The Marranos preferred to live in the cities of Italy—Ferrara, Naples, Ancona, Rome, Venice, Pésaro, Leghorn, etc.—and in the southwestern part of France—Bayonne, Bordeaux—and, in the seventeenth century, in London, Amsterdam, Hamburg, and in distant lands such as Surinam, Pernambuco, Jamaica, Barbadoes, Curaçao, New Amsterdam. These Peninsular Jews we denominate Renaissance Jews because, unlike their brethren who were expelled in 1492, they were nurtured in the national Catholic traditions of both Spain and Portugal. Because the West, on both sides of the Atlantic, reached the heights of power and culture in the past three centuries, there has grown an intensive interest in the Jews of Hispanic origin, for they were great factors in the new transformations. The Jews from Germany and Poland and Russia, upon entering the Western countries that had been closed to them, once acclimatized and in power, were attracted to the germinal communities of the Marranos which had made it possible for their subsequent incorporation. Grateful to their Sephardic brethren, they undertook the task of tracing the Marranic contributions to Western and Jewish history. Following the weakly endowed descendants of the Marranos, such as Lindo, the Germanic or Ashkenazic

Jews like Jacobs, Keyserling, Loeb, Kaufmann, Gräetz and Roth made astonishing discoveries. Two problems confronted them: the marrano communities, their origins and developments; and the Peninsular background of the Spanish Jews. Thanks to a new and powerful awakening of Spanish scholarship favorably disposed towards the Jews, the Germanic Jewish scholars enjoyed great assistance in their researches from men like Llorente, Castro, Amador de los Ríos, Fernández y González, Padre Fita, etc.

The reader must remember, however, that the ballads we have collected in New York were found among the medieval Jews; that is to say, among the heirs of those Jews who upon their expulsion from Spain went to live in North Africa, Egypt, Mesopotamia, Palestine, the Balkans, and Asia Minor. Centuries after a Sephardic community had been established in New York, descendants of these medieval Jews came to live here. Our first and immediate interest is to know the history of these African and Levantine Sephardic Jews. What Western scholar, Jew or non-Jew, writes about them? Since they had ceased to be important in world history, why bother about them? Scattered references to them might be found in certain history books and so there is no need to be ungrateful. Gräetz devotes many pages to their establishment in Safed, Salonica, and to the Sabbatian movement of the seventeenth century. But he too interpreted the four-century history of our people as an incident in Jewish history. Who were these remnants of a once glorious body of people anyhow? In numbers they were insignificant; in achievement, negligible and puny. Russian Jewry, German Jewry, American Jewry, Zionism, these were the absorbing topics in modern Jewish history.

Neither Gentile nor Ashkenazic scholarship devoted much time or effort to the history of the Hispano-Levantine-Moroccan Jews among whom scores of Spanish ballads survived. Ashkenazic Jews have written deeply and extensively on the Jews in Spain and on the Marrano communities in Western Europe and America. Fritz Baer has already published in Hebrew a very thoroughly documented history of the Jews of the Iberian Peninsula. Very fine monographs on specific phases of Judeo-Spanish history, such as Braunstein's *The Chuetas of Mallorca* and Rabbi Herbert I. Bloom's work on *The Economic Activities of the Marrano Jews in Holland in the Seventeenth Century,* have already appeared. The Anglo-Jewish scholar, Cecil Roth, has given us numerous studies on the Marrano communities, and his *History of the Marranos* in particular is very readable and informative. For a comprehension of the pan-Sephardic world all these works are invaluable. The Marrano communities were not hermetically closed to the Levantine Sephardic foci. And for a full understanding of the movements undergone by the Romancero, the history of the Marranos is indispensable. I shall have occasion in the next chapter to avail myself of the above-named scholars' contributions in the building up of the main lines of post-exilic Sephardic history. But meanwhile I must call the reader's attention to the deplorable dearth of historical accounts of the African and Levantine Sephardic communities. There seems to have been no real interest in them among the Gentile or Ashkenazic scholars. The contention here is that without a historical background no real grasp of the function of the *romancero* among the Jews who concern us is possible. Here then is another cause that has deterred me from pursuing my studies in this field all these years.

Fortunately in the very recent past there has been an awakening among Sephardic Jews of Levantine origin which has helped the work interesting us. After S. Rosanes, who wrote in Hebrew on *The Jews of the Near East,* two Salonician Jews, Professor Joseph Nehama and Rabbi Emanuel, independently of each other, have written the history of Salonica with reference to the Jews of that city. Professor Nehama has not yet finished his monumental work. So far the published volumes cover the history of Salonica through the sixteenth century. Trained in France, inheriting the historical style of Michelet, Joseph Nehama is the first to write beautifully and accurately a consecutive account of the Sephardic Jews in the Levant. Utilizing all the materials at the disposal of Jewish historians, such as the *responsa* of the Sephardic rabbis, the *hascamoth* or communal ordinances of Salonica, the Hebraic and Judeo-Spanish writings of the times, and the accounts of sixteenth century travelers, Nehama, having a disciplined mind and imagination, succeeds admirably in presenting an authentic reconstruction of a Sephardic microcosm transplanted to a non-Hispanic environment. Rabbi Emmanuel, trained as he was at Breslau, follows the positivistic school of historical scholarship. His style is dryer and unornamented, but what he says is documented and to the point.

The first to write a history of Levantine Jewry, other than Rosanes, are these two Salonician scholars, both familiar with the Sephardic ethos. Though we regret that they have not written the whole history of the Hispano-Levantine world, we are grateful to them for what they have done. Abraham Galante, from Smyrna, in a less organized way, has contributed to our knowledge of the Hispano-Levantine Jews in his several volumes and brochures written in French and Turkish. Formidable difficulties beset the path of the Sephardic scholar. Since little monographic preparation has been done in the laying of the foundation for the construction of a complete history of Sephardic Levantine Jewry, no one could expect these scholars alone to undertake the whole task. Salonica being in more than one sense the archetype of a Levantine Sephardic community, the establishment, organization, development and eventual decadence of the other communities were on the whole similar to it. If we therefore study the Salonician pattern carefully we can penetrate into the lives of the Sephardic Jews of communities like those of Alexandria, Brussa, Andrianople, Monastir, Gallipoli, Rhodes, Constantinople, Smyrna. Salonica helps us to understand the Hispano-Levantine world for another essential reason. Salonica was a diminutive Jewish republic, made up of plebeians and patricians, weavers, scholars, merchant princes. (And this flourishing Salonica is no more. The Hitlerian hordes destroyed it almost completely.) There was enough learning to give these Jews a historical consciousness that made them aware of their existence and their relationship to the Jewish world as a whole and to the Gentile world in general. Historical awareness is the key to self discovery.

Intermittently, then, I have been working on the Hispanic traditions of the medieval Sephardic Jews for almost three decades. Reluctance on my part to study the ballads as a scholarly exercise has taken me far afield. In lieu of writing a study of the Judeo-Spanish ballads, I ended in completing a work on the *Hispanic Culture and Character of the Sephardic Jews living in the Near East*. I believe that not only I, but anyone interested in Judeo-Spanish culture, will now be prepared to undertake any study concerning that culture with a less hazy notion of what it was. Once this nostalgic book of mine has been read with sympathy my work on the *Muwassaha and the Romance among the Sephardic Jews* will write itself, as it were, since I shall no longer be confused and distracted. For now, thanks to my reconstruction of the Hispano-Levantine culture, I hope to believe the place occupied by *muwassaha* and *romance* in that culture will be clear.

NOTES

1. M.R. Cohen, "History versus Value," in *Journal of Philosophy,* Vol. XI (1914), p. 701 ff.; cf. also by the same author, *Reason and Nature,* New York, 1931, pp. 369-373.

2. For a fine discussion of the thesis that "every order of the real requires by reason of its very distinctness an appropriate mode of investigation," see Etienne Gilson, "Concerning Christian Philosophy, The Distinctness of the Philosophic Order," included in *Philosophy and History,* Essays presented to Ernst Cassirer, Oxford, 1936, pp. 61-76.

3. Jaime Fitzmaurice-Kelly's *Historia de la literatura desde los orígenes hasta el año 1900, etc.,* Madrid (Septima edición), is an excellent illustration of positivism run amuck.

4. See *General bibliography* for works and studies by Abraham Danón and Abraham Galante.

5. For the Spanish literary texts and language used by the *moriscos,* see A. R. Nykl, "Aljamiado Literature," in *Revue des Études Hispaniques,* 1929, pp. 406-611; and by the same author, "Aljamiado Texts in Tunisia," in the same review, vol. 81, p. 254 ff.; also see Jaime Oliver Asin, "Un morisco de Túnez, admirador de Lope," in *Al-Andalus.* I, pp. 409-450. One of the earliest studies on the subject is "Discurso que el Excmo. Sr. D. Eduardo Savedra leyó en junta pública de la Real Academia Española el día 29 de diciembre de 1878, al tomar posesión du su plaza de Académico de número," in *Memorias de la Real Academia Española,* vi, pp. 140-192; and cf. Pedro Longas, *Vida religiosa de los moriscos,* Madrid, 1915.

6. S. M. Stern, "Les vers finaux en espagnol dans les muwassahas hispano-hebraïques. Une contribution à l'histoire du muwassah et a l'étude du vieux dialect espagnol mozarabe," in *Al-Andalus,* XII, 1948, pp. 299-346.

7. Francisco Cantera, "Versos españoles en las muwassahas hispano-hebreas," in *Sefarad,* IX, 1949, pp. 197-234.

8. Dámaso Alonso, "Cancioncillas 'de Amigo' mozárabes, in *Revista de Filologia Española,* XXXII, 1949, pp. 297-349.

9. This is not the place to give an adequate bibliography on the *muwassaha.* Only some important items need appear here for the present. For the works of the great Spanish Arabic scholar, Don Julián Ribera, who did more than anybody else to throw light on this subject that for more than a century baffled

European scholarship see a) A. R. Nykl, *El cancionero de Aben Guzmán*, Madrid, Imprenta de Estanislao Maestre, 1933. Another work of great significance by A. R. Nykl is b) *Hispano-Arabic Poetry*, and its relations with the Old provençal troubadors, Baltimore. Printed by J. H. Furst Co., 1946. c) Martin Hartmann, *Das Arabische Strophengedicht,* 1. *Das Muwassah*, Weimar, Emil Felber, 1897. d) S. M. Stern, Imitations of Arabic muwassahat in Spanish-Hebrew Poetry, (in Hebrew) in *Tarbiz*, XVIII, 1947. c) Idem, "Un muwassah arabe avec terminasion espagnol," in *Al-Andalus*, XIV, 1949, pp. 214-218.

10. *Zejel* is the name given to the poem in this verse-pattern when written in popular Arabic and *muwassaha* is the designation when it is composed in literary Arabic. Which came first, the zejel or the *muwassaha*? Scholars are not agreed on the precedence of either one.

11. For the nomenclature given to the different parts of the *muwassaha*, see R. Menéndez Pidal, *Poesía europea, con otros estudios de literatura medieval*, Buenos Aires, Espasa-Calpe, S. A., 3rd edition, 1946, pp. 18-19; and for the true meaning of *markaz*, cf. S. M. Stern's study in *Al-Andalus*, 1948, pp. 301-302.

12. The outstanding Spanish authority on Hispano-Hebrew poetry is José Maria Millás Vallicrosa. His *La poesia sagrada hebraico española*, Madrid, 1940; second edition, 1949; and *Yehuda ha-Levi como poeta y apologista*. Madrid-Barcelona, 1947, contain indispensable studies on the *muwassaha*. In the second book, pp. 55-57, 59-61, Millás gives translations of two poems by Jehuda Helevi whose *harjas* ended in Spanish, transliterated in the original, of course, in Hebrew characters.

13. For *harja* number nine, see Stern, Cantera and D. Alonso, for all deal with it. The reader interested in the language phase of the *harja* will be considerably agitated over the outlandish forms like *corachón, mib,* tornarád, samarad, *yed,* and the Semitic words, *Rab* and *li-l-habib*. All our specialists take up the morphology involved. Recasting the four lines of this *harja* into a more prosaic mould, Dámaso Alonso gives us: mi corazón se me va de mi, Oh, Dios, ¿Acaso se me tornará? ¡Tan fuerte mi dolor por el amado! Enferma está, ¿cuándo sanará?

14. R. Menéndez Pidal, "Catálogo del romancero judio-español," included in *El Romancero, Teorías e investigaciones,* (Biblioteca de Ensayos, No. 3). Madrid, n.d., pp. 101-124. This study appears in many works by its author. See the several bibliographies of R. M. P.'s works for them.

II

The Sephardic Diaspora
1391 - 1950

The Turning Point in Sephardic History

The turning point in the history of the Spanish Jews is to be found in the fatal year 1391. Whoever is curious can consult Amador de los Ríos or Graetz for the details of that tragic year.[1] It is not for us to exhort or lament but it is our duty to describe the historical background of the Spanish Jews. The massacres and the incendiary acts of the mob aroused by well-meaning ecclesiastics but deprecated by civil and church authorities of the highest rank which spread throughout the length and breadth of Spain, open a new chapter in the history of the Iberian Jews and their Catholic fellow-citizens.[2] There were two consequences of far-reaching significance. Hundreds of Jews imposed exile upon themselves. Jews left the south and the Balearic Islands for the cities of northern Africa, Egypt, Salonica, cities where Jewish communities were already established. These Jews who left Spain a century before the edict of banishment was promulgated by the Catholic sovereigns, were the precursors of the Sephardic spirit throughout the world. The type of communities they founded is important for our synthetic *aperçu;* we shall return to discuss it later.

By far most revolutionary result of the religious riots of 1391 was the emergence of a new kind of Spanish subject, namely, the Marrano. As in all historical events of decisive significance the causes giving rise to the new social class of the Marranos are obscure and multiple. The Church, true to her genius, encouraged the conversion of the Jews to protect them physically from the fury of the populace and to offer them spiritual salvation. Undoubtedly hundreds of Jews accepted Catholicism in sincere conformity with a tendency persistent in Jewish communities finding themselves in cultural configurations of a high level of achievement. This tendency manifests itself in those communities where many Jews feel an irresistible attraction towards the mores of their non-Jewish compatriots. Assimilation is the inevitable consequence whether stimulated by propaganda or by the mere presence of the advantages offered by the non-Jewish society. In Spain the agitation, popular and ecclesiastical, precipitated the conversion of thousands upon thousands of Jews. Many reconciled themselves to the new conditions. In many cases the craving they had to feel they belonged to the ways and manners of the country where their ancestors had been living for centuries was satisfied. On the part of many there was sincere reconciliation, indeed so sincere that at times the neophytes displayed an overzealousness that translated itself through the sense of guilt into a mania to persecute their former co-religionists. While admitting in all fairness the incorporation of many Jews into the ethos of the country, which at that time was a fusion of love of land, language, soil, customs, gestures and belief, in a certain kind of theology, there were nevertheless thousands and more thousands of neo-Christians who felt most uncomfortable to say the least, in the new religion and society opened for their benefit. Their sense of guilt manifested itself in a secretive life. Unable to accept Catholicism in all its implications, torn between the all-absorbing attractiveness of their membership in the new society and the powerful force of the ancestral inheritance, these neophytes began to lead double lives. Hence arose crypto-Judaism.

Under Moorish dominance Jews on the whole had for centuries enjoyed many privileges as tradesmen, merchants, artisans, farmers and members of the learned professions. With the transfer of Spanish lands to the rule of Christian sovereigns, the Jews continued for scores and scores of years to be the benefactors of benevolence and encouragement. Students of Spanish history know how well the Jews were treated by Alphonso VI, who called himself the Emperor of the Three Religions, by Fernando el Santo, conqueror of Seville, and by his learned son Alphonso X. The fratricidal warfare between Pedro el Cruel and his brother Henry of Trastamara interrupted the amicable relationship between Jew and Christian. Slowly the Jews were shedding their Arabic ways and acquiring Romanic manners. The dialects of Latin origin were becoming their daily speech, and their psychology and family life were assuming the characteristics of their surroundings.

By the time of the mass conversions, the Jews of Castile and Catalonia and other regions were in many ways integral parts of the prevalent Hispano-Christian civilization. Conversion gave them futher opportunities to assimilate the Hispanic ethos.[3] Concretely, the constraining forces opened to them fields hitherto sealed to them. They could now engage in activities connected with the Church, the university, the army, the learned professions. In their status as Catholics the neo-Christians were allowed to aspire to enter the oldest aristocratic families of the Peninsula. Clearly their conversion was a windfall. Seduced though they were by all the rewards of their opportunities, these neophytes continued to be true to their former religion. It must be admitted that divided loyalties gave rise to a secretive psychology in the souls of these people now derisively called Marranos by their Christian compatriots. Whereas it had been thought conversion was going to bring about unification, the crypto-Jews, according to students of Spanish history, contributed to the social and political unrest of the fifteenth century, though we deny they were the chief cause. Marranism had formidable after effects. The people in resentment now saw the Marrano as the focus upon which all its discontent could be centered. John II and Henry IV, impotent as rulers, could not solve the new problems: the turbulency of the feudal lords, the encroachments of Portugal, the challenge of the Moorish kingdom of Granada, which was always a reminder that national or Christian unity had not been achieved, and the Marrano elements. Briefly, the Marranos were a new type of Spanish subject with divided loyalties. From the Jewish point of view the Marranos were Jews who showed material advantages, secular culture, emancipated manners that gave them access to a world closed to those orthodox Jews permitted by sufferance to remain in the country. In the fifteenth century the Marrano and the orthodox Jews were contemporaries. By devious channels they were in contact. When the Catholic Sovereigns had recourse to the establishment of the Inquisition (1478) in order to suppress the shameless scandal of the two-facedness of the Marrano so that in time he would come to have the psychology of the true Catholic, they soon found out that as long as the orthodox Jews were living contiguously to the Marranos all efforts to wean the Marranos away from Judaism would fail, notwithstanding the vigilance of the Inquisition. One of the chief arguments for the expulsion of Jews was that they were contaminating sources for the Christians.[4] For the Marrano, observance of Judaism was easier with the orthodox Jews living in Spain.

Free intercommunication between Marrano and Jew prevailed in the fifteenth century. Yet the orthodox Jew continued to live on the margin of Spanish society. For one thing the orthodox Jew on the whole belonged to the poorer elements in the population. The rapid linguistic transformations which were taking place in the upper strata of Spanish society affected the Marranos more than the orthodox Jews. Hernando del Pulgar, don Juan Pacheco, Marqués of Villena, don Pedro Girón, Micer Gonzalo de Santa María, Alfonso de Baena, Rodrigo de Cota, Pablo de Heredia, Alfonso de Zamora, Andrés Helí, Alonso de Cabrera, and many more eminent writers, statesmen, courtiers of Marranic ancestry were far removed, socially speaking from the orthodox Jews who remained faithful to Judaism. It is a characteristic of religions in general and of Judaism in particular to be conservative in almost every respect.[5]

Our aim here is to distinguish these two types of Jews, for in these distinctions we shall find the key to the roles they played after 1492 within the Peninsula and outside it. Feeling themselves aliens, the orthodox Jews could afford to·celebrate their Passover, their Purim, and the other holidays in the archaic Spanish. The continuation of the Spanish of the thirteenth and fourteenth centuries satisfied them for its association with holy things, and the obsolete elements in their speech tended to give cohesion to their mores. They could continue writing their letters and their communal accounts in Hebrew characters, intermingling their Spanish, their Catalonian dialect, their Portuguese, with archaisms and Hebrew expressions. The Jewish communities of Castile holding their council in order to legislate for their closed world redacted their minutes in Hebrew characters in a language both Hebrew and Spanish. The translations of the Bible, of the poems written by Gabirol, Judah Halevy and other Hispano-Moorish bards continued to be read and sung in a Spanish much older than the one prevailing among the Marranos. A careful examination of the Spanish in the so-called Duke of Alba Bible written at the beginning of the fifteenth century by the little known Rabbi Moses Aragel of Guadalfajara will convince anyone versed in the evolution of the Castilian tongue that it is more archaic

than contemporary documents of the Bible, even though this translation of the Bible was destined to be read by a man of the highest nobility
of the land.[6] By their entrance into the new society the Marranos were
initiated into a more evolved speech. By exchanging the Hebrew alphabet for the Latin script they were given access to a great literature then
in the making. Alfonso de Baena,[7] Francisco López de Villalobos,
Antón de Montoro, Rodrigo de Cota and perhaps Fernando de Rojas,
if they were participants in the germinal Renaissance of the Castilian
language, were in turn also contributors to its growth and development.
Right in the midst of the fifteenth century the orthodox Jews differed
from the Marranic Jews. Still profounder differences separated these
two types of Jews. By living in the same world as their Iberian fellow-
citizens, on an equal footing, the Marranos changed their physiognomy
by intermarriage. They were soon behaving like hidalgos of the first
rank. Gestures, manners, looks, language, occupations, aspirations, in
all these categories the Marranos differed from their Jewish brethren. A
century of life as Marranos transformed a large percentage of the Jewish population, preparing it for the inheritance of Western culture as it
was being elaborated in Italy, and in the sixteenth century in France, the
Netherlands, and in England. From this inheritance the orthodox Jews
were on the whole excluded, particularly the Jews who after 1492 went
to live in the Orient and in Africa.

The First Dispersal of the Spanish Jews

This succinct account has shown, we hope, how the Jewish population of Spain in the fifteenth century was bifurcated into two separate
streams. The remnant adhering to Judaism formed part of the fluvial
system of world Judaism. The Marranos on the other hand, were "Jews
in all but name, Christians in nothing but form."[8] They either incorporated themselves completely into the Hispanic nation, thereby effac-
ing all traces of their origin, or preferred, despite subsequent disadvant-
ages with the establishment of the Inquisition, to lead double lives. To
avoid misunderstanding, we must state that the Marranos we have in
mind now are those who kept a complete or a partial loyalty to the
religion of the Patriarchs and the prophets. The fact that, at the beginning of the sixteenth century and thereafter for many decades, they left
the Peninsula in order to observe secretly their Judaism in countries like

France and Flanders where they could not be recognized as Jews, or to revert openly to Judaism in various countries of the world, proves beyond doubt that Marranism was transmitted from generation to generation in the fifteenth as well as in subsequent centuries.

Now that this point is clear we can retrace our steps to 1391 again. There is no hope of ever getting a firm grasp of Judeo-Spanish history unless we reject as too simple the superficial notion that the Sephardic dispersion began the year Columbus discovered America. Jews left Spain on three different occasions.[9] As far back as a century prior to 1492, we learn of a voluntary exodus of Spanish Jews. Although this departure did not have outstanding consequences, yet the problems and the solutions to the problems faced by the immigrants of 1391 in their new environment anticipated in more ways than one those which a century and more later confronted the orthodox Jews who could no longer live in Spain as such.

Scholars working in historiography all over the world where Jewish culture is in the ascendancy are utilizing, more and more, the rabbinical *responsa*[10] as the chief source of Jewish chronology and history. Mr. Epstein of England has written two separate works on the *responsa* of two Peninsular rabbis for the purpose of reconstructing their respective periods. Rabbi Durán's *responsa* enable us to have an idea of what happened to the Iberian Jews who preferred to leave their country in 1391.

The Balearic Rabbi Simon B. Zemah Durán's "Questions and Answers," comprising his opinions, decisions, judgments, and decrees, on careful analysis have supplied enough materials to reconstruct the first period of the Sephardic dispersion. The departure of the first contingent of the Pyrannaic Jews for Africa occurred in 1391. Upon the arrival of the Jews from Catalonia, Andalusia, and above all from Mallorca, in the communities of North Africa, they discovered a very low level of material and spiritual development. From 1389 to 1411 there was considerable political uncertainty. Books were scarce, synagogal scrolls of the Law were in a dilapidated condition, the rabbis of the native Jews were crassly ignorant, and many branches of Hebraic learning were unknown, such as the study of the Talmud. Coming as they had from a land where well being and culture were highly developed, the Peninsular immigrants soon formed their own independent synagogal unities. "Wherever they settled themselves they formed separate groups retaining their former style of dress, their method of organization and mode of speech.''[11] No sooner did they become established than economic conditions began to improve. The curse of the Moroccan Coast, that of piracy, was somewhat mitigated. It did not take long for the Jews who had crossed the Mediterranean Sea to find favor among the authorities of Algiers and other localities. On their behalf the poll tax was decreased. While in their haste these Jews had left Spain, the great majority still remained behind. The immigrants, following the innate impulses of all modern demographic displacements, soon discovered their inseparable attachment to the land of their origin and to their fellow-worshippers. Benjamin de Tudela[12] was one of the few travelers who left Spain in the twelfth century to see for himself what was going on in the Jewish communities. Many other individuals after him wandered from Spain into other regions. By the establishment of the fourteenth century Sephardic communities, Spain and Africa became commercially connected and remained so for over a hundred years. In the three dispersions, that of 1391, that of 1492, and those of the sixteenth and seventeenth centuries, we have evidence that the exiles left relatives behind in the Peninsula. Subtracting what there is of exaggeration and animus in Sombart's[13] theory that the Jews were the founders of modern capitalism, a substantial amount of truth obtains in it. Without international trade no modern commercial system is imaginable. On a small scale then, the Balearic Jews through their business houses in Africa contributed to the ushering in of the new economy. In spite of the risks involved, what with the primitive methods of traveling by sea and the menace of pirates along the coasts of Africa and Spain, the Jews made repeated voyages in the pursuit of their business. For more than a century thereafter the Jews continued the same commercial transactions between the various countries. They organized societies with purposes similar to those of the monarchal units in Christian Spain, namely, to forestall piratical raids and to ransom slaves from pirates and other organizations.[14]

> The wanderers pursued, undisturbed, their own destiny, administered their own affairs, regulated their social and communal relations in an orderliness that distinguished the Jewish communities in the country of their origin.

These Jews provided North African Jewry with a new type of spiritual leadership, learned and enlightened.

What is worthy of note is that the Hispano-Jewish communities administered by men like Durán were almost self-perpetuating social organisms. True to the medieval spirit of allowing corporations of all sorts, guilds, universities, church, the right to rule themselves, the Hispano-Jewish community under the leadership of a rabbi and the laymen elected democratically to various offices, controlled the spiritual, educational, juridical, and economic phases. Disputes arising out of economic friction, matrimonial misunderstanding, religious controversy, were settled before the rabbinical court without recourse to the non-Jewish courts of justice. "The Spanish Jews who formed communities by themselves established their communal organization on democratic lines. They were governed by duly elected 'Ne-emanim' or 'memunim' as they were in Spain; and though the Responsa of Durán supply us with little information on the subject, it can be safely stated that they transferred to their new homes all the remarkable methods of communal administration that distinguished the Spanish *Aljamas*. We even note that they introduced the *sisas* levy, the tax on meat and wine, which as in Spain, was farmed out to one or more individuals for the payment of a lump sum."[15]

One more observation on this aspect. The Hispano-Jewish communities were ruled by documents issued for the purpose of keeping the peace. By means of ordinances called among the Sephardic Jews 'hascama' (the plural: 'hascamoth') these units were ruled.

> The ordinances which covered a wide field in the communal life were enforced by the anathema or *Herem,* which was a powerful weapon vested in the communal chiefs to maintain discipline and enforce obedience to the regulations passed from time to time.

In summary, we may say that the emigration of 1391 which gave rise to Hispano-Jewish communities in Africa, Egypt, Salonica, foreshadowed by a century how the Sephardic Jews were going to manage their affairs. Judaism, by the way, was officially suppressed in Mallorca in 1436, and therefore more contingents of Jews left for the communities established a generation or so before. Economically they were a boon to the cities they reached; while mindful of their connections with the mother country they continued to do business with their compatriots. A new kind of Jewish life was introduced by them with more learning, better manners, and higher standards of living.

NOTES

1. For a workable and reliable bibliography on Jews of Spain consult Abraham A. Neuman, *The Jews in Spain: Their Social, Political and Cultural Life during the Middle Ages,* Vol. II, Philadelphia, The Jewish Publication Society of America. 1942 - 5702; José Amador de los Rios, *Historia social, politica y religiosa de los Judíos de España,* Madrid, Imprenta de Fortanet, 1876, 3 vols; and Heinrich Graëtz, *History of The Jews,* Philadelphia, 1891-98, 6 volumes.

2. The question as to who is to blame for the destruction of the *Aljamas* becomes today a topic of acrid polemics and controversy. Américo Castro in his *España en su historia, Buenos Aires, Editorial Losada, 1946, and in his Aspectos del Vivir Hispánico Espiritualismo, mesianismo, actitud personal en los siglos XIV al XVI,* Santiago de Chile, Editorial Cruz del Sur, 1949, defends the thesis that the common people rather than the privileged classes took the initiative to harass and destroy the aljamas. In support of this point of view read this passage. . . "pues los judíos en España eran muy queridos y honrados por los reyes y principes, y por todos los sabios e inteligentes, *porque los destierros no fueron provocados sino por causa de algunos de la plebe, que pensaban que los judíos y porque habian venido al reino, se habia encarecido los alimentos.* Asimismo fueron ocasionadas las expulsiones por los frailes, los cuales, a fin de mostrar su santidad y hacer ver al pueblo que pretendían honrar y ensalzar la religión cristiana, diariamente predicaban contra los judíos cosas terribles. Mas por las restantes corporaciones cristianas eran los judíos considerados como si habitaran en su propria tierra, y eran muy queridos de ellas, como que era reconocido por los ancianos de España."

This remarkable analysis by Salomón Ben Verga, a contemporary of the final expulsion, up to a certain point coincides with the view that the masses were the mortal enemies of the Jews and the converts. But it goes beyond that too,—See his *Chebet Jehuda* (La Vara de Jehuda), Traducción española con un estudio preliminar por Francisco Cantera Burgos, Granada, Liberia Lopez-Guevara, 1927, page 203.

3. Cecil Roth is the Jewish historian who is considered the specialist on the Marranos. See his *A History of the Marranos,* Philadelphia, 1932, for all the facts, conflicts and controversies dealing with them. A Spanish translation by Aaron Spivak was published by Editorial Israel, Buenos Aires, 1941 - 5701.

The Marranos in the fifteenth century were known under other names, some

neutral, as neophytes or New Christians, and others were derogatory, such as
alboraicos.

"En la villa de Erena, de la provincia de León, fué puesto nombre a los
neófito judaizantes, conviene a saber a los *conversos,* agora ha sesenta años y
más años de la guerra que estonces se hizo en toda España por muerte de
espada, conviene a saber destrucción en las aljamas de los judíos, e los que
quedaron vivos por la mayor parte los bautizaron por fuerza y tomaron ellos
sobre sí un sobrenombre en hebraico *anuzim* que quiere decir forzados. Ca si
alguno se torna cristiano llámanle *Mesumad,* que quiere decir en hebracico
revolvedor, que los revuelve con los cristianos. Y así alguno de este linaje llega
a algún lugar donde hay aquesta mala generación, preguntánle ellos, ¿eres
anuz, cristiano por fuerza, o *mesumad,* cristiano por voluntad? Si responde
anuz soy, dánle dádivas y hónranle; y si dice *mesumad soy,* non le hablan más.
Así como de otros de esa Andalucía y de España sean *anuzim Cristianos,* porque más no pueden hacer, esto es en el nombre, ca non en las obras, guardan-
do sabad y otras creencias judaicas, rezando por libros de judíos, empero porque ellos tienen la circuncisión como moros, e el sabad como judíos, e el sólo
nombre de Cristianos, aunque por la voluntad judíos, pero non guardan el
Talmud nin las ceremonias todas de judíos, nin menos la ley cristiana y por
esto les fué puesto este nombre por mayor vituperio, conveniene saber
alborayco.

Y yo buscando este nombre en la vieja y nueva Ley y en sus glosas, non la
pude hallar, pero hallélo en el Alcoran. Ca Mohamad, caudillo de los moros,
fingió que Alá envió del cielo a lo llamar con el ángel Gabriel, y que para ir
allá, le truxo un animal que así lo llamó Alborayque, en que fué caballero. . .
etc.''

Since the alborayque was neither horse nor mule and its features were in
some particulars those of wolves, oxen, serpents, eagles, etc. the vituperative
epithet was applied to some marranos.

This curious quotation comes from the MS No. 356, fols. 60-70 of the
Spanish MMS section in the Bibliotheque Nationale de Paris. See Isidore
Loeb, "Polémistes chrestiéns et Juifs en France et en Espagne," *Revue des
études juives.* Paris. 1889, vol. XVIII, pp. 219-242.

I owe the above reference and quotation to Seymour Resnick's doctoral dissertation presented at New York University 1950, but not as yet published, entitled *The Jew as Portrayed in Early Spanish Literature.*

4. "Si los reyes de España desean desterrarlos no es porque sean pecadores, sino para que no hagan a sus vecinos pecadores y malvados como
ellos." Salomón Ben Verga *op. cit.* page 271.

5. We must not forget that Fernando de Rojas the author of the immortal
La Celestina and Juan de Mena were members of the illustrious *cristianos*

nuevos. For the Jewish ancestry of Juan de Mena see Américo Castro's *España en su historia.*

6. The "Biblia de la Casa de Alba" is an unexplored philological mine and as a cultural product it has not yet been duly interpreted. Castro is the first to draw some inferences from the fact that a Maestre de Calatrava had requested an obscure rabbi living in Maqueda (Province of Toledo) to expressly translate for him the Old Testament. Castro in his *España en su historia* connects the translation of this Bible with the interest other Castilian magnates were showing in the fifteenth century in cultural matters.

In the first letter to Rabbi Moses Arragel that Don Luis de Guzman wrote he said:

"Nos el Maestre de Calatrava embiamos mucho saludos a vos rabby Mosé Arragel, nuestro bassalo en la nuestra villa de Maqueda, Como aquel para quien honra e buena ventura queríamos. Es nos dicho que soys muy sabio en la ley de los judíos, e que ha poco que ende venistes morar. Lo qual a nos copo en placer por seer sabio, e vos entendemos fazer merced: Rabby Mosé: Sabed que auemos cobdicia de una biblia en romance, glosada e Ystoriada, lo qual nos dizen que soys para lo fazer assy muy bastante."

Antonio Paz y Melia studied on behalf of the Duke of Alba this Bible. For his study see *Homenaje a Menéndez y Pelayo.* Estudios de erudición española, ·Madrid, 1889, 2 vols. A shorter account by the same author appears in Volume I of *Biblia (Antiguo Testamento)* Traducida del Hebreo al castellano por Rabí Mosé Arragel de Guadalfajara (1422-1433?) y publicada por el Duque de Berwick y de Alba, Madrid, Imprenta Arística, 1920, (2 vols.).

7. On Alfonso de Baena and other distinguished converts, see Cecil Roth, op. cit. pp. 25-26.

8. Cecil Roth, ibid, pp. 27-28. Here we are given the origin of the word marrano.

9. For the expulsion of Jews from Spain under the Visigoths, see Salomon Katz, *The Jews in the Visigothic and Frankish Kingdoms of Spain and Gaul,* Cambridge, Massachusetts, The Medieval Academy of America, 1937.

10. Isidore Epstein, *The Responsa of R. Solomon ben Adreth of Barcelona (1235-1310) as a Source of the History of Spain,* London, 1925;—, *The Responsa of R. Simón b. Zemah Durán as a Source of the History of the Jews in North Africa,* London, 1930.

11. Isidore Epstein, The Responsa of R. Simon - - - - Durán, *passim.*

12. Benjamin of Tudela, *The Itinerary of Rabbi Benjamin of Tudela.* Translated and edited by A. Asher, 2 vols., London and Berlin, 1840 -41;—*Viajes de Benjamin de Tudela, 1160-1173.* Por primera vez traducidos al castellano con introducción, aparato crítico y anotaciones por Ignacio González-Llubera. Madrid, V. H. Sanz Calleja, 1918.

13. Werner Sombart, *The Jews and Modern Capitalism.* English translation with notes by M. Epstein, London, 1913.

14. We all know how Miguel de Cervantes was ransomed by the Trinitarian friars in Algiers. Jews likewise had their societies for ransoming slaves. It was a religious prescription known as *Pedion Shivuyim* highly respected by the Jews of Spain and by the exiled communities. See Joseph Nehama, *Histoire des Israélites de Salonique,* T. I. (140 av., J. C. à 1640) Thonon 1936, Paris, Librairie Lipschutz, p. 224.

15. Both quotations in Isidore Epstein, *The Responsa of R. Simón b. Zemah Durán,* London, 1930.

III

Far-Flung
Marrano Settlements

The attention of the reader has been repeatedly called to the emergence in the fifteenth century of a new type of Jew in Spain, or, straining the point somewhat, a new kind of Christian. In the fifteenth century the Jewish problem shifts its emphasis: from being an irreducible opposition to the Jew, it now becomes a determined hostility to the Marrano. Involved in the maladministration of Álvaro de Luna's ministry and in other affairs of the State, the Marranos aroused such popular resentment as to give rise to bloody riots in Toledo and elsewhere in 1449 and in 1467. The problem called for a statesmanlike solution.[1] The Church's experimentation in the conversion of the brothers of Christ could not be renounced, the wrath of the populace could not be appeased by ecclesiastical benedictions; obviously the universality of the Brotherhood of Man through the Church and the concrete difficulties of the country had somehow to be reconciled. The establishment of the Inquisition was thought to be sufficient to obliterate the accusation that the neo-Christians were not sincere in their profession of Christianity. If by admonition, coaxing, threats, and punishment, the Marranos could be made to enter the scheme of things, sloughing off their way by adopting an agrarian, feudal mentality, then the social opposition to them would disappear. An echo of the continuous opposition to the Marranos was finally summarized in the pride of racial purity, *limpieza de sangre,* a boasting most repugnant to the spirit of Catholicism.[2]

A quotation from the chronicle on the Catholic Sovereigns of the Curate of Los Palacios (Ms. Chapter 43) as translated by Prescott[3] gives us in compact form the reasons and feelings of the Spaniards concerning the Marranos, manifesting the underlying causes for their treatment. A bit of truth made clear in recent times by first-rate thinkers who have dealt with problems of cultural patterns, is that whatever we may think of the relevancy and cogency of the beliefs of past civilizations is immaterial. The fact is that whatever those people thought constituted their ideology. Hence we need not stop to confirm or disprove the sentimental reactions of the Castilians of the fifteenth century. It is enough to know that this is how they thought and what they thought is what concerns us. The Marranos were hated because they were reluctant to comply with the religious rites of Catholicism, and they preferred to celebrate their holidays in secret. The culinary practices of the Marranos were quite different from those of the Christians. Their disrespect for Christian institutions, such as monastic life, and their profanation of that life was another charge against them. They were accused, on the economic level, of being very ambitious and grasping. They lacked the feeling of solidarity and cooperation with their fellow Christians. Finally, as a result of their excessive wealth, the Marranos succeeded in marrying into the aristocratic families of the land. Sentimental, religious, psychological reasons were at the bottom of the popular antagonism to the Marranos.[4] Curiously enough, a Hebrew Chronicle of the sixteenth century gives a searching and profound analysis of this antagonism, going into the charges coming from Castilian sources. Without sharing the feelings of the opposition, nevertheless the Chronicler admits the charges and tries to give a rational explanation of the woes and tribulations visited upon the Jews and the Marranos.

> Por que hay tres clases de envidias importantes: la envidia de la religión, la de las mugeres y la de las riquezas, y todas tres se encuentran en Israel con los demás pueblos; pues por el continuo trato y habían comenzado los judíos en España a poner sus ojos en las hijas del país . . . La envidia de las riquezas, por que entraron los judíos en los oficios y negocios de los cristianos. . . se envanecieron algunos de nuestro pueblo y pensaron mandar sobre los cristianos, los habitantes del país, siendo estos señores.[5]

The establishment of the Inquisition and the expulsion of the Jews in 1492 were the inevitable consequences of the policy adopted by the Catholic Sovereigns, namely, to attain internal peace through the thorough assimilation of the representatives of the money economy. In time the Castilian purposes were fulfilled to a remarkable extent.

Through the machinations of circumstances and world politics, the Marrano problem that arose in Castile changed its locality. In the previous section we failed to say that over six hundred families of Castilian Jews received the right to reside permanently in Portugal upon the payment of a tax. But about a hundred thousand Jews entered Portugal, each adult paying eight escudos, with the promise that they were to leave the country before completing a year of residence there. It is pathetic to see how countries imitate ideologies from their neighbors when their needs are not similar. Portugal was forced to expel the Jews by the dynastic marriage of Manuel and Isabella, daughter of the Catholic Sovereigns of Spain, one of the stipulations of this marriage being that the Jews were either to be converted or expelled. Unlike Castile Portugal was not consistent. The Jews were not allowed to leave the country in accordance with the agreement binding the King of Portugal when he admitted them into his country. What was extraordinary in the case of the Castilian proposition to the Jews, that they were either to remain by becoming Catholics or leave the country, was not to be found in the treatment the Portuguese meted out to their guests. By trickery and chicanery, all Jews, the native Portuguese as well as the Castilian Jews were compelled to adopt Catholicism, willy nilly. Cecil Roth, the modern historian of the Marranos, says:

> The expulsion from Portugal is thus, as a matter of fact, a misnomer. The number of those who were able to emigrate was so exiguous as to be negligible. What put an end to the residence of the Jews in the country was a general conversion of unexampled comprehensiveness knowing almost no exceptions, and carried out by means of an unbridled exercise of force.[6]

The vacillating policies of Portugal made it possible for Marranism to grow into a very sturdy underground religious movement which was never destroyed. Since as Jews the Marranos could not leave, as Christians they might theoretically be entitled to travel at will. Again Portuguese theory and practice were ambiguous and inconsistent. By 1499 laws were passed prohibiting the emigration of Marranos. But after the bloody riots of 1506 in Lisbon, the previous promises that the Lusitanic neo-Christians were to be left alone, unsupervised by ecclesiastical authorities, were renewed with the additional guarantee that thereafter they could transfer themselves and their possessions wherever they wished. These two privileges accorded to the Portuguese Marranos had world-wide repercussions and consequences. In the first place the marranos of recent conversion in whose blood remained an irresistible push toward their ancestral religion, at the first opportunity left Portugal for the Sephardic communities in Africa and the Levant. The so-called "Portuguese" congregations in Salonica, the Balkan cities, Smyrna, and Constantinople sprang up on the arrival of the Castilian Marranos at this time. Because as yet the Inquisition was not established and because there was considerable guarantee against inquiring into one's faith, many Castilian Marranos left Spain to join their brethren in Portugal.

A result of these favorable circumstances was the beginning of a new migratory movement of the Portuguese Marranos toward Italy, France, and Flanders. Now as "Portuguese" they had the right to establish themselves in those countries without having to fear any supervision. Even after the establishment of the Inquisition in the thirties of the sixteenth century (1536), the Marranos were constantly seeking opportunities for business transactions and relative freedom from persecution.

Once the Inquisition began to function in Portugal, it was natural for the thinly-veneered neo-Christians to hurry away from that land. And examination of the correspondence exchanged in the forties of the sixteenth century between Charles the Fifth and his beloved sister Marie, Queen of Hungary, on the financial dealings of the Marranic family Mendez, shows how apprehensive the defender of the Catholic Faith had become of the intrusion of the Jews in Flanders and elsewhere under the disguise of Christianity.

Quant aux nouveaux cristiens qui viennent *journellement* de Portugal en Anvers, ils passent continuellement du dit Anvers en France et de la (comme lon dict) vers Ferrare, sans que scet riens alleguer contre icelx entant quilz se dent bons cristiens et scavent generalement respondre de la foy cristiene, combien que la presumption soit grande qu'ilz ne se retirent du dit Portugal en si grand nombre, sans estre grandement suspectz. *Et quant on les interroge, porquoy quilz retirent, disent quilz le font pour avoir melieure commodite de vivre, non sachans gaigner leur vie au dit Portugal que n'est vray semblable.*[7]

Merchants of Antwerp when questioned by Queen Marie of Hungary as to their attitude towards the Portuguese merchants, gave as their opinion that it would be a good idea to make them wear a badge of distinction like the Jews of Germany. The remarks of the Emperor's sister show fully the idealism and disinterestedness of the championship of Catholicism by Spain.

> Car silz sont Juifz vostre Majeste ne les vouldroit tollerer en vos pays mesmes les avoir fait retirer de Geldres et *silz estoint cretiens on leur feroit tort faire porter marcque.*[8]

At Flanders the authorities realized that the Portuguese merchants were using the country in many cases as a passageway to the cities of Italy where the Marranos were tolerated as such and even accepted as professing Jews. Flanders also served as the connecting link between the West and cities like Salonica.

> Monseigneur il y a grand presumption contre eul qui sont Juifz, qui petit a petit se retirent vers Salonique.[9]

It would be impossible to attempt a synthetic resumé of the establishment of Marranic communities through the world, and trace their contributions to the culture of the countries where they went to live. Against all odds we want to get the bare outlines of these extraordinary people who in so many ways were the precursors of the modern Jews. There were many types of Marranic existence. Fortunately we can encompass the Marranic life under various divisions and subdivisions:

Peninsular Marranos. The Marranos of Spain proper start their crypto-Judaism in the last decade of the fourteenth century. A variegated chapter with a tragic strain can be detected in the Balearic Islands.[10] Whenever the Inquisition discovered traces of Judaism and brought the culprits to trial, we logically infer the existence of Marranos. Already the history of the Marranos in Mallorca has been written. The conversion of the Balearic Jews presented a new variety of Catholic. A racial boycott enabled the neophytes of those islands to preserve their blood stream free of admixtures with the blood of the natives. The *Chuetas,* the Catholics of Jewish origin, to protect themselves from the hostile environment developed an extra-orthodox religious feeling which did not offer them immunity from social discrimination but gave them the right to live on the Island of Mallorca.

Many Marranos fled from Spain to the Canary Islands to be away from the highly explosive atmosphere of the Peninsula. A study of the records of the Holy Office shows how many neo-Christians went to live on Spanish soil free from the constant social pressure exerted upon the Marranos.

Thanks to the investigations of scholars like Keyserling and others, we know that the Marranos of Aragón and Andalusia made direct contributions to the discovery of America.[11] Notwithstanding the laws of the sixteenth century discouraging the emigration of Marranos to the West Indies and the lands of Tierra Firme, many Marranos finally succeeded in reaching Mexico and Peru.[12] The ubiquitous Holy Office ferreted the Marranos out of their underground religious practices.

The second chapter that must be written on the general history of the Marranos will have to treat the *Lusitanic Marranism*.[13] Portugal, as hinted above, became the classical land of the Marranos. Not only did she become the reservoir of Marranos, supplying contingents for the foci that spread all over the world for over two centuries, but Portugal and her oceanic possessions continued to have Marranos down to our present time.[14]

The most interesting chapters by far concern the Marranos in the non-Hispanic lands. Three different phases must be distinguished. The "Portuguese Nation" as they came to be known abroad, for decades formed small nuclei in Catholic lands, such as Flanders, France, and Italy.[15] In cities like Bordeaux and Bayonne, the Marranos had their children baptized and their dead buried in accordance with Catholic practice, for the sake of appearance. Readily the ecclesiastical authorities there connived at this strange behavior, and they were kind enough to forgive these people who appeared to be law-abiding and acceptable in every other way. Connivance at their crypto-Judaism continued for a long time in communities of that sort, but with the early eighteenth century the Marranos of southwestern France were permitted to profess their Judaism publicly.

Another type of Marranic community developed in the middle of the sixteenth century in Ferrara which, in due time, became the prototype of other similar units in Italy and elsewhere. The Italian princes of cities like Ferrara, Leghorn, Venice, recognized as a *fait accompli* the Judaism of these so-called neo-Christians. As Jews these Peninsular Marranos who had behind them two or more generations of training in the Catholic faith displayed a psychology and a culture so profoundly modern, European, that they were allowed to enter civil life in entire freedom. In Ferrara we see the pattern of the Marranic Jewish community. The famous Bible of Ferrara was published in Latin characters, unlike the Pentateuch that appeared in Constantinople in three languages, Hebrew, Greek, and Spanish, side by side on each page, each transliterated in Hebraic characters. It was likewise in Ferrara that Usque (originally the family came from Huesca) published in the classical language of sixteenth century Portugal his lamentations and defense of Peninsular Judaism: *Consolations for the Woes of Israel.* Communal organizations, the utilization of Spanish and Portuguese for religious and domestic purposes, the publication of religious works in the Peninsular tongues, and the composition of original works in the literary fashions of the Peninsula were some of the traits distinguishing the new type of Jewish community.

These Jewish communities of Marranic origin spread, as a result of Italy's loss of commercial supremacy in the seventeenth century, and even before that loss, to Holland, Hamburg, London, and the New World. A fascinating book could be written on the Jewish centers in Surinam, Curaçao, Jamaica, Barbadoes, New Amesterdam, Newport, and even Saint Thomas.

> Un signe exterieur commun a toutes les communautés marranes étaient la culture de la littérature espagnole et portugaise, édité non en caractères hebreux commes les Sefardim orientaux mais d'une manière intelligible à tous les nouveaux arrivés parmi les emmigrants.

If we read the works of Menasseh ben Israel, Immanuel Aboab, Isaac Cardoso, the apologists of Judaism in a Castilian pure and crystal-clear like the best written in Spain, or the paraphrases of the Psalms, or the poems of all categories composed by Enrique Gomes, or Barrios, we become convinced that linguistically speaking these Jews were inseparable representatives of Peninsular culture as it developed in the two centuries subsequent to their expulsion. Like the victims of Nazi Germany, the Marranos established literary academies under the patronage of a man like Belmonte who had achieved inclusion in the aristocratic hierarchy of Europe. As far as their language was concerned, they did not speak dialects but rather the highly polished speech of Portugal and Spain as spoken in the high social circles there, in the university, the church, the army, and on the stage. Many of the Marranos before they reverted to Judaism (in many cases in their old age) had been university trained. Physicians, jurisconsults, astronomers, dramatists, poets, philosophers, theologians, rabbis, merchant princes, army officers, and many representatives of other callings were found in great numbers among these people. Recently the social upheavals everywhere have made investigations into the structure of society an imperative duty. As a result of these investigations we know now that society is made of the masses and the minorities ruling them. Applying this discovery to the Marranic communities, we are surprised to notice a preponderance of leading minorities without the masses to lead. One reason among many that might explain the eventual obliterations of these communities may be found in the absence of the masses to serve as centripetal forces sustaining the community.

The Marranos sacrificed much in order to have the liberty to practice the religion of their fathers freely and unashamedly. Thousands found abiding satisfaction in the release from a religion they could not completely assimilate. Whatever people may say to the contrary, it seems that Catholicism is more than religion. Like Judaism it is an all-embracing mode of life. It hurt the Jews deeply to change their *Weltanschauung*. But Catholicism in many ways had wrought wonders. It had transformed the Marranos so radically that Judaism seemed pale and insubstantial to many of the Marranos who went abroad. No wonder then that many were happy to return to the Peninsula and others remained Catholics wherever they might be. Still many who had difficulties in assenting to the symbolism and mystery of Catholicism found Protestantism nearer to the Hebraic tradition and readily accepted the new form of Christianity.

Bordering cases of Marranos who were torn between the old and the new religions can be illustrated in the tragic life of Uriel da Costa.[16] He ran away from Portugal because mysteriously he heeded the call of his forefathers. His perverted interpretation of Catholicism made him seek in hallucination, as it were, the religion of the Bible. To his amazement Judaism was far removed from the religion he envisaged in his dreams. The virus of modernity ate his heart up. Religion he forgot was all-binding in all the activities and phases of life. Torn between his satanic sense of freedom and his all-consuming thirst for spirituality, he could not tolerate the mores of the synagogue. His submission to the discipline of the synagogue after being anathematized cut into his sensitive pride so corrosively that in despair and shame he committed suicide. Of a more serene outlook was Baruch de Spinoza. His scruples made him avoid the dogmas of the clashing religions of Holland. Thanks to his aloofness, to his ascetic mode of being, and to his sense of independence, he was able to create one of the immortal philosophies of Western Europe. Through the tortured soul of Uriel da Costa and the Olympic calmness of Baruch de Spinoza we see Marranism ushering in the age of modernity. Out of its training in the Renaissance finally came the Romantic dissolution, and the promise of a new dawn still very distant and now hardly visible.

Not long ago philosophers and scholars thought Spinoza a fresh start in modern thought. The work of Professor Harry Wolfson, *The Philosophy of Spinoza* (Harvard University Press, 1934), has dispelled all doubts as to the interconnectedness between medieval Jewish philosophy and the Cartesian contributions. As far as we are here concerned, we see the best of Judeo-Hispanic thought incorporated in the meditations of modern metaphysics. This synthesis of medievalism and modernity discernible in Spinoza is the pinnacle of the Marranic contribution to European civilization.

The Swan Song of Western Sephardism

More than once in this synthetic summary of Sephardic history we have hinted at the *hidalguism* of the Marranos who reverted to Judaism in the various countries on both sides of the Atlantic Ocean. A few instances of how this *hidalguism* manifested itself will be given here. Here then are additional traits to round up the sketchy account of the hidalgo Jew.

Sephardic scholars like Michael Molho and I. S. Emmanuel[17] who have studied the sepulchral stones of the Salonician Jews have reported that in the majority of cases the inscriptions on the tombs are in Hebrew and usually without any ornamentation. The Marrano cemeteries on the other hand reveal hidalgo vanity in all its grandeur and pettiness.

> Les armoiries des hidalgos de la Péninsule commencèrent à apparaître sur les pierres tombales du Lido ou l'hebreu devient presque exceptionnel.

The same author observes this about the cemetery at Leghorn:

> Beaucoup portent des armoiries surmontées de casques de chevaliers... Celle du fameux rabbin Isaac Ergas se pare aussi de cette distinction, bien qu'elle soit accompagnée d'une inscription entierement rédigée en

hebreu. Ce fait rend probable la supposition qu'il était lui aussi d'origine marrane.

This hidalguism that pathetically became ostentatious in the House of Life, as the Hebrew expression designates the graveyard, was so impressive that the Germanic Jews who came in contact with their Hispanic brethren imitated them in this vanity as in other ways.

Reciproquement, il est remarquable que des familles d'origine germanique recente et incontestable, telle que celle des Worms, *ont subi a tel point l'influence de leur entourage que les inscriptions funeraires sont redigées en espagnol.*

Painters like Rembrandt who came to know the Marrano Jews intimately immortalized some of their types. A full gallery of these exceptional men and women has to be put on review for us to get a whole notion as to the extent of their achievement. Suffice it to transcribe here the description of a Sephardic Jew in the eighteenth century English colonies on this continent by President Ezra Stiles of Yale University:

On 28th of May did that amiable benevolent, most hospitable and very respectable gentleman *Mr. Aaron Lopez* Merchant, who retired from Newport Rhode Island in these Times resided from 1775 to his death at Leicester in Massachusetts. He was a Jew by Nation, came from Spain or Portugal about 1754 and settled at Rhode Island. He was a Merchant of the first Eminence; for Honor and Extent of Commerce probably surpassed by no Merchant in America. He did Business with the greatest Ease and Clearness, always carried about a Sweetness of Behaviour, a calm Urbanity, an agreeable and unaffected Politeness of manners. Without a single Enemy and the most universally beloved by an extensive acquaintance of any man I ever knew. His Beneficence to his Family connexions, to his Nation, and to all the world is almost without a Parallel. He was my intimate Friend and Acquaintance! Oh! how often have I wished that sincere pious and candid mind could have perceived the Evidences of Xty, perceived the Truth as it is in Jesus Christ, known that Jesus was the Messiah predicted by Moses and the Prophets! The amiable and excellent Characters of a Lopez, of a Menasseh Ben Israel, of a Socrates, and a Gangenelli, would almost persuade us to hope that their Excellency was infused by Heaven, and that the virtuous and good of all Nations and religions, notwithstanding their Delusions, may be brought together in Paradise on the Xtian System, finding Grace with the all benevolent and adorable Emmanuel, who with his expiring breath and in his deepest agonies prayed for those who knew not what they did.[18]

Discounting the eulogy that is due to the dead, still enough is given in the New Englander's diary to show how at home in the Gentile world men like Aaron Lopez could be. No one can gainsay that his Sweetness of Behavior, his calm Urbanity, his agreeable and unaffected Politeness of manners, could have had its source other than in the Peninsula. This indelible aristocratic breeding was one of the many gifts Spain gave the Marranos. A more illustrative case of a Marrano Jew could not be thought of. Notice the Hebraic and the Hispanic so harmoniously combined in the name of Aaron Lopez.

Literally thousands of examples could be chosen to show the thoroughness with which the hidalgo type came to be the product of Marranic Sephardism. The negative qualities of the hidalgo inevitably came to be associated with the Jew too. Prosperity made Jews in time disdain work. According to Van Praag, the Dutch scholar, many families lived in Holland, whose male members for generations did not have to do a stroke of work. Pride of ancestry went so far as to make them refuse intermarriage with Ashkenazic Jews. Pusillanimity and selfishness betrayed many of them into a policy of intra-family breeding that in time thinned their blood, producing unlovely specimens of humanity. Their anxiety to preserve their family fortunes intact led kin to marry closely related kin. Besides the inbreeding which made for stagnation and even degeneracy there were other factors that determined the petering out of this stock once so sturdy and vital. Their training in the Christian ways, the delusions that came in the aftermath of the bursting of the Messianic bubble in the seventeeth century, the various inducements, monetary, social, and intellectual, to drift away from Judaism, and other more subtle factors, contributed to the collapse of Marranic Sephardism. Two more fundamental causes in their negativeness explain the weakening and well-nigh obliteration of Marranic Sephardism. For generations the Marranos preserved a sort of pan-Hispanic society. Intercommunication among the various centers established by them and the uninterrupted contact with the Peninsula gave their world a cohesion. Their sense of martyrdom, their adventurous spirit which made them risk life and limb by having all kinds of relations in Spain, their material connections with the Peninsula, were the forces making for unity. With the decline of Hispanic culture and commerce, and the corresponding ascendancy of the former enemies of Spain and Portugal, came the inducements to abandon the old and accept the new. Full participation in the politics of the countries where they resided as a result of the French Revolution likewise helped to wean them from their Hispanic traditions. Nationalism in France, Holland, England, Germany, Italy, the United States, demanded complete homage to the local gods. The cultivation of the native tongues broke the Hispanic cohesion. With the abandonment of Spanish and Portuguese as the synagogal and domestic languages, the pan-Sephardic community deteriorated. Western Sephardism did not receive any reinforcements from the Hispano-Levantine and Hispano-African communities. What the Marranic communities lacked—the medieval sense of Judaism and the masses—were unprocurable, and what is more probable not wanted.

If they were unwilling to call upon their Sephardic brethren because of so many difficulties entailed by such invitations, they were not very eager to welcome and rejuvenate themselves when, voluntarily, thousands and even millions of Ashkenazic Jews arrived in their countries. The Sephardic Jews were in a very, very small minority in the Western World. They would have been overwhelmed in time no matter what they did or refrained from doing. It would be a pity to forget that by being pioneers they had prepared the new lands for their Germanic and Slavonic brethren. The new Jews in the West have reaped where the others have sown.

NOTES

1. José Amador de los Rios, *op. cit.* vol III, chapter III.

2. There does not exist as yet a scholarly work on this most important topic of purity of blood. Any student of Spanish history and culture could if he wanted to, concoct a more or less plausible theory as to the origin of this monstrous social reality: *limpieza de sangre*. We have a guess at the riddle. Briefly (a) if the little anonymous people were the shaping agents of Spanish policy at the end of the XVth century.

(b) if the expulsion of the Jews brought peace to the land and the Inquisition succeeded in part in keeping the Conversos under control, then we know that

(c) the power and prestige of the Marranos did not seem to diminish, the further removed they were from professing Jews, the harder it was for the authorities to verify their origins;

(d) *Hidalguism* became the highest desideratum for all.

(e) Symbolic hidalguism without an economic basis would have been mere gesture.

(f) Something of a more coercive nature was needed...

(g) the envidious stigma of not being a *cristiano viejo* soon was found to be effective in humbling and degrading the proud hidalgos of Marrano origin.

For centuries the *limpieza de sangre* motif played a dissonant note in the Spanish ethnic composition. Valeriu Marcu, who is not an authentic scholar, in his most readable *The Expulsion of the Jews from Spain* (translated from the German by Moray Firth), New York, The Viking Press, 1935, devotes a whole chapter to the subject: *The Struggle for Purity of Blood* (pp. 86 - 102).

"La manía de *limpieza de sangre* llegó a un punto risible. Cabildos, Consejos, hermandades y gremios consignaron en sus estatutos la absoluta exclusión de todo individuo de estirpe judía, por remota que fuese. En este género, nada tan gracioso como el estatuto de los pedreros de Toledo, que eran casi todos mudéjares, y andaban escrupulizando en materia de limpieza. Esta intolerancia de los relapsos, fué en adelante semillero de rencores y venganzas, piedra de escándalo, elemento de discordia. Sólo el progreso de los tiempos pudo borrar esas odiosas distinciones en toda la Península. En Mallorca duran todavía." M. Menéndez y Pelayo, *Historia de los Heterodoxos;* reproduced in an anthology made of selections from his work: *Historia de España* (Seleccionada en la obra del maestro), Madrid, 1934, p. 128.

Cervantes satirized most deliciously the boasting connected with racial pretentiousness in his most delightful farce: *El Retablo de las Maravillas.*

Albert Sicroff, a former student of the writer, is now working on a doctoral dissertation on this subject under the direction of Marcel Bataillon of the Sorbonne. Bataillon's scholarship is so highly thought of, that anything approved by him would be reliable.

3. William H. Prescott, *The History of Ferdinand and Isabella, the Catholic.* (Edited by John Foster Kirk) Philadelphia, J. B. Lippincott Company, 1872, Vol I, p. 339, and Vol. II, Chapter XVII, pp. 134-151.

4. Américo Castro has boldly approached the subject of why Jews and Marranos were so vehemently disliked in XVth Century Spain. Zealously and desperately he attempts to dig deep into axiological causes. A few short quotations will hint at Castro's thesis.

"Iberia con Castilla por centro dinámico, una vez casi acabada la Reconquista se lanzó a la tarea colectiva con su desnuda espontaneidad..., sus armas fueron el ímpetu, el gusto por las actitudes, las utopías y los sueños. Con escasa atención para las razones, porque estas escinden al hombre en su interior y truncan su visión del mundo.

"No siendo de su voluntad y de sus creencias el español se creía seguro, y asi realizó creaciones de maravilla y eternidad casi siempre en "tempo" de tragedia. De ahí el despego por sus travesuras de la mente, la técnica—mécanica o intellectual—, que envilecé cuando se convierte en trabajo manual, y relega el puro ímpetu a lugar secundario." Pp. 93-94

"El exterminio de los hebreos y su secuela la Inquisición, no son fruto de la intolerancia de los reyes, sino un gran capítulo en la tenaz defensa del espíritu popular hispano, secundado por el rencor defensivo de muchos conversos." P. 95.

"La verdad es que, además de deicidas, los hebreos fueron para los cristianos unos testigos tan imprescindibles como enojosos ... La tragedia de Israel fué no haber desaparecido al haber dado vida a su retoño cristiano." P. 103.

Castro's impulsive enthusiasm and his anti-rationalism or supra-rationalism give rise to serious doubts as to how much credence one is willing to lend to his views and interpretations.

The above quotations in his *Aspectos del Vivir Hispánico,* Santiago de Chile, Editorial Cruz del Sur 1949.

On the presence of Marranos in religious orders see chapter in above work: "Conversos y Jerónimos." Originally part of *Lo hispanico y el erasmismo* in *Revista de Filología Hispanica,* Buenos Aires, (1941-1942).

5. Salomon Ben Verga, *Chebet Jehuda* (La Vara de Juda). Traducción española con un estudio preliminar por Franciso Cantera Burgos. Granada, Libreria López-Guevara, 1927 pp. 65-66. Compare the following with Castro's views:

"Jamás he visto que un hombre inteligente de verdad odie a los judíos. Solamente son odiados por el bajo pueblo. Y esto último tiene su razón justificante: el judío es soberbio y apetece siempre mando: no piensan que ellos son unos pobres desterrados y esclavos que andan echados de nación en nación; antes bien procuran presentarse como señores y gobernantes, y por eso el común del pueblo los aborrece...cuando los judíos entraron en nuestros dominios, venian como siervos y desterrados, vestidos de andrajos, y continuaron muchos años sin vestir trajes preciosos y sin mostrar deseo alguno de ensalzamiento sobre los demás. Y de aquel tiempo no ha podido escuchar nuestro señor que fueren inculpados los judíos de beber sangre (de cristianos); porque tal hecho, de haber ocurrido, hubiese sido consignado en las Crónicas de los reyes de España, según la recta y buena costumbre de consignar tales sucesos para enseñanza en lo futuro. Por lo que se ve que en aquel tiempo en que los judíos no despertaron la envidia del común del pueblo fueron queridos por éste....

"La segunda razón del odio a los judíos es porque éstos, cuando vinieron al reino de nuestro señor eran pobres y los cristianos estaban ricos y ahora sucede lo contrario; pues el judío es inteligente e ingenioso para conseguir su pro-

vecho, además de que se han enriquecido grandemente por las artes de la usura. Vea nuestro señor que las tres partes de los campos y heredades de España están en manos de los judíos, gracias a la onerosa usura que ejercían."
(The apocryphal King sees no wrong in the economic exploitation but...):
"Todavía creo yo que existe otra razón de tal odio: la gran diferencia que los separa de los cristianos en su comer y beber; pues no hay cosa que más aproxime los corazones de las gentes como la costumbre de comer unos con otros en igual trato íntimo."

6. Cecil Roth, *op. cit.* Chapter III. "The General Conversion in Portugal" pp. 55-73; in particular page 60.

See for a contemporary traveler's opinions on the Jews of Portugal at the end of the XVth century, Jerónimo Münzer, *Viaje por España y Portugal en los años* 1494 y 1495. Versión del Latín. Noticia preliminar y notas por Julio Puyol. Madrid, 1924, p. 110 (For the Latin text of this book, see *Revue Hispanique,* 1920. Here are Münzer's words "Los judíos de Lisboa poseen cuantiosísimas riquezas; son los receptores de los tributos que han arruinado al rey; muéstranse harto arrogantes con los cristianos y temen mucho al destierro, porque el rey de Castilla ha pedido al de Portugal que expulse a conversos y judíos o rompa con ellos las hostilidades. El monarca portugués imitando el ejemplo castellano ha mandado que antes de la fiesta de Navidad salgan de su reino todos los Conversos; ya les están embarcando en una hermosa nave llamada *Reina,* y antes de médiar diciembre saldrán rumbo a Nápoles. En cuanto a los judíos, el rey les ha dado término de dos años para que en este tiempo vayan saliendo ordenandamente de la tierra y en atención a ello, son numerosísimos los que cada día marchan a países extranjeros en busca de lugar y casa para establecerse."

7. Jacob Resnick (J. Ha-Rosin) *La Duc Joseph de Naxos. Contribution a l'Histoire Juive du XVIe siècle,* Paris, Libraire Lipschutz, 1936. p. 71. passim.

8. *Ibid.* p. 71

9. *Loc. cit.*

10. A. Lionel Isaacs, *The Jews of Majorca* (The First history of the Jews of Majorca ever published"), London, Methuen & Co., 1936.

The history of the Jews in the Balearic Islands is an anomalous one. Whereas all traces of Judaism disappeared from Peninsular Spain, yet the religious and social ostracism of the converts there has no parallel in any other section of the Hispanic world. Racially the converts known as *Chuetas* have been forced to live their own lives as Catholics without being admitted as equals by their fellow islanders. Even to this very day they are forced to seek wives and husbands in the Peninsula. All attempts to find out whether the *chuetas* have any living memory of their ancestral religion have failed.

"It is impossible to discover if any remains of Judaism still exist among the *chuetas* of Majorca. In Portugal families have been found in certain northern districts, descendants of the sixteenth century Jews, who secretly practiced a form of Judaism handed down through the centuries by oral tradition...In the course of time, it naturally became much changed and reformed, but the spirit was there, and those peasants guarded with tenacity and heroism the belief of their predecessors." (Lucien Wolf, *Report on the "Marranos" or Crypto-Jews of Portugal,* London, 1926; S. Schwartz. *Os Christáos Novos em Portugal no século XX,* 1925; also, in the *Menorah Journal,* XII (1926), pp. 138-149, 283-297).

"If anything similar exists in Majorca the secret is kept jealously, for all en-quiry, even the most discreet, produces a blank imperturbability. The descen-dants of the ancient converted Jews resent all inquiry and all questions. The usual reply is that they are Catholics, their parents were Catholics, and their grand-parents were Catholics, beyond that they know nothing." A. Lionel Isaacs, *op cit.,* pp. 212-213.

Vincente Blasco Ibáñez wrote a fine novel, *Los Muertos Mandan,* in which factually and imaginatively he presented a living account of the strange ex-istence of the Jewish-Catholics or Catholic Jews of Majorca. Their blood stream has changed but little during the centuries, yet in orthodoxy the chuetas are irreproachable. Gabriel Alomar, the fine essayist who lived in Majorca, told the writer of these notes (in 1924), that when it came to the question of defending them against the discrimination they suffered, the chuetas themselves were his worst enemies.

"Blasco Ibáñez, treating of the social status of the chuetas of Majorca, wrote as recently as the year 1908: "The ancient population of the island was divided into various social classes, isolated and unmixable. At the top were the *butifarras* ("Butifarra is a species of sausage; the nickname is applied to the highest Majorcan nobility in allusion to their stiff attitude and blown-up pride..."), the quintessence of arrogance; then the nobles, the *massoms,* a kind of intellectual middle-class comprised of lawyers, doctors, etc., and after them the shopkeepers, workmen, and countrymen who cultivated the land....'"

"Undoubtedly after those Majorcans, nobles and commoners, came in order of respect, the pigs, dogs, donkeys, cats and rats, and at the tail-end of all these animals of the Lord, the hated inhabitants of the Calle, the *chueta,* the cursed descendant of the Jews. This social order still exists. He who is of the *calle* must live and die with those of the *calle.* It matters not if he be rich or intelligent.... But the most extraordinary part of the hatred that continues in spite of modern progress is that the *chuetas* are not Israelites by religion, but

Catholics, and fanatic Catholics with a fervent and blind faith..." *Apud* A. Lionel Isaacs, ibid, p. 205. Another work on the same topic, B. Braunstein, *The Chuetas of Majorca: Conversos and the Inquisition of Majorca,* Scottsdale, Pa., 1936.

From an unpublished article *Los chuetas de Mallorca* sent to the author (February 8, 1936) from Palma de Mallorca by Sr. Francisco Aguiló we will extract a most interesting passage of the vituperative epithets applied to the Conversos of Mallorca. As far as it is known to us no one else has published anything similar on the subject.

"No tan sólo han sído llamados *chuetas* los descendientes de conversos, sino que aún, les han hechado (sic!) como expresiones de rencor varios apóstrofes:

Chueta que viene del catalán "chuya" era el epíteto más común usado para molestarles. Los cristianos no ignoraban que la carne y grasa de cerdo, *chuya,* es la carne vedada por la religión judía. Y ella es la misma expresión "marrano" en España, y el "schwein" alemán. De esta palabra hay la variación "chuetó" [Compare with A. Lionel Isaacs' explanation, op. cit. p. 191: "It was about this time (17th century) that the descendants of the conversos received the appelation of *chuetas,* or *chueytas,* which is derived from the word *Xuhita* or *Xuhueta,* meaning a little Jew applied as a term of contempt or derision (the letter X in Majorcan or Catalán, is pronounced *j*). A second, but incorrect, explanation of the origin of the word is from *chuya* meaning rind of pork, in allusion to the Jew's abstinence from the flesh of the pig; this name of derision still exists at the present day."]

De la calle. Asi fueron llamados por dos razones. Una por tomar apellido los conversos del siglo XV de personas cristianas muy conocidas. En Mallorca *des carrer* o de la calle, quiere decir, sin nombre, del arroyo. Y la otra por vivir retirados en varias calles, en casas de su propriedad, siguiendo reunidos remedando la Aljama, regida por los consejos de viejos sabios y prudentes.

Macabeus: En castellano Macabeos. A la vista salta que querían molestarles, al citarles los nombres gloriosos de la Historia Hebrea antigua: Los Macabeos. Por cierto que, con este título, a mitad del siglo XIX, aun corrían unas listas de apodos que cómo costumbres pueblerinas, se aplican apodos que llegan a ser más conocidos que el apellido mismo, *juen* o judío. Son el castellano judío o judía.

Melej: Este nombre que creo que quiere decir "rey" en hebreo era comúnmente empleado. Hoy es rara vez citado. *Codafet:* Ignoro el exacto significado y desconociendo si viene del hebreo, expongo gratuitamente, ni quisiera decir venal. Es conocido un pájaro en Mallorca parecido al gorrión, por el nombre de *codafet.* Como este animal vuela a trechos cortos se aplicaría a los conversos sus cortos vuelos, por sus presuntas herejías; cosa no siempre exacta!

Neo. Lanzada esta palabra para decir *"cobarde"* no quiere decir tal cosa, sino *nuevo.* Y por ello, podemos darle el mismo valor que converso.
Nuevo en religión. (May it not be cristiano nuevo)!
Final note from Sr. Aguiló: ¿Cómo responden a su pasado? Es fácil suponerlo. Tienen una tradición, pero no la practican. . . . Se hizo tan popular el reírse a sus barbas, con cualquier apodo de los citados que se han vuelto recelosos y desconfiados, cuando se les pregunta con insistencia: ¿Es Ud. judío? . . . La mayor parte de las veces contestan mal, creyéndolo ofensa, mas si se hacen amigos de ellos, algunos los encontrarán simpáticos y originales. No demuestran externa simpatía ni apatía por los turistas hebreos ni los conocen. *Es fácil conocer sus rasgos faciales; los de aquí con los de Turquía se complementan."*

Un dato curioso: En las elecciones del año 1933 españolas, en Mallorca, muchos de los que citamos votaron la coalición centro o izquierda por haber dicho, en un mitín, el Sr. Gil Robles: Hay que hacer una España nueva sin masones ni judíos.''

11. (a) For the Marranos in the Western world see C. Roth, op. cit., Chapter XI.

(b) Also consult Meyer Keyserling, *Christopher Columbus and the participation of the Jews in the Spanish and Portuguese discoveries.* Translated by Charles Gross, New York, 1894.

(c) Cecil Roth's book is of 1932 and since then two very important works have been published on the Carvajal clan of Mexico which contribute enormously to the history of the Marranos in Mexico during the 16th century: *Procesos de Luis de Carvajal (El Moxo)* (Publicaciones del Archivo General de la Nación, XXVIII.). México. Talleres Gráficos de la Nación, 1935, 357 pages, and Alfonso Toro, *La Familia Carvajal,* Estudio histórico sobre los judíos y la Inquisición de la Nueva España en el siglo XVI, basado en documentos originales y en su mayor parte inéditos, que se conservan en el Archivo General de la Nación de la Ciudad de México, México, D. F. Editorial Patria S. A. 1944, 2 vols.

Luis de Carvajal, *el mozo,* is perhaps the first Mexican mystic. His passion and zeal were expressed in deeply felt poems that now are considered worthy of being included in Mexican Anthologies of Verse. The poem we quote, in Alfonso Toro's work, Vol. I p. 333, reminds the student of Spanish literature of *A Cristo Crucificado.* Here is not the place to use the following poem for a study of the Marrano's anguished soul

> Pequé Señor, mas no porque he pecado
> de tu amor y clemencia me despido,
> temo según mi culpa ser punido,

y espero en tu bondad, ser perdonado
Recélome según me has aguardado
Ser por mi ingratitud aborrecido
Y hace mi pecado más crecido,
el ser tan digno tú de ser amado.
Si no fuera por tú, de mi qué fuera,
Y a mí de mí sin tí, quién me librara
Si tu mano la gracia no me diera
Y a no ser tú Señor, quién me sufriera,
Y a tí sin tí mi Dios quién me llevara.

12. For the Marranos in France see

(a) G. Cirot "Les Juifs de Bordeaux. Leur situation morale et sociale de 1500 á la révolution." *Revue Historique de Bordeaux,* II-XXXII (1909-39), 14 installments.

(b) Henry Léon, *Histoire des Juifs de Bayonne,* Paris, 1893.

Of major importance for the history of Western culture is the fact that Montaigne's mother was of Marrano origin. See A. Castro, *Aspectos del Vivir Hispánico,* pp. 156-157.

"La madre de Montaigne, Antonia López, pertenecía a la segunda generación de judíos en su forma esencial de vida. Esa familia López procedía de Aragón y se había enriquecido en Toulouse comerciando con plantas tintóreas. El padre de Montaigne tenía en alta estima a su mujer, y en su testamento la juzga capaz de administrar su hacienda. La acción de Antonia López en Montaigne debió ser muy efectiva, y junto a ella aprendería a conceder importancia a vivir sintiéndose y expresándose a sí mismo, porque eso es lo español."

Likewise see for documentation on subject Paul Courtault: "La mère de Montaigne," in *Mélanges de Littérature, d'Histoire et de Philologie* offerts á Paul Laumonier, Paris, 1935 page 311 ff.

13. Samuel Usque, *Consolaçam as Tribulacoens de Israel,* Ferrara. 1553.

14. For an extensive bibliography on the Jews of Holland, see Henry V. Besso, *Dramatic Literature of the Sephardic Jews of Amsterdam in the XVIIth and XVIIIth Centuries,* New York, Hispanic Institute, 1947, and Cecil Roth, *A Life of Menasseh Ben Israel: Rabbi, Printer, and Diplomat,* Philadelphia, The Jewish Publication Society of America, 1934.

15. Cecil Roth, *History of the Marranos,* Philadelphia, 1932, Chapter XII, *Some Marrano Worthies.*

16. Uriel da Costa, *Die Schriften des Uriel da Costa.* Edited and translated into German by C. Gebhardt, Amsterdam, 1922. Uriel da Costa's tragic autobiography was written in Latin: *Exemplar Humanae Vitae.* English translation by Whiston: *The Remarkable Life of Uriel Da Costa,* London, 1740.

17. Michael S. Molho, *Contribución a la Historia de Salonica,* 5692 - 1932 (In Judeo-Spanish, printed in Rashi characters).

18. F. B. Dexter ed., *The Literary Diary of Ezra Stiles,* New York, 1901, III, 14-25. June 8, 1782.

IV
Sepharad Ha Ghedola[1]

The Sephardim in the Near East

Without entering at this juncture into the reasons and diplomatic maneuvers[2] making the expulsion of the Jews in that most memorable of all memorable years in modern history, we shall again remind the reader of the migratory movements that forced the Sephardim[3] to leave the Spanish Peninsula at different times before and after 1492. Under the Visigoths many Jews left Spain because of unfavorable legislation against them. The most important exodus of Israelites in the twelfth century occurred in Islamic Andalusia under the menace of the Almohadic tribes from across the Straits. Families like that of Moses ben Maimon, after wandering in the Christian cities of the Peninsula, finally went to live in Fez, where they could not find an atmosphere of toleration. In the last section we analyzed in some detail the establishment of Sephardic communities after the religious riots and conversions of 1391. The most momentous date in modern Jewish history, if not in general Spanish history, was the expulsion of the Sephardic Jews from the land where they had lived uninterruptedly for more than a thousand years. Some historians have compared the departure to the exodus after the conquests of Palestine by the Babylonians and Romans in different epochs. The dispersal of the Spanish Jews affected the life of the exiles as well as the life of the peoples among whom they were soon to find themselves. We cannot here do more than touch upon the salient features of the settlements and colonies they established all over the world.

It took the Jews many years before they found places of refuge. Contrary to general belief, all the Sephardic Jews did not leave the Spanish Peninsula in that fateful year. Many devious schemes were attempted by them before they renounced the land of so many enthralling and heartbreaking memories. The Jewish evacuation was never complete, and consequently a reference to the distribution of the Jews from 1492 on is imperative. Attachments of all kinds, economic, social, intellectual, sentimental, obliged a large percentage to remain in the country by complying with the *sine qua non* provision, namely, conversion. To the Marranic elements were added new contingents in the eleventh hour. At first Navarra and Portugal seemed to be places of refuge. Soon the Jews were either expelled or forced to join the Christian faith. As for Portugal, about two thousand families had received the privilege of settling in that land. In round numbers, one hundred thousand Jews entered Portugal, too, believing they could induce the authorities to permit them to remain. Dynastic considerations, diplomatic motives, economic factors, ecclesiastical pressure, and other facts compelled the Jews to enter the Christian faith without the moral choice as in Castile of either departing as Jews or remaining as Catholics. Whereas in Portugal no Marranism had evolved in the fifteenth century as in Castile, soon in the absence of the Inquisition crypto-Judaism flourished strongly, and when the laws prohibiting emigration were modified, Portugal became both the source of Jewish migrations, and the depository of Marranos for the communities to be established by them in the sixteenth century, one or two generations after the Castilian and Aragonese Jews had formed their nuclei in Africa and in the Orient.

As will be shown in this section, the Jews who left Spain in 1492 and Portugal before and after 1506, were in the majority the representatives of what we choose to call the medieval Jew. On the whole they formed the rank and file of the Jewish masses. The alternative given and taken compelled them from the very beginning of their departure to adhere to the Mosaic community. As an act of their free will, they left because they were not wanted as Jews and they wished to remain Jews. The leadership belonged naturally to the spiritual heads of Spanish Judaism. Unsuccessful in their endeavor to have the edict of expulsion rescinded, the Rabbis said to their congregations: "Whatever befalls, let us surmount every calamity for the honor of our *nation* and our *religion* by a brave endurance...If they leave us our life, we will live; if they take it from us, we will die; but never let us violate our *holy law,* the fullness of our affections or the counsel of wisdom. Or rather...let us abandon our settlements, and seek for homes elsewhere."[4]

Purposely *nation, religion, holy law* were underlined to indicate how at the outset the medieval Jew left Spain with the determination to re-create communities dedicated to the Mosaic tradition. It did not take them long to join the Jewish nuclei already in existence in the lands of their unknown destination. True to the impulse that made them aban-don fatherland and hearth, they created the medieval Jewish theocracies of the the type they had had in Spain for centuries. But the theocracies established in cities of the Levant, in the absence of an encroaching, transforming, most vital culture foreign to the spirit of their traditions, became perfect types of their kind for the weal and woe of Sephardic Judaism. The point here suggested is important and needs elaboration. When they were in Spain, the culture of the land was not entirely alien to them. The Jews had been so profoundly moulded by that culture that they were daily participants in the richness it had to proffer.

Africa from 1391 on had definitely distinguishable Sephardic com-munities. The Arabic-speaking Jews from Granada were the first to leave Spain in the defeat of Boabdil. Lage numbers settled in Tunis, Al-giers, and other cities opposite the Straits of Gibraltar. Political condi-tions in Italy were unsettled. Big contingents lived temporarily in Naples, Genoa, Rome, and other cities. Sicily had a relatively large Jew-ish population, but Sicily being a Spanish possession, the Sicilian Jews likewise had to seek new lands. Turkey, successful in destroying Byzan-tium in the fifteenth century, encouraged immigration to populate the devastated regions in Macedonia, Thrace, and the territory around Constantinople, the Gallipoli peninsula, Adrianople, Rodosto, etc. By the first decade of the sixteenth century, Jews from Spain, Portugal, Provence, Sicily, and Italy had established themselves in numerous sec-tions of the Turkish Empire.

Where heretofore haziness existed about the creation of the Levan-tine communities by the Spanish Jews, we now have a coherent picture of the most successful Sephardic city, that of Salonica. Again and again references will be made to Salonica because its history is in the process of being written with the help of all the resources of modern scholarship.

Very appropriately we might review here the equipment and inherit-ance the Spanish Jews took along with them as they left the Peninsula. Our interest at this point is in the medieval Jew with tinctures of Ren-aissance culture.

Obviously their origins, languages, character, economic preparation, their religious and cultural achievements are some of the aspects that might be considered. "The Jews and Christians there lived together on terms of friendship and tolerance, unparalleled in Europe; regarded as aliens and treated as such, they were in many respects placed on an equal footing with their Christian neighbors. They enjoyed the favours of the kings and nobles; they were protected against undue violence and arbitrary oppressions by means of privileges and immunities granted to them from time to time. They formed an *imperium in imperio*. Within the walls of their Jewish quarter (aljama) they lived according to their own administration and managed their communal affairs. Their number in Spain at that time was greater than in any other country in Europe. Settled in towns, especially the great ones, employed in all kinds of trade, as well as money-lending and mortgage transactions, many of them acquired considerable wealth and power. They became the owners of extensive estates and landed property."[5] Though Rabbi Epstein has in mind the Hispano-Jewish world of the fourteenth century, what he says in the above quotation also applies rather accurately to the Spanish Jews up to the time of the expulsion, notwithstanding the civil war in the fifteenth century and the growth of crypto-Judaism. The processes of Hispanization were accelerated in the subsequent century to such an extent that in every hamlet, village, town, city, throughout the length and breadth of the Peninsula, Jews were to be found in small or large numbers. Jewish writers for example were born in the following localities:[6]

Alba de Tormes	Calahorra	León	Monzón
Alcolea	Calatayud	Lérida	Murcia
Alcalâ de Hena-	Córdoba	Lorca	Ocaña
res	Carrión	Lucena	Pamplona
Albazón	Coimba	Lunel	Peñafiel
Arévalo	Denia	Mâlaga	Ronda
Avila	Daroca	Maqueda	Sevilla
Baena	Gerona	Medina Celi	Soria
Barcelona	Granada	Medina del Campo	Tarragona
Béjar	Guadalajara	Monreal	Toledo
Briviesca	Illescas	Montalbân	Tolosa
Burgos	Jaén	Montilla	Tordesillas

Tudela	Valencia	Zaragoza
Ucles	Valladoid	

Once in foreign territory, nostalgic for the Peninsular names which had a powerful attraction for them, they designated their synagogues and their communities by them. Salonica which at one time had over thirty synagogues boasted such names as Castile, Aragón, Portugal, Catalonia, Evora, Lisbon, etc. And family names of Nájera, Toledano, Alcalai, Sevilla, Lorca, Mallorca, Burgos, Carmona, León, Medina del Campo, Tudela, etc., pointed to the Peninsular origins of those families.

What gives cohesion and character to a people is its language. Its language admirably reflects, in turn, the dominant traits of the people who use the language. When we come to the case of the Spanish Jews, we find that the most precious possession they took with them in their exile was the two or three main languages of the Peninsula with a variety of less extensive dialects. Without exception the Castilian modality of the romance languages of Spain triumphed in less than fifty years on foreign soil, among the medieval Jews as well as among the Renaissance Jews. As yet scholars have not taken the trouble to point out in detail the features distinguishing the Spanish of the Jews prior to 1492. A sensitive writer like Joseph Nehama is under the impression that the Spanish spoken at Salonica in the sixteenth century was a language free of admixtures and in general rather pure. Because a man like Almosnino wrote faultless Spanish, and because some university-trained Marranos settled in the Orient in that century, the inference is innocently made that a Spanish of the same texture and grain as that spoken in the cultivated circles of Spain was current at Salonica. The failure to distinguish the Marrano Jew from the medieval Jew gives rise to this confusion. Were we to adhere to this view entertained by Nehama and others, we would not understand why Levantine Spanish came to be so archaic.[7]

The Jews of the Peninsula, it must be borne in mind, were not Hispanized; did not enter the heritage of Romania *at once*. After the Arabic conquest, most of the Jews lived under Islamic rule. Poor and insignificant Jewish communities existed, however, in remote León in the ninth and tenth centuries.[8] With the Reconquest more and more Jews came under Christian domination. The Castilian-Leonese capture of Toledo in the eighties of the eleventh century signalizes the beginning of the wide and deep Hispanization of the Jews. The fact that the Toledan Judah Halevy, in the eleventh and early twelfth century, wrote in Arabic and Hebrew shows how slowly the Jews were acquiring the unhewn and uncouth idiom offered them by their new masters.[9] A symbolical significance can be seen in the presence of Jews, Moors, and Christians in the first literary monument of Castilian culture, the *Poema de Mio Cid*.[10] The author of *Disciplina Clericals*, Pedro Alfonso, had Alfonso I of Aragón for his godfather when he was baptized.

By the middle of the thirteenth century all of Spain with the exception of a small strip of land around Granada in the south was under Christian rule. As hinted above, the persecution of the Jews under the Almohades in the twelfth century had made the Andalusian Jews penetrate in large numbers the Western, Central, and Northern lands under the rule of Castile, Portugal, and Aragón. By the fourteenth century the Jews were so neo-Latinized that they were compelled to follow the Holy Scriptures at home and at the synagogue with the help of translations in Castilian and Catalan,[11] and perhaps in other dialects such as Aragonese.

> In the fourteenth century the Book of Esther was read on Purim in Spanish from a translation for the pleasure of the women, in various parts of Spain. The rigorous purist, Isaac ben Sheshet, was scandalized to find this custom in force at Saragossa, when in the middle of the fourteenth century, he was appointed Rabbi to that congregation. Local Rabbis were more complacent than the new arrival, who set himself with the aid of Nessim Gerundi to crush the custom which had been in existence for a third of a century.[12]

Further evidences of a progressive Hispanization of the Peninsula Jews can be attested by the participation of the Sephardim in many literary undertakings. At the school of translators started in the twelfth century under the patronage of the Primate Rodrigo, in Toledo, many Jews were engaged in translating Arabic works into Latin. Alfonso the Learned in the thirteenth century employed for his encyclopedic ambitions many Jews who helped in translating this time Hebrew and Arabic books into Castilian, the idiom of which he supervised and corrected. The first literary triumph of the Hispanized Jews was the highly praised poet Sem Tob de Carrión.

Independently of the literary activities of the medieval Spanish Jews and apart from the complete assimilation of Castilian culture by the converts, there soon developed a liturgical and domestic form of Spanish among the Jews that remained with them for centuries. It has already been said that the language of the Bible of the House of the Duke of Alba is more archaic than the corresponding literary expression of contemporaries of Rabbi Moses of Guadalfajara. That Bible was finished in the first third of the fifteenth century. From internal and other evidence we conclude that the Jews had oral translations and perhaps manuscript redactions in the fourteenth century. The language of liturgical anthologies, such as the Spanish translations found in the Prayer Book of the Oriental Sephardic Congregation or in the Passover books, etc., was very much older than the dialect spoken. In the fifteenth century, as soon as printing was introduced into Spain, the Jews began to print their works. On the authority of Professor Salo Baron of Columbia University, it can here be stated that over forty Hebrew incunabulae came off the presses before the edict of expulsion. To judge by a document of the Inquisition, a Jewish master-printer, who sold his books in Andalusia though he printed them in Castile, by the eighties of the fifteenth century had already printed a prayer book in *romance* or in Spanish which his daughters at least made use of.[13] Knowing as we do the nature of the translations that have survived, we may be certain that the Marranos must have adhered, too, to the archaic versions then current.

From Babylonian times at least, Jews have been in the habit of translating the languages of the countries where they happened to dwell, besides their national tongue, in Hebrew characters. This tradition was transferred to the composition of letters, documents, treaties, and literary works in the languages of the Peninsula.[14] The Statutes of the Jewish Castilian communities that met at Valladolid in 1432 were redacted in Hebrew characters, the languages used being Hebrew and Castilian.[15]

> "Le document est écrit en caractères hebreus et dans une langue ou l'hebreu l'espagnol se mêlent constamment et forment la plus singuliere mosaique. Il ne faudrait pas s'imaginer que ce fut la langue courante des Juifs espagnols; dans la conversation ils mettaient, surements beaucoup moins d'hebreu. Cette langue est une espèce de langue litteraire, si l'on peut s'exprimer ainsi, c'est le style de la chancellerie juive..."[16]

In the Peninsula, then, there began with the gradual incorporation of the Jewish aljamas under Castilian control the development of a language among the Jews that differed considerably from that spoken and written by their Christian contemporaries. Linguistic differentiations seem always to have existed in the vernacular spoken by the Jews when compared with those of the Gentiles whose mother tongue they had learned for all purposes. In intonation, vocabulary, sentence structure, semantics, the Castilian, say, of the Jews of Toledo, differed from that of the non-Jewish Toledans in all these respects. Out of this account must necessarily be omitted those ever-growing sections of the Jewish communities who, through conversion, intermarriage, and close contact with the secular life of Spanish society, were being thoroughly assimilated. Who knows but that the Marranos might not for generations have liberated themselves from those linguistic differentiating elements? According to Professor Van Praag, the Dutch of the Castilian and Portuguese Jews still differs from the autochthonous modulation.[17]

The phonological range of the Jews was more extensive than that of the Spaniards, irrespective of localities. From the Arabic-speaking regions of Spain, they brought to Castile modulations of voice, a certain repertory of sounds, and modes of thinking foreign to the central and northern Iberian language habits. The deformations, transformations of sound that occurred were transmitted. Certain quirks of Arabic expression were translated into Spanish. Bilingual habits of speech so far apart as Arabic and Castilian were the result. In order not to complicate the discussion more than necessary, the reader must remember that the Jews while living in Arabic-speaking Córdoba continued with their Hebraic tradition which overlapped or went beyond Arabic-Moorish culture. The Jews of Toledo then had really three sets of language habits for many decades: Hebraic, Arabic, Castilian. Many motives prompted the Toledan Jews to conserve Arabic. They dropped it in time, but their retaining two sets of language habits in the meanwhile caused their Castilian to suffer changes.[18]

Since the Jews were surrounded by danger and pressure of all kinds, the Arabic and Hebrew expressions could be used as a defense mechanism: as a secretive language for communication among coreligionists. Another fundamental cause tending to give the Jews a Spanish that was different is to be found in their religious needs and customs. Their pattern of life, particularly at home and at the synagogue, gave the Jews a distinctive culture. That culture expressed itself in gestures, celebrations, and in song and speech. Dietary laws, culinary traditions in the different festivals, and the corresponding nomenclature; the utensils at home, the objects at the synagogue, and the spiritual references peculiarly Hebraic, demanded a technical language in the vernacular. Religion being conservative, translations of Holy Scriptures and selections from the great poets of the Sephardic schools were handed down without changes from generation to generation. No attempt was made to have the old language keep up with the linguistic changes through which the Castilian language was going. Besides, the translations were literal versions of the Hebrew; and there was no desire to use the evolving Castilian syntax. Here are two examples as remembered by the author from his boyhood. One is a stanza rendered in a cantilatory fashion, coming from the famous poem on the story of Esther as interpreted by Judah Halevy:

> Echó mano en el goral espandió
> y vido que en *Adar* murió
> Padre de la ley,
> y no se acodró que era la hora del nacer,
> Dolores de la que pare, vengan a él.[19]

The other is from the Seder ceremony on Passover eve:

> Siervos fuimos a *Paró* en *Ayifto*
> y sacónos *Adonay* de allí,
> con poder fuerte y con brazo tendido.
> Y si nos sacara, el Santo Bendicho Él
> A nuestros padres de Ayifto
> *Aínda,* nos y nuestros hijos,
> hijos de nuestros hijos,
> *sujeftos* éramos a Paró en Ayifto
> y *afilu* todos nos sabios,
> todos nos entendidos etc.[20]

The Castilians of the fifteenth century were aware of the Spanish spoken by the Jews having a flavor and an emphasis all its own. Many a wag satirically expressed the feeling of strangeness by interpolating in his own poems some of the Hebrew expressions current in the vocabulary of the Jews. Here are a few verses of the famous poet of the century, Alvares de Villa Sandino, written in a mocking tone against Alfonso Ferranded Semuel, "el mas donoso loco que ovo en el mundo":

Ffase su testamentario
Para cumplir todo aquesto
Un judío de buen gesto
Que llaman Jacob Cidaryo,
Al qual manda ssu sudario
En señal de *cedaquá*
Porque rreze *tefylá*
Desque fuere en su fonsario.[21]

Indubitably the greatest cultural inheritance which the Sephardim brought with them was the language of Castile. It is needless to repeat here what has been stated and suggested already, namely, that the Jews of Castile, for example, had two forms of the Spanish language, one for domestic and synagogal usage, and the other, more contemporaneous, for communication with the non-Jews at the market place and in social contacts. There was no uniformity in their speech when they left, as there is none in the Castilian spoken even today, despite all the leveling processes of modern times. But the Castilian language, in spite of all regional differences, had enough unity to give it a distinctive cohesion and a conquering power, due to the achievements in the literary field in the Middle Ages and its pushing power looking to the future. Gonzalo de Illescas in his *Historia pontifical* (Barcelona, 1606, p. 106) remembers having seen Peninsular Jews in his travels.

Pasaron muchos a Constantinopla, Salónica o Tessalonica, el Cairo, y a Berbería. *Llevaron de acá nuestra lengua,* y todavía la guardan y usan della de buena gana, y es cierto que en las ciudades de Salónica, Constantinopla, *y en el Cairo y en otras ciudades de contratacion y en Venecia no compran, ni venden, ni negocian en otra lengua sino en español.* Y yo conocí en Venecia judíos de Salónica hartos que hablaban castellano, con ser bien mozos, tan bien y mejor que yo.

Gonzalo de Illescas might have spoken to Salonician Jews of Marranic origin, and even if they were descendants of the medieval category the fact that they were in Venice made them free of the theocratic environment and enabled them to be influenced more readily by the renovated Castilian of the sixteenth century as spoken by the Marranos and the Spaniards sojourning in Italy. Perhaps we shall never know to a nicety the exact stage attained by the speech of the Sephardim in the sixteenth century. If we judge retrospectively we find that the speech of Morocco has retained a resiliency and purity putting to shame the Balkanized dialects of the Levantine Jews. Within the Levantine area we find two large sections, the speech of the region around Constantinople and the speech of Salonica and its environs. Isolated communities like Monastir present a form of speech much more archaic than that of Salonica or Constantinople.[22]

Now we enter another phase of the Sephardic dispersion. For the above-mentioned reasons, Salonica became the prototype of the Sephardic community. On account of its depopulation Salonica was chosen as a place of refuge. From Pauline times and even earlier, there had been Jews in Salonica. When Salonica fell into the possession of the Turks, the Greek population was almost annihilated. Landing at Salonica, the struggling families arriving in 1492 found there small communities of Greek-speaking Jews, Yiddish-speaking Jews, and even a community of Catalan-speaking Jews from the Balearic Islands. It did not take long for the word to fly proclaiming the attractiveness and quietude of Salonica.[23] Unceasingly ripples and waves of the Sephardic immigration beat upon the shores of the Salonician gulf. Had the Peninsular Jews been quiescent and conforming they would have accepted the law and customs of the resident Jews. Their particularisms, their Iberic recalcitrance to strict discipline, their tendency to form small nuclei, asserted themselves, giving rise to the the creation of communities characterized by their separatism and independence. In brief, the Peninsular Jews formed separate units almost self-sufficient. Round their synagogues they had their schools, their libraries in some instances and the various societies for the care of the poor, the sick, and the dead. One example from many will suffice to show the Iberic tendency to disintegrate.

"The Aragonese and the Catalonians, although they travelled together, did not mingle at all with each other. From the very beginning they separated into two communities, very different from each other. The Aragonese who had lived in the interior of Spain were adherents of the past, traditionalists, suspicious of their independence, rights, and privileges, and at the same time instinctively domineering, proud to excess, on the border of stubbornness, often sulky, cold, self-centered, sombre, and almost taciturn, rough in their manners, of an exaggerated circumspection and of a rugged and meticulous honesty. The Aragonese were little prone to exert much effort and little inclined to work; indeed they were lazy and apathetic. The Catalonians, on the other hand, were a people from the seacoast, alert and mobile, friends of novelty, gay, communicative, of smooth and polished manners, of vivid intelligence, penetrating in their enterprises, self-willed in their projects; the Catalonians were all activity, exuberant in their vitality. Skillful in their work, the Jews hailing from Barcelona, from Gerona, from Tarragona, and from the Valencian coasts, were hard workers, unrelenting in their industry. *Los Catalanes de las piedras sacán panes,* the Catalonians are capable of getting bread out of the very stones. And as they were, despite all that, refined people, cultured conversationalists, good dialecticians, they were not wrong in recalling in their behalf the praise-giving proverb current among Spaniards: *El aire de Cataluña agudece,* the air of Catalonia makes one nimble-minded.

A few families came together from Galicia and established themselves on the *cortijos* of the poor; cortijos that joined each other in a row. They were simple folk, unmannerly, ignorant, long-suffering, and sober. Accustomed to servile conditions, they were disciplined and willing even to fulfill voluntarily the humblest, lowest types of work. Their rural dialect, rich in gutturals and nasals, is akin to Portuguese. They spoke loud and had great difficulty in being understood by the Castilians, Aragonese and Catalonians. A distant echo of the difficulty which they experienced at the beginning in making themselves understood is found in the popular saying still in circulation in Salonica: *Somos Gallegos non nos entendemos.* The Gallegos were not numerous enough to form a community of their own. A little while after their arrival they were assimilated with the immigrants from Lisbon whom they most resembled linguistically."[24]

To their fellow Jews in Safed, Tetuan, Sofia, Damascus, Salonica, Adrianople, and in scores of other cities, the Peninsular Jews presented a compactness, a homogeneity due to their manners, behavior, gesticulation, and psychological traits that was a source of admiration, fear and emulation. And this external appearance was an all-conquering force nothwithstanding the obvious existence of clashing heterogeneous elements among the Peninsulars. A French traveller who saw them sympathetically and studied them closely said: "Ils ont tant de difficultéz entreux et de schismes que plusieurs sont d'opinion contraire les uns aux autres."[25] Their secular and religious superiority over the African Jews, over the Mesopotamian Jews, over the Byzantine Jews, over the Germanic Jews was so great that in two or three generations they were capable of overwhelming them by their sheer worth. The first reaction of the native Jews to the Peninsular Jews was expressed in their efforts to print their traditional book of prayers and communal regulations. The various synagogues or communities known as Romania,

Ashkenaz, Castile, Catalonia, Aragon, Italy, published their *Mahzors* or prayer books, but it was love's labor lost. Professor Idelsohn, the great authority on Jewish music studied from original documents the clashes and conflicts of the various Jewish communities trying to free themselves of the Sephardim. Translating freely, we get this imposing picture of what finally transpired:

> In this struggle the Castilian modality won and it was then that the Sephardim showed their superiority over the native Jews in culture, intelligence, and numbers, especially in the Balkan communities and in the north of the Turkish Empire. At Plevna there were three small communities, Sephardic, Germanic, Hungarian, the last two were assimilated by the Sephardic Jews, in the same fashion as in Nicopolis, Vidin, Belgrade. About 1620 there were a Greek-speaking, a Sephardic, a Germanic, and a Hungarian Jewish community. Soon they merged with the Sephardic. At Angora there was a Castilian and a Portuguese community; in Magnesia there were three: Toledo, Shalom (Peace), and Lorca; at Patras, a Greek, a Sicilian, a Sephardic, and a Polish one; at Tricola there was a Greek, a Sephardic, and a Sicilian; at Orto there·were four: Corfu, Calabria, Puglia, and Sicily, and in Lefantes there were a Greek, a Sicilian, and a Sephardic community. All these gradually incorporated themselves with the Sephardic community. At Salonica the community of the Greek-speaking Jews joined the Sephardim about 1570. "And the Jewish world submits to the Sephardic rite because the Sephardic constitute the majority in this kingdom, and their liturgical rite is beautiful and rich, and that is why all or the majority give up their own ritual and join the Sephardim, only the Ashkenazic community conserves its ritual" (Responsa 34 of Samuel de Medina del Campo).[26]

Culturally speaking the linguistic triumph of the Castilian tongue was the most significant happening that occurred in the transplanted Hispanic world. Ritual triumphs after all did not alter the Jewish religion. Except for pronunciation, liturgical reading matter, marriage contractual customs, procedures followed at the slaughtering houses to determine the acceptability of the animal slaughtered, communal administrative schemes, the *Sephardization* of the native Jews did not go very far or deep in the transformation of the religion which they all professed. The universal elements of Judaism remained all binding and unchanged. But when it came to the language habits of the natives the changes effected by the triumph of the Castilian tongue introduced unaccountable phenomena. Why should Spanish have triumphed over the Peninsular dialects and over Sicilian, Italian, Provenzal, Yiddish,

Greek, Arabic, etc.? The prestige of Castile could not exercise any in-fluence in those remote communities. No governmental power, no rul-ing class forced it upon the non-Hispanic Jews. Still more, no economic advantages forced the issue. Because Professor Nehama has caught the spirit and significance of the triumph of Castilian Spanish and because his felicitous language expresses most adequately this phenomenon we give this rather long quotation which deserves immortality:

The Triumph of the Castilian Language in Salonica

"Soon the Castilians give the tone to everything, extending to the whole population their customs and their manners. This task is rather easy for them. They are by and large the most numerous, and exert over all the activities of life considerable influence. After all who is there to question their superiority? These haughty hidalgos are at home in all the sciences. Splendidly generous, employing gestures befitting aristocrats, they have lived in the surroundings of the Court and of the grandees of Spain, and they have kept the sentiments and manners of those sur-roundings. Often they themselves have worn the cape and sword of the hidalgo and have occupied the highest positions. They enjoyed emoluments and prestige. They look down upon people and are trained in the art of leadership. Imbued with the sentiment of honor arising out of the feudal aristocracy of Spain, they are courteous, brave, scrupulous in keeping their pledged word, and persevering in their undertakings. The contrast between them and the others is most apparent. Aragonese, Catalonians, Majorcans, all bow before their superiority and permit themselves to be eclipsed. The Portuguese themselves, in their great ma-jority of Castilian origin, though rich and cultivated, are the last persons on earth to deny a supremacy which they share. Italians, Sicilians, Calabrians, Apulians, resist somewhat. They try to counteract that in-fluence. The people from Otranto, above all, are proud of their own ancestry. For a long time they marry only in their own group and meticulously observe their own customs.

The people who delay most in yielding are the Ashkenazic Jews. They do not mingle with the Sephardic Jews; they do not marry the daughters of Sephardic Jews who are denied to them, anyhow, as if they were of another race. Sephardic and Ashkenazic Jews do not eat at the same table; the former do not eat the meals prepared by the latter and vice ver-sa because they consider the others' meats impure and they would there-fore be committing a sin in indulging. Customs, prayers, liturgy, every-thing differentiates them. The Sephardic Jew looks haughtily down upon this poor, small Jew from the North; the latter accustomed to wretched-ness and oppression as he is, effaces himself, humbles himself to avoid conflict; this type had always lived walled in, with doors and windows closed to the outer world, in the *Judengassen,* in a hirsute isolation, removed from all social contacts, from the possibility of forming friendships with the non-Jews; this Eastern European Jew, harassed and hounded, lived here and there like a very nomad, ready always to pick up his knapsack and his wanderer's staff.

In his turn the Ashkenazic Jew looks upon the Sephardic Jew with suspicion. He does not question his superiority but regards him as a kind of non-believer. He does not wish to be subjugated, he chafes and grumbles. After ten centuries of separation these brethren in Israel have stopped acknowledging each other. Their encounter does not occur without friction. They are not far from considering each other strangers.

On all these disparate elements, upon these Greeks, these Italians, the natives of Provence, these Portuguese, and these Germanic Jews, the speech of Castile imposes itself as the official language. Among themselves the people of the same origins use their own regional dialect. The Byzantine Jews speaks Greek; the Ashkenazic Jew, Yiddish; the exiles from France, Provençal. The true Italians persistently speak Italian in their homes and in their temples because they read and write their native language in the texts redacted in Latin characters, and their intellectual formation is often of a high order. Thus, in 1512, the Calabrians renounced the ministry of the famous rabbi, Jacob ben Habib who had founded their congregation, in order to have a preacher in the Italian tongue,—David Messer Leon, son of the celebrated physician and rabbi, Judah Yahiel Messer Leon, of Naples (1450-1490), an Aristotelian philosopher, who was besides one of the most perfect Latin scholars of his time.

But above the dialects and the jargons dominates the Castilian language, known by the majority of these men, almost all of them cultured and often remarkably well versed in Belles Lettres.

For communal acts, for announcements, for sermons, for business transactions, for the interrelationship among the people of the different provinces, they have recourse to Castilian. Even the Greeks and the Turks of the city learn it and make use of it voluntarily as a kind of *Volpuk* in their contacts with the Jews.

The haughty Castilians contemplate this rapid triumph with great pleasure. Is there in the whole world, according to their view, a more harmonious and more noble language than theirs? Castilian enjoys the highest prestige in all Spain where a cohort of writers and scholars, encouraged by the princes, have raised it to literary dignity. The Sephardic Jews who are to spread in a period of one hundred and fifty years over all the vital points of the earth adopt it as in Salonica. It is thus that Tunis, Nice, Amsterdam, London, Hamburg were to conserve the Spanish of Castile for a long time as a living relic of the lost fatherland..."

(Joseph Nehama, *Histoire des Israélites de Salonique,* Tome II, *La Communauté Séfaradite* Période d'Installation (1492-1536, pp: 39-41)[27]

We wish we could claim for our ancestors greater deeds, more glories, than they actually achieved in the African and Levantine worlds where they found themselves. Belittling is as much a form of exaggeration as boasting, as Tartarin de Tarascon's sad experience proved. The medieval Jew did much that deserves recording. Hebraic literature as was to be expected flourished for a whole century. Spanish culture was so much in the blood of the Sephardim that they went so far as to trans- late into Hebrew the popular novel of the day *Amadis de Gaula,* and the first modern work of genius in the Castilian language *La Celestina.*[28] Unquestionably the most enduring contribution to Western civilization made by the orthodox Jews of Spain was the *Dialogues of Love* by Judah Abrabanel, a book so seminal that through its three Spanish translations it had the privilege of fertilizing the finest genius of the Golden Age of Spanish literature. Very rich bibliography exists on the subject. It would prolong our analysis unduly to say anything other than that the Abrabanels were encouraged to produce in behalf of civil culture because they were in Italy. More we need not say.[29] Italy in some respects was so liberal that the Abrabanels could lead very cultured lives within orthodox Judaism. Had the Jews of the Levant had a propitious ambient, they too would have been induced to give fruits of their genius to realms of the spirit other than religious. So far no work, if ever printed in Spanish written in Latin characters, has survived among the Hispano-Levantine Jews.[30]

Orthodox Sephardism can show with pride the extraordinary attain- ments of the Abrabanels and can even be indulgent toward their family pride claiming direct lineal descent from King David. Isaac Abrabanel was a rabbi of the first water, a scholar of no mean order, and a diplo- mat and financier besides, having had access in Portugal, Spain, Italy, to the highest circles. His two sons, Judah and Samuel, were worthy of their illustrious father. Refinement and culture were the heirlooms of these children. Still more amazing however was the presence of Sephar- dic women who were the equal if not superior to the unusual feminine types of the Renaissance.

"De más que el señor don Semuel Abravanel era dotado de excelentes virtudes como habemos dicho, fué venturoso en tener por compañera una de las más nobles y generosas matronas que hubo en Israel despues de nuestros esparzimientos; tal era la señora doña Benvenida Abrabanela; dechado de honestidad, de piedad, de prudencia y valor... Mientras que estubo en Napoles, siendo alli Visrey don Pedro de Toledo, quiso que su hija doña Leonor de Toledo, se criase debaxo de la disciplina de la señora Benvenida, y en su casa, y despues que casó con el Serenisimo gran Duque Cosmo de Medices, y vino a ser gran Duqueza de la Toscana, siempre en sus casas se valía de la señora Benvenida que habitaba en Ferrara, a quien llamaba madre y como a tal la trataba y veneraba."[31]

The Abrabanels, in brief, combined the best features of medieval and Renaissance Sephardic Judaism: by their Hebrew culture, their familiarity with and attainments in the vernacular of Portugal, Spain, Italy, their material successes, their training in finance and diplomacy, their good fortune in having educated women in their midst, their unswerving devotion to Judaism and their Jewish brethren; by these traits and by their dedication to the highest values, the Abrabanels epitomized the glories of Sephardism.

"Wo immer eine aufblühende Stadt entstand findet sich gleich eine Jüdische Gemeinde".[32] The Jews who went to Turkey did not only seek a place of refuge; true to their commercial instincts they chose that country because there the opportunities for material well-being were as favorable 'as for the exercise of their religious ways. Two French travelers, Pierre Belon and Nicolas de Nicolay, both connected with the Foreign Office of France, visited Turkey about the middle of the sixteenth century, at the time when Turkey was a formidable empire, challenging the Mediterranean hegemony of the Italian states and of Spain particularly. Both of them accompanied ambassadors to Constantinople when France was attempting to use the Ottoman Empire as a counterbalancing force against the Spanish Empire. It is appropriate to mention here that there were no Jews in France in the sixteenth century other than the neo-Christians scattered here and there and a small contingent in Avignon. In the absence of first-hand information about the Jews, it is remarkable how accurately these highly polished Frenchmen recorded some of the outstanding features of the Hispanic Jews in the Ottoman Empire. The Marranic dispersion had already begun by the time they visited the Near East, and whatever they put down is ambiguous for our thesis but very illuminating in all other respects. Uppermost in the minds of these "Scholar-spies" was the economic activity of the Jews in Turkey. Gold and silver, for example, had begun to shake the financial status of Europe; what has come to be known as the Price Revolution had begun to transform the structure of European economy.[33] Pierre Belon made a special trip to the gold mine exploited by Sephardic Jews at Siderocapsa. Spain was uppermost in his thoughts as he described the mining processes of Siderocapsa which was not very far from Salonica. France and other countries, say England, were anxious to find new sources of wealth.[34] "Les ouvriers metallaires qui y besongnent maintenant sont pour la plus part de nation Bulgare. Les paisants des villages circonvoisins qui viennent au marche, sont chrestiens et parlent la langue servienne et Grecque. *Les Juifs en cas pareil y sont si bien multipliez qu'ils on fairt que la langue Espaignolle y est quasi commune: et parlants les uns aux autres, ne parlent autre langage.*"[35] Still more astonishing is what he tells us about the mines being idle on Saturday.[36] The Hebraic tradition in religion and the Spanish language as a commercial instrument are the two outstanding facts about the Sephardic exploitation of the mines at Siderocapsa.

Less sympathetic to the Jews was Nicolas de Nicolay, "lord of Arfeuile, chamberlain and geographer in ordinary to the king of France." Discounting the distorting perspective he took, we get some valuable information from him.

"The number of the Jews throughout all the cities of Turkey and Greece and principally at Constantinople is so great that it is a thing marvellous and incredible; for the number of these, using trade and traffice, of merchandise, like money and usury, doth there multiply so from day to day that the bringing of merchandises which arrive there from all parts, as well by sea as by land, is such that it may be said with good reason that at this present day they have in their hands the most and greatest traffic of merchandise and ready money that is in all the Levant. And likewise the shops and warehouses, the best furnished with all sorts of rich merchandise, which are in Constantinople, are those of the Jews.

"Likewise they have amongst them workmen of all arts and handicrafts most excellent, and especially of the *Maranes,* of late banished and driven out of Spain and Portugal, who to the great detriment and damage of Christianity have taught the Turks divers inventions, crafts, and engines of war, as to make artillery, harquebuses, gun-powder, shot and other ammunition; they have also there set up printing, not before seen in those countries, by which, in fair characters, they put in light divers books in divers languages, as Greek, Latin, Italian, Spanish, and the Hebrew tongue: they have also the commodity and usage to speak and understand all other sorts of languages used in the Levant; which serveth them greatly for the communication and traffice which they have with other strange nations to whom oftentimes they serve for dragueman or interpreters."[37]

The geographer and chamberlain to the king of France, notwithstanding his prejudices, was very much interested, as a feudal lord, in the economic role played by the Jews. They were the agents of international trade, dealers in goods from all over, the intermediaries between the local merchants and the traveling salesmen from abroad. From other sources we know they were, as in Spain, for the Turkish government farmers of taxes and other fiscal transactions.[38] Money, fast becoming the sinew of modern trade, sustained them. Merchandise, the concretion of commercial values, passed through their hands with greatest of ease. Skill in foreign tongues was at their fingertips, as it were, because both international trade and the heterogeneous demographic conditions of the Near East demanded it. As a diplomat he saw very acutely into the contributions made by Hispanic Jewry. Gunpowder transformed medieval warfare. The Marranos brought knowledge and skills in the making of instruments of war and ammunition and put them at the disposal of Turkey. There might be some miscalculation in the import of these contributions, but that they were of considerable significance is attested by their being referred to again and again by many other observers. Some of the things mentioned by Nicolas de Nicolay can be checked up. The introduction of printing is proved by the books that have survived. The Jews who brought presses from the Peninsula, such as Guedalia, and from Italy, such as the Soncinos, printed Hebrew books and Spanish works in Rashi characters in various cities, Salonica, Constantinople, Safed, etc. Pierre Belon besides confirming his fellow countryman's analysis supplies us with more details. Medicine and the trade in drugs were a practical Jewish monopoly. As good physicians the Jews relied on empirical knowledge and were weak in theory. This was the fact even two generations after their arrival. Often, however, doctors trained at Salamanca and Coimbra went to Turkey. The most illustrious example was that of Amatus Lusitanus, alias Joao Rodriguez de Castel-Branco, who at the end of his life went to Salonica and there died.[39] Jews owned slaves too, and to judge by what Christians have reported about their treatment of their slaves, they were considerate and kindly. Piracy was the blight of the Mediterranean routes. At Venice, Salonica, and other Sephardic communities, societies existed for the ransoming of Jewish slaves. Their being slave owners was one of the compensations for their own sad fate of being slaves in turn.

Passing allusion has already been made to the existence of various communal centres in the Levant established by the Sephardic Jews in conjunction with their other Mediterranean brethren. The triumph of the Castilian tongue and the usages that prevailed in Castile have been examined. When it comes to the economic activities of the Peninsular Jews and the Sephardized coreligionists, the evidence of their importance is obtained from European travelers. The sixteenth century being what it was, the germinal knowledge of geography and anthropology in currency precluded any thorough understanding of foreign peoples on the part of diplomats and their aides. Men like Pierre Belon and Nicolas de Nicolay could not be expected to be in a position fully to describe the life of the Jews. Even with all the good will in the world, yet they could not examine closely the Jewish communities, and they had many other things to occupy their attention as they entered the kaleidoscopic world of the Near East. Other sources have to be consulted if an approximate picture is to be drawn of the Sephardic Jews in that most vital of centuries, the sixteenth. Diplomatic documents relating to the economic activities of the Jews in Belgium, Venice, Turkey, have in recent years been recovered. Aside from these letters, treaties, and correspondence on matters of state, the *Answers and Questions,* the *Responsa,* or the *Consultations* of the Rabbis (all these terms apply to the same authoritative statement of opinion), are now the great mine whence all kinds of facts, details, and ideas may be obtained on the life of the Sephardim. Furthermore, the ordinances passed by the Jewish Communities of the Near East, known as *ascamoth,*[40] supply very much needed information on the internal organization of those microcosmic units.

By the help of these documentary sources we now have a more satisfactory idea of many phases of Sephardic life. We cannot in this historical examination avoid recognizing the existence and functioning of minute states within the larger state of Turkey. Moses de Almosnino denominated his native city the *Republica de Salonique.* Taken literally *Republic* suggests a civil government independent of monarchical and ecclesiastical authority. In this sense Salonica was not a republic. A government must have the last word in ultimate decisions; that is what sovereignty amounts to. Likewise in this sense Salonica was not a republic. Excluding these two limitations: the exercise of supreme sovereign rights and freedom from kingship and church, then Salonica was a society extraordinarily compact and self sufficient. If we may coin a new word, we might say that Salonica was an *ascamatarchy* or an *ascamotocracy*. An ascamotocracy is a Jewish community ruled by freely elected officials who run the affairs of their society in conjunction with rabbinical authorities. The latter govern that society according to Jewish law, the source of which is the Talmud and books of codes derived from the Bible and the Talmud. Through the issuance of decrees or ordinances the community comes to have an inner organization which attends to all the affairs of Synagogue, Talmud Torah, the home, and the market place. All phases of life are regulated. In our day and age we feel the lack of a planned society. *Laissez-faire* has brought as much bad as good in its trail and we fear lest a collapse of our world may ensue. Many have been the suggestions and practices in recent years to bind us into a coherent body, realizing as we must that our spiritual needs cannot be divorced from our material urgencies. Whatever the outcome of the new legislation may be, so far as our study is concerned one thing is positive, and that is that the ascamotocracy of Salonica in the sixteenth century, true to the mercantilism of the age, created a body of laws which regulated the commercial and industrial activities of that city.[41] Weaving of woolen cloth became the chief industry in Salonica, and to judge by the technical terms used, such as *telar, batanero, tundidor, prensador, manteo, ropero*,[42] etc., scholars conclude that the weaving industry was brought over from Spain. By the middle of that century Salonica made an agreement with the Turkish government to pay the collective taxes owed in cloth goods. This provision, in effect for over two centuries and a half, provided a special reason for further *ascamotal* legislation. Salonica had a proletariat made up chiefly of weavers. Looms were even run by the synagogue to supply the sufficient number of rolls of goods each year to be delivered to the Turkish authorities, who used them for uniforms for the Janissaries. The wool industry was a complicated industry connected with other branches of economic activity, such as dyeing, tailoring, etc.

To protect the wool-trade the rabbis sharpen their wits, to perform miracles through the means of legislative inventions. They multiply the ascamoth in order to regulate all the details relating to the cloth business. They prevent outbidding in the purchase of raw wool, put a brake to over-production, do away with sales at a loss, and stop the lowering of prices. The authors and works of the time swarm with juridical and economic considerations relating to the innumerable depositions arrived at to deal with the effects of heedless competition in the manufacturing and sale of cloths. The jurisprudence formed by the ascamoth promulgated with this view in mind, and some of which go back to the very start of the establishment of the exiled Jews from Spain, is one of the most complete and closely knitted that rabbinical activity has ever produced in the city of Salonica.[43]

The ascamoth or ordinances on the woolen and dyeing industry show clearly how well united were the Jews of the sixteenth century in everything they undertook. After the World War, everywhere in Europe and in the United States, acute housing problems arose making us realize the discomfort and exploitation that go hand in hand with overcrowding and rampantly insolent landlordism. From very early days the rabbis of the West were cognizant of housing problems. Under Rabbi Duran in Africa ascamoth were passed to protect the tenant. Through religious sanctioning the tenant was protected by endowing him with the right of occupancy in contradistinction to the right of possession by the owner of house or store occupied by a Jew. This extraordinary privilege is known under the name of *hazakah*. In Italy the term hazakah was translated as *Jus gasaqa*. The hazakah or the right of preferential tenancy was transmissible: children could receive it as a legacy or dowry.[44] As long as rent was paid, eviction was impossible. As soon as the Sephardim arrived at Salonica, they promulgated and renewed often the *ascamoth* on *hazakah*.[45] The provisions were on the whole obeyed because they all understood the protection they received from this rabbinical legislation on housing. The Sephardic communities had their *Beth Din* or religious courts. Conflicts and quarrels were settled at the Jewish Court of Justice where judgments were given practically free of charge, there being no expense attached in the way of lawyers' fees and other legalistic paraphernalia requiring payment. The recalcitrant was made to obey by all kinds of social pressure. Punishment of supreme rigor was in the form of excommunication. The ceremonies in the synagogues when anathema was pronounced upon the disobedient were awe-inspiring and terrifying. Biblical and Zoharic imprecations were formulated in the ascamoth to imbue the faithful with the sense of awe. Considering that the sovereign power lay with the Turkish authorities, we are amazed at the great success achieved by the medieval communities in conducting their *ascamotal* form of government.[46]

It has been said that the diplomatic archives of the chancelleries of Europe have been consulted for possible information on the role played by the Jews in the sixteenth century. A great amount of documents are now available. On the credit page of Sephardic culture in the sixteenth century must be recorded: the Bible of Ferrara, published by Abraham Usque; the *Dialogues of Love* of Leon Hebreo; the printing of the *Zohar;* the compilation of the Jewish code by Joseph Caro known as the Shulhan Aruh; Safedic mysticism; Moses Almosnino's *Regimento de la vida;* and the extraordinary adventures in finance and diplomacy of Don Joseph Nassi.[47] It is particularly on Joseph Nassi that we possess documents in Turkish, French, Spanish, and Hebrew. His historical role was unique and extraordinary. Many governments sought his help and others endeavored to undermine his prestige for good. Success and failure characterized their diplomatic moves.

It is our suspicion that the Sephardic Jews were most productive in the sixteenth century because they came from a country burgeoning with creative sap and entered a region under the domination of a Power at the zenith of its conquests. Italy was the point of intersection where the conflicting forces in peace as in war balanced one another. In the germ plasm of the Sephardim were the vitality of Spain, the energy of Turkey as a nourishing force, and the propitious climatic surroundings of Italy. Disregarding the metaphor, the reality of the interconnection of Spain, Turkey, Italy, is exemplified fully in the life and works of the Mendez family. The Mendez were bankers who had branches at Antwerp, Lyons, Venice, Constantinople, etc. Natives of Spain, Francesco Mendez in Portugal and Diego Mendez in Antwerp were international financiers who made loans to Charles V and the King of France. The death of the brothers made Doña Gracia, wife of Francesco, head of the firm. Bienvenida Abravanel was a fine type of a matron in Israel. Doña Gracia or Beatrice de Luna, the other name by which she was known, is the first business woman in modern Europe, a worthy contemporary of Catherine de Medici.[48]

As might have been surmised, the Mendez were Marranos. When Doña Gracia began to have difficulties in Portugal, she transferred herself, her daughter and her relations to Antwerp, far away from the electrified religious atmosphere of Portugal. In Belgium her daughter became the cause for Don Francesco Aguilar to promise a loan to Charles V on condition that he intervene in his behalf and get Doña Gracia's consent to his marriage proposal. Rumors circulated throughout Antwerp that John Miguez, a nephew of Doña Gracia, had eloped with his cousin. Whatever truth behind this rumor, the Mendez were soon living in Venice. Brianda de Luna, sister to Doña Gracia, denounced her as a crypto-Jewess. Brianda's agents in turn betrayed their mistress to the ecclesiastical authorities. As a consequence the wealth of the Mendez ran the danger of confiscation, and the reconciled sisters might have suffered punishments by the Holy Office if, in the meanwhile, Don Joseph Nassi, alias John Miguez, had not gone to Constantinople and there through letters of recommendation from the French ambassador and help from Dr. Amon,[49] chief physician to the Sultan, obtained the cooperation of the Sublime Porte on behalf of his family. For diplomatic reasons the Venetian authorities released the two sisters and returned their wealth to them. After some peregrinations in Italy, the Mendez family reached Constantinople in pomp.

> Un dia una señora portuguesa que se llamaba doña Beatriz Mendez muy rica entró en Constantinopla con cuarenta caballos y cuatro carros triunfales, llenos de damas y criados españoles. La gran señora habia estipulado desde Venecia con el gran Turco, que permitiera a todos sus criados no traer tocados como los otros judíos, sino gorras y vestidos a la veneciana; y luego doña Beatriz dejó con todo su cortejo el mal impuesto cristianismo y mudó su nombre por el de 'Doña Gracia de Luna'. No tenía más que una hija, a quien daba de dote 300,000 ducados y tras estos fuese, l'año siguiente de 1554, un sobrino de la señora fastuoso tambien, diestro en armas y bien leido; y hay pocos hombres de cuenta en España, Italia, y Flandes que no le conociesen y llamabase don Juan Micas; circuncidióse, después vino con su prima y mudó el nombre por el de Josef Nasi. Los gentiles hombres suyos, uno se ponia don Samuel, otro don Abraham, y otro Salomon.[50]

Under Selim II, Don Joseph Nassi excited and frightened the chancelleries of Europe by his manoeuvers. The French government had to endure humility when, through his intervention, French merchantmen were detained at Turkish ports and their cargoes confiscated as retaliatory measures for the refusal of the French to acknowledge their debt to the house of Mendez. The excuse made for the refusal was that the Mendez turned out to be Jews and, according to the law of the times, the government had a right to get possession of the wealth belonging to a renegade. Joseph Nassi was made Duke of Naxos. His power benefited his fellow Jews in Turkey and elsewhere. He was instrumental in proclaiming the first economic boycott of modern times against the city of Ancona where some Marranos had to pay the last penalty for, their crypto-Judaism. Within Oriental Judaism there was no consensus on the advisability of continuing the boycott. Economic interests and conflicting trends of thought made the boycott a partial success. Some rabbinical authorities were of the opinion that the condition of the Jews would worsen by the economic warfare started by the Levantine cities. The city of Tiberias was conceded for Jewish settlement to Don Joseph Nassi. The fine wools of Spain were imported, for some time, for cloth weaving on Spanish looms. These deeds and activities of Joseph Nassi illustrate, in concentrated form, the interlinkage of Western Europe and the Near East through the mediation of Italy.

Inextricably textured with the economic life of the communities were the spiritual pursuits of the deracinated Jews, to which the foreigner did not have any access. Aside from the usual studies of Bible and Talmud in the great Yeshivahs of Salonica and of the other communities, the Peninsular Jews in the sixteenth century were going through very exciting mystical and messianic experiences which heightened and deepened their lives. The roots of their mystical explorations, like many of their other spiritual possessions, are found in the subsoil of Spain.

Spiritually speaking Sephardic Jewry developed various currents of thought during five centuries of creative activity. Rabbinical Judaism through custom and law, festival, sanctification, inculcated encouragement, succeeded in preserving the aljama in a well-knit structure. On account of the philosophical challenge of Aristotelian philosophy in Arabic-speaking Spain, men like Judah Halevy restated the position of orthodoxy in books like *Al Kusari*. Judaism without national aspirations had always been inconceivable. Dreams and hopes mystically fused in a tense nature produced the awe-inspiring Zionistic poetry of Judah Halevy. The overwhelming genius of Maimonides injected into rabbinical Judaism the fermenting germs of rationalism. So overpowering was Maimonidean rationalism that Judaism became fraught with danger because the life-giving irrational elements of the Mosaic tradition were slighted. There were two forces of reaction. Rabbis like Salomon Ben Adereth, recognizing the dangers of Aristotelianism as enemies of faith, decreed against the study of Aristotle before the age of thirty or thereabouts.[51] Divisions and clashes ensued between the followers of Maimonides and the arch-orthodox. Many dreaded the disruption of Judaism. With the compilation and composition of one of the greatest books in Israel, namely, *The Zohar*[52], developed a compensatory reaction to rationalistic Judaism in Spain. There have been many doubts concerning the origin of this mysterious book. Moses de Leon's claims have been disputed. Regardless of the pros and cons, one thing is certain, and that is that there was no Zohar before the Castilian rabbi issued the book in the thirteenth century, and nothing like it has appeared in Israel ever since. Two centuries of existence made the book circulate throughout the Jewish world. There were many copies, and groups appeared in the Jewish communities for probing into its arcana. The Sephardic expulsion caused the book to travel far and wide. Once published in the Orient, the Zohar became the most esteemed possession of Jewry. Rabbinical adherence to the Talmud, to the legislative provision of Jewish law was not weakened in the Sephardic Diaspora. On the contrary, the urgent necessity for agreements on the government of the communities made interest in the codes primary. Theocratic rule held great sway in the Sephardic nuclei, and no theocracy could be run without canon law. Canon law in the Jewish religion corresponded to the rabbinical legislative enactments. The genius of Sephardic Jewry reached its sublime heights in *The Shulhan Aruh,* the code of laws produced through an unusual organizing mind like that of Joseph Caro.[53]

Concurrent with interest in the Jewish codes we find in the Sephardic Mediterranean world an accelerated and all-transforming absorption in the mystical mode of existence. Perhaps not since the days of Philo in Alexandria was mysticism so popular, so widespread, and so consequential as in the sixteenth century among the Sephardic Jews. Eastern Jewry has known in the form of Hassidism, a popular folkish mysticism that sweetened life and ennobled sentiments. But prestige and universality were denied to Hassidism. Sephardic mysticism on the other hand became all embracing. The elite and the masses, the rabbis and the workers, Ashkenazic and Sephardic geniuses, poets, Talmudists, all were drawn into the mystic realm. As in the case of the Spanish mystics like St. Theresa of Jesus and St. John of the Cross, Sephardic mysticism was harmoniously combined with unimpeachable orthodox purity. Joseph Caro, the creator of the greatest code of Rabbinical law, was a student and devotee of the *Zohar*.[54]

The *Zohar* is a Sephardic creation not only because it was cradled in the mystic tradition of Jewish-Arabic and Christian Spain, but also because in its pages the Sephardic exiles found depth, consolation, and great promise in the strange lands where they established their homes.

> And even as the exiles from Judea took the Bible as the treasure of all the wealth that had been theirs in the Holy Land, so, too, did the exiles from Spain take the Zohar as their capital for the dark days ahead of them. And even as the Bible and the Talmud proved adequate for the exiles in helping them to withstand the destructive forces that threatened the Jew on every hand, so, too, did the Zohar prove adequate in saving the Sephardic groups in the various countries to which they were obliged to readjust themselves from falling into the pit of despair.[55]

The wonder of wonders in Sephardic mysticism was the creation of a mystic city, a unique abode for the seekers of God through intuition and ecstasy. Salonica in the sixteenth century was a perfect theocracy. Safed in upper Galilee was the City of God. Perhaps it was a mere coincidence that mystic Safed should have been at its zenith in the very years when the Peninsular geniuses were seeking God through action, prayer, meditation, mystical union with God. The coincidence of such close parallelism between mystic Avila and mystic Safed would not be possible without a common source. Sephardic mystics and Spanish mystics had one undeniable bond at least. Both were heirs of medieval religion as nurtured in the Peninsula. Sephardic tradition triumphed in the Mediterranean Basin on the strength of its greatness. Of equal significance was the immediate spread of the *Zohar* and of the mode of life recommended by the believers in esoteric secrets. Safed is to be credited to the Peninsular inheritance of the Sephardic Jews.

> Ever since the destruction of the national center in Jerusalem the genius of the people aspired to create for itself a dwelling place, as a gathering focus and organizing center, where it could develop its spiritual values, whence as in the form of rays could reach all the communities of the splendid body of the folk, that they might be illuminated, encouraged, taught, and be fused into a mystical unity.

Safed became this energizing and unifying center. Just as Salonica was preferred by Sephardic Jews because it was excluded from the centers of strife, so Safed was chosen because it was most distant from populous cities, Sephardic Jewry deliberately looked to this city on the hills of Palestine. Even in the nineteenth century it was still hard to reach.

The road up to Safed is as bad as anything called a road could be—a steep climb of two hours over sharp stones, among tall weeds and briars, —but it is cheered by a background view of the lake Tiberias, which seems to be nearer and nearer as you leave it behind, until at Safed it looks from end to end right under your eye. The situation of this town is superb, commanding from the ruined citadel a full view of the lake, a fine prospect of the Mediterranean, and a glance of Meron, the upper lake of the Jordan, about five miles long and three broad, and some ten miles north of Tiberias.[56]

Only the sensitive soul can enter into the secret of the God-intoxicated mystics. Ariel Bension, a descendant of the Judeo-Spanish mystics, true to the inheritance was able to understand their ways. Of this sacred city he wrote:

For Safed, apart from its clear and healthy air, had a special attraction for the mystics. It was very close to the little village of Meron, which was both the birthplace and the tomb of the hero of the Zohar, Simeon ben Yochai. And Safed became the center of this Jewish mysticism. Safed became the legendary city of signs and wonders. Safed, we are told, has a special sort of air which helps men to grasp the secret mysteries with greater ease than anywhere else...And there arose a center that was high in the culture and in moral value, and from which went forth creations that enriched mankind's spiritual treasure, not only in the hidden mystical teachings but also in the revealed truths, to which men adhered.[57]

Safed became a city of Sephardic saints and scholars. As in other cities to which they migrated there was awaiting them at Safed a more or less developed Jewish communal group.

Their numbers were so increased that they considered themselves strong enough to attempt to force their special usages with regard to the regulating of dowries upon other sections of the community. *The Spanish language, the vernacular of the Sephardim became soon the teaching medium in the schools, suppressing all other languages.* They quickly won, both by their numbers and by the distinction of their leaders, such an exceptional position that we find men of importance and standing among the native Jewish population vain enough to call themselves Sephardim, the name common to Jews hailing from Spain and Portugal.[58]

Numerous motives prompted the Sephardic Jews to go to Safed. Some have been mentioned: proximity of Safed to the birthplace and deathplace of the father of Jewish mysticism; remoteness of Safed from danger spots in the Near East; healthy climate of that city in the hills of upper Galilee. Notwithstanding its inaccessibility, Safed was within the circuit of the trade routes. It could be reached by sea from the port of Sidon, and Damascus was not far away. Seclusion did not prevent Safed from becoming a commercial and industrial center. It must not be thought of as a city of refugees escaping from the world. Judaism is inimical to the transcendentalism of Oriental religions like those found in India. Anchored in reality, Jewish mysticism had to deal with family life, with synagogal practices, with the demands and duties of economic transactions. Talmudic tradition encouraged occupation in trade for the sages if they would give themselves to study and meditation. Sephardic Zoharism was no exception. The late professor Schechter claimed that never in the history of Judaism since the Destruction of the Temple, had a more diversified galaxy of scholars, mystics, saints, legists, and God-fearing men in Israel lived in the same locality as could be found in sixteenth century Safed. But their achievements in study and in exercises toward perfection did not make them look askance upon work.

> None among them was ashamed to go to the well and draw water and carry home the pitcher on his shoulders, or go to the market to buy bread, oil, and vegetables, all the work in the house was done by them.[59]

We now know more than generalities about the economic life of Safed. Safed grew from an insignificant village into a booming town of thirty thousand people by the beginning of the seventeenth century. Schools and colleges sprang up. Above every other economic activity, the trades connected with the production of clothing engaged most of the Jewish workers:

> Trade in Safed was based mostly on the manufacturing of clothing. Not only was the garment prepared in Safed: cutting, sewing, but all the other necessary skills: including spinning, weaving, dyeing of the materials

were carried on in Safed. There were spinners, weavers, fullers, shearers, dyers, cutters. *The Spanish exiles who came to Safed brought with them the art of weaving wool and sewing clothing, till gradually this occupation became a Jewish occupation in all the lands of Turkey.*[60]

A very significant story is told of a Jewish rabbi who was a clothing manufacturer in Safed. The towering personality of the mystic Luria made the pious in upper Galilee tremble and despair of ever attaining perfection. One day the rabbi-clothier asked Luria whether he could detect any revelation of imperfection in the features of his face. Luria reluctantly admonished the pious rabbi for not scrupulously following the precepts of justice. The rabbi, alarmed at this warning, called his factory hands together and implored them to express any complaints they might have. Only a woman worker asked to be paid more for her work.[61] Thus work and worship went hand in hand in Safed.

What particularly characterized Safed was its population of men determined to purify themselves, and through their immaculate lives in accordance with the teaching of the *Zohar,* help to save the world in spite of its discord from going to pieces.

> ...the impression the Safed of the sixteenth century leaves on us is that of a revival camp in permanence constituted of penitents gathered from all parts of the world. Life practically meant for them an opportunity to be only occasionally interrupted by such minor considerations as the providing of a livelihood for their families and the procuring of the necessary taxes for the government. Prayer was the main and universal occupation.[62]

With prayer went other practices of a purgative nature. Purgation took all forms. Moses de Cordovero, the most fertile commentator on the *Zohar,* author of *The Garden* in which he gives a very clear analysis of Cabbalistic mysticism, recommended among many other things meetings among the pious for discussing spiritual matters and for receiving and giving accounts of a confessional nature. It is a well-known phenomenon that accentuation of mysticism within the frame of orthodox religion begets usually lyrical prose and lyrical verse. Santa Teresa's prose is as melodic as a Gregorian chant and soars similarly toward the heavens. The poems of St. John of the Cross are the hymneal outpourings of a transfigured heart. In Safed Jewish mysticism produced some of the finest poems in Hebrew ever written since the Golden Age of the

Andalusian and Castilian poets of Israel. The orthodox nature of Safedic mysticism is proved by the fact that some of the hymns composed in Safed have been accepted by the Ashkenazic and Sephardic communities for their prayer books. One poem immortalized in that way is the hymn sung on the Sabbath, *Leha Dodi*.[63] Written in Hebrew, this Sephardic song, following the millenial tradition of personifying the Sabbath, compares the day of rest with a bride and Israel with the bridegroom going to meet her. Solomon Halevi Alcabez caught the yearnings of Israel, superbly imbuing his composition with the incandescence of the Safed landscape. Israel Najara was the poet who incorporated the mystic tradition of Safed into a popular poetry discarding the archaic modes adhered to by other poets. He brought as a singer a lyrical sensuousness to his hymns which made them suspect of worldliness. In 1579 Safed was attacked by an Arabic tribe. Israel de Najara left, with his family, for Gauhar, a small town near Damascus. The fertility and luxuriant vegetation of Gauhar so influenced Najara as to make his poetry romantically erotic. Professor Israel Davidson, of the Jewish Theological Seminary, has collected over a thousand poems by Najara (or attributed to him). Najara interests us not only as the last great poet of the Sephardic Hebraic tradition but also as a composer of Hebrew hymns modelled after Greek, Turkish, Arabic, and Spanish poems.[64]

Safed, the holy city of work and worship, was the focus of mysticism, it was the center of learning and poetical creativity as well. The Greek-speaking Jews at Salonica and Constantinople were encouraged to explore the realm of culture. The Yemenite Jews at Safed through example and precept were similarly inspired toward literary activity. Unlike Hispanic mysticism, Safedic mysticism had another dimension making for heroism, agitation, and dismal failure from a practical point of view. The Sephardic diaspora was such a vital experience that it awakened dormant aspirations for messianic redemption. Israel receives its dynamics because it feels incomplete. The Messiah as an imminent actuality becomes a compelling force at various times. Catholic mysticism emphasized the individual, personal perfection and the fruits of a pure life in good deeds. Jewish mysticism also emphasizing purification and charity was carried away by the messianic hopes aroused by visionaries cropping up everywhere. Zoharic speculation had as such no political repercussions. Messianism however acquired

momentum from the time David Reubeni and Solomon Molho started
to spread the tidings of the Redeemer's coming till the glorified
preaching of Sabbetay Sevi and his ignominious failure in the seventeenth century. Diego Pires, a Marrano Jew from Portugal, under the
influence of the Ethiopian Reubeni, circumcized himself and changed
his name from Pires to Molho and traveled to the Sephardic communities of the Near East. Joseph Caro, the level-headed codifier, had a
tremendous love for this Marrano visionary who tried to hasten the
coming of the Messiah. Handsome and persuasive, he was so forgetful
of self and personal safety that he scorned to spare his life by recanting.
Molho courted martyrdom, and indeed, in 1532, he was burned at Mantua for being a relapsed Catholic. In the Sephardic world messianism
and mysticism fused together.

Sephardic Contacts with Spain

The synthetic review of the Sephardic inheritance given thus far com-
prehended the language equipment, the institutional plans developed on
foreign soil, the economic techniques and activities begun in the Peninsula and elaborated abroad, the cultural achievements in Italy and the
Levant, and finally the Zoharic and messianic mysticism blooming at
Safed. All these indicate the depth and extent of the spiritual wealth of
the Spanish Jews when they commenced their migrations from Spain.
Superficial knowledge of the Sephardic Jews and their history has made
many believe that the Jews broke off completely with the Peninsula in
1492. The recognition of the Marranic dispersal as a continous exodus,
at one time in small numbers and at another time in larger contingents,
covering a period of over two hundred years, has made us see that the
African and Levantine communities were not isolated from Spain. A
large body of rabbinical legislation at Salonica dealt with levirate marriages. According to Mosaic law, as is well known, a widow left without
children was bound to marry her brother-in-law to carry on the family
tradition of the deceased. Think in this connection of Henry VIII of
England marrying Catherine of Aragon. Only through a certain
ceremony harking back to Biblical times could the widow be freed of
this obligation of her husband's family. Many women in Salonica
found themselves in an ambiguous situation, since their brothers-in-law
were presumably Catholics living abroad in Spain or America. The rab-

bis had therefore to decide upon the advisability or inadvisability of freeing the widows so they might marry without the consent of their husbands' brothers.[65] Venice had a Ponentine and a Levantine community which cooperated many times on problems of mutual interest, such as the ransoming of slaves. Men like Nicolas de Nicolay and Pierre Belon and others had called attention to the presence of Marranos in Constantinople and Salonica. The arrival in Turkey of the Mendez, as described in the *Viaje de Turquía* can supersede many pages of historical reconstruction: We know definitely that for decades the influx of Marranos considerably increased the Sephardic population in the Near East. However meager their influence may have been in matters of language, certainly in other matters, such as folklore, they brought many new specimens of the latest creations. The messianic-mad Marrano, Solomon Molho[66] lived a few years in the Hispano-Levantine communities where he was initiated into Cabbalistic traditions. Visits like that of Molho, shorter or longer in duration, must have been common from the first century of the Expulsion. The Ancona boycott[67] mobilized the Marranos and the medieval Jews in the middle of the sixteenth century. Venice, upon becoming the center of Sephardic printing, supplied the book needs of the Peninsular Diaspora without regard to individual origins. Commercial dealings on a large scale as carried on by the Marrano Jews included transactions with parts of the Turkish Empire. For more than a century Western and Levantine Jewry met constantly. Sephardic Jews who had for generations lived in Turkey travelled to the cities of Italy for business purposes. They traveled also to Austria and even further West, enjoying in many cases immunities and privileges as Turkish subjects denied their Ashkenazic coreligionists.[68] In Venice they were treated with a great deal of considerateness, and in the eighteenth century, when native Jews were excluded from the Austrian capital, they were allowed to live in Vienna. The Marranic communities continuously were renovated by the arrival of new refugees from Spain, their cultural status was consequently more or less of the same level as that in the Peninsula. The contacts possible between the Hispano-Levantine Jews and the Marrano Jews enabled them to share, to a small extent, in the evolved and modernized Spanish language.

Although the Marranos regarded themselves as of hidalgo stock and so in a civil sense different from their medieval brethren, yet in religious matters they considered themselves inseparable from the Sephardic

traditions as cultivated and preserved among the Hispano-Leva
communities. Referring to the rabbis of the Orient, Imanuel Aboab, of
Marranic extraction himself, acknowledges them as the leaders of
Israel, of Sephardic Israel.

> Ahora nos toca dezir como sobre todos sus discípulos floreció el
> eminente señor Rabenu Joseph Caro, el qual sucedió en su lugar (i.e., of
> Jacob Berab, the chief rabbi of Safed) y fue Ros Yesiba, o general
> maestro de *nuestra gente*...*Gobernonos* siempre con mucha prudencia,
> severidad y amor; y era de todos amado como padre universal.[69]

Even with the establishment of communities in the North of Europe,
their sense of belonging to the brethren in the Near East did not entirely
leave them for some time. Sabbatian messianism shook the Jews of
Amsterdam as well as the Marranos of the Christian world as much if
not more than their Sephardic coreligionists in Morocco, Macedonia,
Mesopotamia, and Asia Minor.[70] A careful study of the synagogal
minutes of congregations like those at Amsterdam, Saint Esprit,
Bordeaux,[71] Hamburg, New York, Newport, Philadelphia, Curaçao,
Surinam, Jamaica, Barbados, etc., would reveal that appeals for money
either through letters or through specially designated messengers were
complied with for the relief of distress and poverty among the Hispano-
Levantine Jews. Many institutions have bound together the discrete
Jewish nuclei scattered throughout the world. The messenger, or
shalliah,[72] who is sent to the communities of Universal Israel, has been
an institution for many centuries. Whoever has lived in a small Jewish
community abroad has known the reverence and esteem bestowed upon
this bearded stranger who, hailing from the Holy Land, equipped with
bona fide documents as credentials, solicits funds in the name of God.
He is usually invited to the homes of the *Ghebirim,* or the eminent
members of the congregation. He was expected to deliver a sermon on
the Sabbath.

There is on record the coming of these *shelihim,* or messengers from
the Holy Land, to the English colonies in America in the eighteenth century. The oldest synagogue in the United States, Shearith Israel (The
Remnant of Israel) in New York, did not fail to lodge and shelter many
a shalliah, and probably never permitted the messenger to leave without
a generous contribution from the Sephardic merchants.[73] Mordecai M.
Noah, who at one time wanted to solve the Jewish problem by creating

settlements of his brethren in this country, gave as a good argument for favoring these messengers, the services rendered by Palestinian Jewry in preserving the continuous attachment of Israel to the Holy Land. "The pious attachment of the resident Jews of the Holy Land gives them the highest claim on our charity and protection"[74]. Ezra Stiles, who knew the Jews of Newport very well, has left a vivid description of a remarkable *shalliah* in his diary. This messenger, Rabbi Isaac Hayim Carigal,[75] travelled all over the Sephardic world. Born in Hebron, a town in Palestine, into a rabbinical household, he was the heir to orthodoxy, piety, good breeding, and great learning. From Ezra Stiles we learn that Carigal was a Sephardic scholar, versed in the old and modern languages. From his attire we conclude that he was a genuine representative of Sephardic Palestinian Jewry. True to the tradition of the *shalliahate,* he came for money to be used among the needy. Bringing credentials from other Sephardic communities, he was respected and honored by the Jews of Newport and New York, and consulted on many matters pertaining to Jewish lore and law. He enjoyed the honor of seeing the sermon he delivered in Spanish translated into English, on the holy day of the Pentecost, 1773, and published in Newport the same year.[76] Men like Carigal undoubtedly brushed up on their Spanish before facing the Marranic communities in Italy, France, Holland, England, the Carribean Islands, and the English colonies. How much the *shalliah* took back with him in terms of Hispanic culture to spread among his Hispano-Levantine coreligionists is very hard to say, but certainly some influence must have been exerted by the institution of the *shalliahate.*[77]

The Sephardic world maintained some form of unity and cohesion for more than two centuries. This cohesion and unity was effectuated through immigration, commercial transactions, residence on the part of Hispano-Levantine Jews in Marranic communities: through the incorporation of Marrano Jews into the nuclei of the Near East, in Palestinian cities, in Aleppo, Damascus; and elsewhere; through the circulation of Hebrew books; through the engagement of Afro-Levantine Sephardic rabbis for the Western cities; through cooperative activities among the medieval and Renaissance Sephardim for the purpose of ransoming slaves, helping the destitute and the orphaned, and providing dowries for poor girls of Israel; and finally through the travelling *shalliah*. This analysis makes one fundamental idea stand out; namely, the unity of Sephardic Jewry in matters of religion, philanthropy, mysticism, and messianism. Admission of this unity does not in any way damage our contention that culturally speaking the Jews of the minute theocracies in the Near East differed substantially from the Jews who had gone through the Catholic tradition and who were ultimately admitted in the pattern of Western civilization.

The *inter* Sephardic and *intra* Sephardic communal contacts in all the points singled out above establish certain general trends characterizing the Peninsular Jews abroad: The medieval communities by their theocratic form of government excluded a direct relationship with Catholic Spain. We now know positively that the Marranos were a vital branching out of Peninsular life for many decades. Saturated with Peninsular culture, the Marranos, as hinted above, were up to date in the ways of polite society. Little or much of this cultural attainment permeated the medieval units. There are scattered evidential facts that show that for over a century the Spaniards and Portuguese came to know the exiled Jews in their new homes. Memorable is the case of a Castilian boy who, at the age of eight, left with the banished as a Jew, and after wanderng all over the Mediterranean cities, returned to Spain despite the law of 1499 which prohibited the entrance of Jews even though they might be willing to submit to baptism.[78] The law of 1499 proves that the boy of Illescas was no exception. Many Jews must have found life far from their ancestral home unbearable. The report must have been moving that was given by the native of Castile who, in 1514, upon cross examination before the Inquisition, confessed to having had intercourse with Jewish life among the Peninsular Jews in Italy, Africa, Egypt, and in cities like Salonica, Adrianople, Constantinople, Brussa, etc. In a score of years the Jews of Spain had already formed their communities in exile.

> E que de alli este confesante se fué a la ciudad de Adrianopoli, que está dos jornadas de Salonique; e que estuvo allí quince dias por judío e entre judíos; y que vió allí muchos judíos naturales de Toledo e de Torrejon, e Madrid, e Guadalajara, que se habían ydo cuando la general espulsion, e habló con ellos e les dixo quien era, e como yba; e que comió un sabado con un judío que le combidó, e comieron carne e cerezas.[79]

Among the many incidents related by the blind beggar from Illescas is that artisans like weavers from Valencia were living in Turkey and that people who had been Christian in Spain were now Jews there. Most decidedly then many Jews must have returned to Spain to live their last years among the living and the dead of their native land.

In the Sixteenth century Italy was filled with Spaniards—soldiers, statesmen, scholars, prostitutes, merchants, priests, authors, actors. El Gran Capitan, Garcilasso de la Vega, Don Pedro de Toledo, Juan de Valdés, Torres Naharro, Cervantes, were among the numerous distinguished Spaniards who lived in Italy for shorter or longer periods. The Abravanels had acquaintances in the most distinguished society. On account of public opinion at the time, those who had liberal minds and generous hearts could not show tolerant feelings toward the Jews in Spain proper, but once away from Spain they had no scruples in associating with their fellow-countrymen who happened to belong to the Mosaic tradition. Only from this point of view can we understand the readiness with which a Spanish grandee like Don Pedro de Toledo allowed his daughter to be brought up by Bienvenida Abravanel, the wife of the orthodox Jew, Samuel Abravanel. Numerous other contacts must have obtained between the Jews and the Catholic Spaniards in Italy and elsewhere.

It is both amusing and curious to see how the characters in the picaresque novel *La Lozana Andaluza*, which purports to be an account of Spanish rascals and whores, feel solidarity with the Spanish-speaking Jews at Rome and disdain toward the German and Italian speaking Jews:[80]

> *Lozana:* Que es aquella casa que tantos entran?
> *Rampin:* Vamos allá y vello has; esta es sinoza de catalanes y esta de abaxo es de mujeres, y alli son tudescos, y la otra de franceses, y esta de romanescos o italianos que son los mas necios judíos que todas las otras naciones, que tiran al gentilico, y no saben su ley; *más saben los nuestros españoles que todos, porque hay entre ellos letrados ricos, y son muy resabidos...*[81]

Spanish solidarity abroad manifested itself in two ways: on the one hand the Catholic Spaniards were ready to help their Spanish-speaking fellows born in the covenant of Abraham, and on the other, whenever possible, the Iberic Jews were willing to assist Spaniards in distress. In the *Viaje de Turquía* we find a sad and amusing story of a Jew who upon seeing the narrator as a slave in Constantinople overburdened with work, went to relieve him of his hard work. The guards spying the meddler gave him a good beating for his good intentions.

...habíanme hecho un dia cargar dos ladrillos que eran de solar aposentos de un palmo de grueso y como media mesa de ancho, de los cuales era uno suficiente carga para un hombre como yo; y yendo tan fatigado que no podía atener con los otros, ni vía, por que el grande sudor de la cabeza me caía en los ojos y me cegaba, y los palos iban espesos, alcé los ojos un poco y dije, con un sospiro bien acompañado de lágrimas: 'Perezca el dia en que nasci!' Hallóse cerca de mi un judío; que como yo andaba con barba y bien vestido, y los otros no, traía siempre infinita gente de judíos y griegos tras mi. Como maravillándose, deciendo uno a otros: 'Este Algun rey o gran señor debe de ser en su tierra'; otros: 'Hijo o pariente de Andrea de Oria.' En fin, como tamboriero andaba muy acompañado, y...no sé que me iba a decir.

Mata: Lo que os dijo el judío cuando se acabo la paciencia.

Pedro: Ah!, dice: 'Ánimo, ánimo, gentil hombre, que para tal tiempo se ven los caballeros!' Y *llegóse a mi y tomome el un ladrillo y fuese conmigo a ponerle en su lugar*. Respondile: 'El ánimo de caballero es, *hermano,* poner la vida tablero cada y cuando que sea menester de buena gana; pero sufrir cada hora mil muertes sin nunca morir y llevar palos y cargas, más es de caballos que de caballeros.' Cuando los guardianes que estaban en la segunda puerta de la casa, vieron dentro el judío, maravillados del habito, que no le habian visto trabajar aquellos dias, preguntaranle que que buscaba: dijoles como me habia ayudado a atraer aquella carga por. que yo no podía; respondieron: *Quien te mete a ti donde no te llaman?* Somos tan necios que no sabemos si puede o no? Y diciendo y haciendo con los bastones entre todos, que eran diez o doce, le dieron tantos, que ni el, ni otro no oso mas llegarse a mi de alli adelante.[82]

Captain Domingo de Toral was saved from captivity at Aleppo in 1634 by a very learned Jew. He was so well acquainted with the poets of the sixteenth and seventeenth centuries that he could quote with pleasure from their works. His knowledge of literature and his years of residence at Madrid concur in making us surmise that he was a Marrano.

> Era tan sabio en la lengua castellana que en abundancia de vocablos y en estilo y lenguaje podía enseñar a muchos muy presumidos, repitiendo a cada paso muchos versos de los insignes poetas de España, como Góngora, Villamediana, y otros...[83]

The vicissitudes of war and traveling evoked much mutual assistance between the Sephardic Jews and the Peninsular Catholics. Don Sebastian's defeat in 1578 on African soil reduced many Portuguese nobles to slaves for sale on the market.

> Allí acabó la flor de Portugal y los que quedaron fueron llevados a Fez, donde fueron vendidos, a voz de pregonero, en las plaças donde habitaban los judíos... Y me contaba el Sabio David Fayan, vecino de Alcazarquivir, y discípulo del Rab Yehuda Aboab, arriba nombrado, que tenían mayor consolación aquellos desgraciados, que ser vendidos por esclavos a los judíos, conosciendo su natural piedad.[84]

NOTES

1. The Jews of Spain chose to identify the name Sepharad that appears in the Bible (*Obadiah,* 1:20) with the Spanish Peninsula. Just as the various peoples living in Spain despite their variety could be designated by a single name, so the Jewish people who entered Spain from various parts of the world finally showed enough characteristics in common to warrant a single appellation. Sepharad was the name for Spain, for all Spain, for all the people in Spain. The interests of the Jews of that country demanded a name to differentiate them from the Jews of Germany and from those who came to be Germanized in accordance with the traditions and rites of the Germanic Jews. In the Middle Ages the name Ashkenaz that appears in *Genesis* (X:3) and elsewhere in the Bible was appropriated for the Germanic lands. As the Jews at different times left Spain and lived among the Jews of Africa, as did Maimonides in the XIIth century, they felt the necessity of calling themselves by the name of the country of their origin. Maimonides took pride in calling himself Sephardi, i.e., the Spaniard. Since words existed in Hebrew to designate the Christians in general, the word Sephardi came to be reserved only for the Jews of Spain.

Sephardi, then, is the Hebrew word for Spanish Jew, and Sepharad for Spain. Curiously enough, Sepharad did not mean the land of the Spanish Jews but Spain in general. Without entering further into the philological implications and consequences, we wish to justify the name given to this section. From earliest times the Jews in Spain availed themselves of the term Sephardi and Sepharad to call attention to themselves and to their land. The historical perspective compels us to find a term that will refer to the expansion and establishment of Sephardic communities all over the world. In the course of this part of the book and elsewhere we have drawn a line of demarcation between the Medieval and Renaissance Jew of Hispanic origin. But in reality the worlds created by these two types were not completely isolated from each other and uninfluenced by each other. The communities of the Levant, of Africa, of Western Europe, and of America, had so much in common that they formed a spiritual community. Seen as a whole the Sephardic world might be called the

Pan-Sephardic Community is a part and parcel of the Spains. From the Jewish point of view, it is an integral part of the Covenant of Abraham. As a cultural expression the Sephardic communities constituted a unit, and we chose for it the Hebrew expression *the Great Sephardic World.* Here Sepharad no longer means Spain but that form of Spain created by the Jews hailing from it.

The latest contribution on the meaning and the origin of Sefarad we find in the articles by A. I. Laredo and David Gonzalo Maeso. "El nombre de *Sefarad*" and "Sobre la etimología de la voz Sefarad" in *Sepharad, (Revista de la Escuela de Estudios Hebraicos)*, Madrid, 1944, año IV, Fasc. 2; pp. 349-363.

Jonathan ben Uziel, a pupil of Hillel, translated the Bible into Aramaic. It was he who gave *Ispania* or *Aspania* as the equivalent of Sepharad. In the Babylonian Talmud, tractate *Nida 30* we find this proverb *"Adam yashen kan/v'roe halom be' Ispamia:"* "A man sleeps here but he sees Spain in his dream." Spain as the legendary land where impossible wishes are fulfilled is then, as old as the Talmud.

2. For the fairest and finest interpretation of Queen Isabel's motives in expelling the Jews, read the chapter devoted to her in Waldo Frank's *Virgin Spain* (New York, 1926).

3. No word exists for the Jews of Spain or of Germany. What is the word for the Yiddish-speaking Jews? Since there is no single word that can be used to designate the Ashkenazic Jew, we are compelled in English to use Ashkenazic adjectivally. The renewed interest of the Spanish-speaking world in the Jews that came from Spain has happily supplied the noun for the purpose. *Sefardi—sefradíes,* or *sefardita* and *sefarditas.* No longer do these words sound foreign to the Spanish ear. Recently the English Jews of Hispanic derivation have been employing *Sephardi* and *Sephardim.* The *i* ending in the singular and the *im* in the plural show that the words have not yet been Anglicized and become naturalized. For the use of this terminology, see "Le discours du Rev. Bueno de Mesquita" given in English, May 25, 1935, in *Le Judaisme Sephardi (Organe Mensuel de l'Union Universelle des Communautés Sephardites)*, July-August-September, 1936, published in Paris.

4. Isaac Abrabanel in his preface to his commentary on the Books of Kings, quoted by James A. Huie in *The History of the Jews,* Boston, 1844, p. 177.

5. Isidore Epstein's "The 'Responsa' of Rabbi Solomon Ben Adreth of Barcelona (1235-1310), as a Source of the History of Spain." *Studies in the Communal Life of the Jews in Spain as Reflected in the "Responsa,"* London, 1925, pp. 1-2.

Read in this connection: "En todas las ciudades de España habitaban Hebreos tanto en el tiempo que el Imperio Romano la dominaba, como después que los godos la ganaron, y assí después que los moros passaron de Africa y la tomaron a los godos. I vivián los Judíos debaxo del dominio de los Reyes Moros y debaxo de los christianos que iban recuperando los Reynos de España de poder de los Moros. *En todas las partes adonde estaban los Hebreos en aquellas Provincias, tenian sus casas heredades, y negocios con privilegios, y prerogativas honradas, que las concedian aquellos Reyes.*" Imanuel Aboab, *Nomología o Discursos Legales...Estampados a costa y despenza de sus herederos, en el año de la creación,* Amsterdam, 5389 (1629). Second Part, Chapter XXVI, p. 289.

6. For the authors born in those places, cf. Joseph Jacobs' *An Inquiry into the Sources of the History of the Jews in Spain,* London, 1894.

7. See note 27.

8. See Claudio Sánchez Albornoz, *Estampas de la Vida en León durante el siglo X. Con un prólogo sobre el habla de la época por Ramón Menéndez Pidal.* Tercera edición, Madrid, Espasa-Calpe, S. A., 1934.

9. "El primer poeta castellano de nombre conocido (¿quién lo diría?), es muy probablemente el excelso poeta hebreo Juda Levi, de quien consta que versificó, no solamente en su lengua, sino en árabe y en la lengua vulgar de los cristianos. Yo no he visto hasta la fecha composición suya entera en verso castellano, porque su copioso Diván, nunca ha sido enteramente publicado; pero en los extractos y traducciones parciales que de él se han hecho, no es raro encontrar palabras y aun versos enteros castellanos extrañamente mezclados con el texto hebreo. Sirvan de ejemplo aquellos dos que en la edición de Geiger (*Divan des Castilier Abjul Hassan,* pag. 141) se alcanzan a leer, aunque desfigurados por un copista probablemente italiano que confundió el *dalet* con el *resh.*

> *Venit, la fesca uvencennillo*
> *¿Quem conde meu coragion feryllo?*

Así conjeturo que pueden leerse estos versos, cuya interpretacion es realmente difícil. *Uvencennillo* parece un diminutivo feminino al modo provenzal: *joven-cita y si festa* es error del copista por *fresca,* del lo cual no respondo, parece que estos dos versos, de los cuales el segundo es gallego más bien que castellano, dan este sentido:

> *Venid, fresca jovencita.*
> *¿Quién esconde mi corazón herido?*

M. Menéndez y Pelayo, "De las influencias semíticas en la literatura española" in *Estudios de crítica literaria* (Madrid, 1895), pp. 382-383.

This note has to be amended considerably to bring it up to date in so far as new discoveries have been made in the scholarly world. H. Schirmann, the contemporary authority on Hebrew poetry, in an article written in Hebrew: "Efo nolad Yehuda ha-Levi," in *Tarbiz,* X (1930), pp. 237-239, came to the conclusion that the city of birth of Judah Halevi was not Toledo as had been believed for centuries but Tudela. It seems that through a mis-reading in the *Poetics* of Moses ibn Ezra (Kitab al-muhadara) *tolitali* (the Toledan) was read instead of *tuteli* (the Tudelensis). Even the authority of Schirmann is not compulsive enough, for we have discrepant views expressed by Francesco Cantera and Professor S. Speigel of the Jewish Theological Seminary. Professor Spiegel told the author he rejects Schirmann's conclusions and admits that no one knows where our poet was born. See José Millás-Vallicrosa, *La Poesía Sagrada Hebraico-española.* Madrid, Publicaciones de la Escuela de Estudios Hebraicos, 1940, p. 97.

We leave intact Menéndez y Pelayo's quotation for it will serve us considerably in Book II, (Continuation of this book, See Introduction), where we shall discuss most extensively the great discoveries that have been made in recent years around the *Muwassaha.* In a sense unsuspected by the great "polígrafo" the first sentence of the quotation still holds true. Judah Halevy was the *first great* poet of the three languages of the Spain of his days: Arabic, Hebrew, and Mozarabic Spanish. See *Notes to Introduction* for bibliography on the *New Discovery.* Dámaso Alonso's article deals with Jehuda Halevy's *harja.*

In Seymour Resnick's *The Jew as Portrayed in Early Spanish Literature* [Doctoral dissertation accepted in New York University (1950)] as yet unpublished, we find a whole chapter on the *arcas de arena* episode. Castro in his *España en su Historia* has some curious notions on this incident of Raquel y Vidas. For one thing he believes it shows how the Castilian warriors despised the Jew and everything associated with him, in this case, money. Resnick points out that *in no place in the Poema are these money-lenders called Jews.* An extravagant interpretation of the coffers of sand is to be found in *"El humor en el engaño de las arcas,"* pages 112-118 of Eleazar Huerta's *Poética del Mio Cid,* Santiago de Chile, Ediciones Nuevo Extremo, 1948.

10. For the episode of the coffers, see Menendez Pidal's popular edition of the *Poema de mío Cid* (in the Clasicos Castellanos series), pp. 33-37.

11. From a letter (December 31, 1936) of Professor Alexander Marx, scholar and Librarian of The Jewish Theological Seminary of America to the author: "I do not know of Jewish translations collected in other dialects except Castilian and Catalan. Bible glossaries in the latter language prove that the Bible was taught in that language. Fragments of prayer books in Spanish have come to light and are referred to in an Inquisition case about 1480."

12. Israel Abrahams, *Jewish Life in the Middle Ages,* New York, 1917, p. 345.

13. "Dixo ansi este testigo que el tuvo a las manos un libro que se llamava *Geturi* (Sidur, a prayer book) de oraciones, de judíos, en romance, en el cual libro cada dia bueltas a la pared, dixo, este testigo que vido muchas vezes rezar a las dichas donzellas, fijas del dicho Juan de Lucena..." apud *Un Typograph Juif en Espagne avant 1482* by S. Mitrani Samarian, in *Revue des Études Juives,* vol. 54, 251. See also Fidel Fita: "Fragments de un Ritual hispano-hebreo del siglo XV" in *Bol. R. Acad. Hist.,* XXXVI, (1900), pp. 85-89 (Fragments found in Cairo).

Our conjecture receives a tell-tale confirmation in Menasseh Ben Israel's *Origen de los americanos:* Esto es Esperanza de Israel Prólogo de Ignacio Bauer, Madrid. Compañia Ibero-Americana de Publicaciones, n.d. We take at random a passage which shows that all Biblical quotations are in archaic Medieval Spanish and in a syntax closer to the Hebrew than to Spanish:

"Sigue pues el Propheta diziendo: *y alsará pendón a las gentes y apañará los empuxados de Israel, y los esparzidos de Jehuda, Congregará de las quatro partes de la tierra:* donde se debe notar, que a los israelitas llama (*nidahim) expuxados,* y a los de Jehuda (*nephussim) esparzidos:* y la razón dello es, porque los (sic!) Tribus habitan no solamente muy lexos de la Tierra sancta, mas aun en qualquiera parte que están, viven en las extremidades y partes mas remotas de aquellas comarcas, pobladas de gentiles; mas no se halla que habiten en la Europa: assi que solamente los dos tribos están derramados por todo el mundo, y desto que se incluen en Geuda: dize que los apañará de las quatro partes de la tierra, como sea que ya oy, tienen synagogas en la America." p. 70; and see Cecil Roth, *A Life of Menasseh Ben Israel,* Rabbi, Printer and Diplomat, Philadelphia, The Jewish Publication Society of America, 1934.

14. a. "...La lengua hebrea, aun continuando este nombre al dialecto caldeo y arameo, no fué jamas lengua viva, a lo menos desde el siglo IX, en las regiones de Occidente, donde los hebreos han acostumbrado a escribir hasta los tiempos de su expulsión de la Peninsula ibérica, sus cartas familiares en el idioma dominante en el país donde estaban domiciliados, alterado, en verdad, no rara vez con la introducción de algunos giros, palabras y frases de la lengua santa, que el rezo y las prácticas devotas vivas en su memoria. Francisco Fernández y González: "Tres manuscritos rabínicos del siglo XV," in *Boletín de la Real Academia de la Historia,* 1884, Vol. V, pp. 299-307.

b. For a document written in Portuguese but transcribed in Hebrew characters see David S. Blondheim's "Notes on a Portuguese Work on Manuscript Illumination" in *Jewish Quarterly Review,* 1928-29, Vol. XIX, pp. 97-137, and 1929-30, Vol. XX, pp. 89-90 and 283-284. For the original text see *Livro de como se fazen as cores* in *Todd Memorial Volumes,* Philological Studies, New York, 1930. Vol. I, pp. 73-83.

   c. For a literary work in Castilian likewise in Hebrew characters, see *Coplas de Yocef: A Medieval Spanish Poem in Hebrew Characters* (edited with an introduction and notes by Ignacio González Llubera), Cambridge University Press, (England), 1935.

   15. Francisco Fernández y González: "Ordenamiento formado por los procuradores de las aljamas hebreas, pertenencientes al territorio de los Estados de Castilla, en la Asamblea celebrada en Vallodolid" in *Boletín de la Real Academia de la Historia,* 1885, pp. 145-189 ff.

   16. From Isidore Loeb's summary of the above epoch-making study in *Revue des Études Juives,* vol 13, 1886, p. 188.

   17. J. A. Van Praag: "Restos de los idiomas hispanolusitanos" in *Boletín de la Academia Española,* 1931, pp. 177-201, passim.

   18. Many of the problems touched upon here are admirably treated by José Benoliel in his "Dialecto Judeo-hispano Marroquí o Hakitía" in *Boletín de la Academia Española,* Vol. XIII, 1926, pp. 206-233.

   Castro ubiquitously appearing in these notes, in his so many times quoted *España en su Historia,* shows how even the language of the Castilians became organically impregnated with Arabic modes of expression which are decidedly foreign to the genius of the Romance morphology. For example, in good Spanish we say "amanecio con un fuerte dolor de cabeza" y "anocheció sintiéndose muy bien." *Amanecer* and *anochecer* used in a personal sense is Semitic in ancestry. In French or standard Italian it is impossible to find the equivalents of these verbs in this personal sense. For further examples see Castro's work.

   19. Compare this stanza with the following English version given by Dr. David de Sola Pool and notice how the compactness of the Spanish translation is expanded and the syntax is true to the genius of the English language:

> He set the time by lot-Adar
> Ill omened month of Moses' death
> Eke Moses birth month, he forgot
> His scheme's birth pangs would rack him.

Book of Prayer; According to the Custom of the Spanish and Portuguese Jews. Edited and translated by David de Sola Pool, New York, 5695-1936, p. 326.

   Since Sephardism in many of its ramifications is the theme of this book, it is not out of place here to record the author's participation in the singing of this marvelous poem on the Saturday preceding the celebration of Purim. Out of the dim past a gleam shines in his memory, and he sees himself dressed in a colorful tunic, wearing slippers and a Turkish fez. The synagogue attended by my father was on the second floor of a building sunk deep in a courtyard. The rabbi who taught us Hebrew used to select a group of boys between the ages of nine and thirteen and train us many weeks before the event in chanting the Hebrew text of the poem and its Ladino version. After certain phases of the Saturday services, the team of boys was escorted to the *Tevah* and in the silence and attention of the congregation, in a beautiful sing-song fashion, they would tell with Toledan intensity the story of Esther, of Mordecai, of the villain Haman, and the Persian King. Only fragments of this venerable poem flash now in my mind, redolent of the most tender feelings of a childhood spent on the shores of the Hellespont.

20. Paro—Pharoah, Ayipto—Egypt. Adonay—the Lord. aínda—still, yet, sujeptos—subjected, afilú—even though.

21. See *El Cancionero de Juan Alfonso de Baena* (of the fifteenth century), Madrid, 1851, pp. 133-134. *Cedaqua*—a misleading spelling of the word pronounced *sedacá* meaning charity, mercy. A perfect example of a poem literally bristling with Hebrew words is No. 501 in the above-mentioned work. Cf. note on this poem on page 697 of the *Cancionero*.

José Benoliel, *op. cit.,* gives a poem of the same nature as the above in Portuguese by Luis Anrriques, pp. 207-209.

An excellent specimen of the use of Hebrew words in a Spanish poem is the supposed answer of the Rabbis to the Marrano poet Pero Ferrus when he complained of the noises that awoke him at the sleeping quarters of the Synagogue at Alcalá de Henares. Among other things the Rabbis say:

"El pueblo e los *hasanes*
Que nos aquí ayuntamos
Con todos nuestros afanes
En el *Dio* siempre esperamos
Con muy buena devoción
que nos lieve a remissión
Por que seguros bivamos" (*Cancionero de Baena,* p 334)
hasanes—precentors. *Dio*—the Spanish-Jewish form for *Dios.*

22. "Many betook themselves to Constantinople, Salonica or Thessalonica, Cairo and to the Barbary coast. They brought from here our language, and still they preserve it very willingly. To be sure in the cities of Salonica, Constantinople, Cairo and in other commercial cities and in Venice, they do not buy or sell, nor do business in any other language but Spanish. And I knew many Jews at Venice from Salonica who spoke Castilian tongue through mere lads as well if not better than I."

Judeo-Spanish as spoken by the Sephardim of the Mediterranean countries has been carefully studied by scholars such as M. L. Wagner, Max A. Luria,

José Benoliel and C. M. Crews; in their respective works, there will be found the necessary bibliography on the subject: M. L. Wagner, *Algunas observaciones generales sobre el judeo-español de Oriente* in *Revista de Filología Española*, X (1923), pp. 225-244; Max A. Luria, *A Study of the Monastir Dialect of Judeo-Spanish based on oral material collected in Monastir, Yugo-Slavia*, New York, Instituto de las Españas, 1930; C. M. Crews, *Recherches sur le Judeo-Espagnol dans les pays balkaniques*, Paris, Librairie E. Droz, 1935; J. Benoliel, *Dialecto judeo-hispano-marroquí o hakitía* in *Boletín de la Real Academia Española*, XIII (1926), pp. 209-233, 342-363, 507-538; XIV (1927) pp. 137-168, 196-234, 357-373, 566-580; XV (1928), pp. 47-61, 188-223.

23. For a contrast between Constantinople and Salonica in the sixteenth century, see this account written by the most cultured Rabbi of the latter city. Rabbi Moses Almosnino was sent with other delegates to Constantinople to procure a charter from the Turkish government guaranteeing the Jews of Salonica their right to stay and be protected. Originally the work was written in Rashi characters and in the seventeenth century it was transliterated into Latin characters.

"Andando, navegando en el golfo del mar de los trabajos que padecen los que se ocupan, en negocios en esta nobilísima ciudad de Constantinopla, corte del gran Señor, donde resido por mis pecados, y adversa fortuna, que todo se juntó para tirar contra mi sus ponçoñosas saetas, *sacándome de mi continuo estudio, y estable contemplación* estando al presente de noche y de día en continuo movimiento, con el zelo y amor que se requiere para efectuar el intento deseado en beneficio de nuestra *República de Salonique*, como tal comisario, intentando los medios convenientes para adquirir el fin de semejantes negocios, me fué fuerza comunicarle con diferentes personas, delatándose por ordinacion divina con remision de un día para otro, y harto *que sentía en mi haber salido de una extremada quietud, tranquilidad, y fixo estado de delectable estudio, y dulce contemplacion* a servicio de Dios y beneficio de su sacra escritura (Alivo para passar esta vida, que mañana acaban, para alcançar la verdadera, permanente y perdurable)." (Prólogo del autor in *Extremos y Grandezas de Constantinoplo*. Compuesto por Rabi Moysen Almosnino. Hebreo. Traducido por Jacob Cansino,...Madrid 1638) (*Traducido* here means transliterated).

Moses Almosnino of Aragonese origin through his father was one of the great rabbis and scholars of XVIth century Salonica: I.S. Emmanuel, *Histoire des Israélites de Salonique*, pp. 176-184.

24. Joseph Nehama, *Histoire des Israélites de Salonique*, Paris 1935. Vol. II, pp. 26-7.

25. Pierre Belon de Mars, *Les observations de plusieurs singularitez et choses memorables, Trouvées en Grèce, Asie, Judée, Egypte, Arabie, et autres*

pays estrangères, redigées en trois livres, Paris, 1553. Book III, Chapter XIV.
26. A. Z. Idelsohn, *Gesänge der Orientalischen Sefardim*...Jerusalem, Berlin, Wien, 1923, pp. 1-9.

For Medina del Campo's Responsa: Samuel B. Moses de Medina ...Responsa 4 pts., according to the arrangements of Jacob B. Asher's *Turim,* Salonica, 1797-98.

Samuel de Medina était né à Salonique en 1506...Dès sa jeunesse, il s'était distingué dans l'étude du Talmud et à l'âge de 25, il était rabbin.

"Il ne fut pas heureux dans sa famille. Il perdit tous les siens...Il fonda à Salonique une école dont la reputation grandit rapidement. Ses élèves, devinrent des rabbins célèbres qui firent connaître le nom de leur maître bien au delá des frontières de Salonique. Nous connaissons sa methode d'enseignement: il chargeait ses élèves de commenter les ouvrages fondamentales et dirigeait ses explications. Un des manuscripts conservé à la Bodleienne nous donne une idée de son système: Il repartissait les chapitres d'un traité du Talmud entre ses disciples et chacun devait donner son interpretation par ecrit. Lui-même en donnait une de son côté, puis on discutait le commentaire de chacun en présence de tous les élèves. Cette méthode permettait de se rendre compte de qualités et des defauts de chaque étudiant de les approuver ou de les critiquer. [Is not this a fine system for a University Seminar?] Dans ces differents postes, il fit môntrer de remarquables qualités morales, etc.," I. S. Emmanuel, *op. cit,* Chapter V.

27. Though we very much like this purple passage, yet we must call attention to the erroneous impression it leaves. Naturally Nehama is carried away by the achievements in lay culture of the Marranos and imperceptibly attributes their Renaissance culture to the medieval Jew. The Marranos were hidalgos, were cultivators of pure Castilian, and had a very high culture, but unfortunately the same cannot be said on the whole of their more humble brethren who had not the benefit of Church, Court, and University contacts. Nehama is on the whole right: the Castilian language triumphed even though it was not the Castilian tempered in the fires of Garcilaso, Fray Luis de León, Cervantes, Lope.

28. a. See *Encyclopedia Judaica* for translation of the *Amadis* in Hebrew.

b. Joseph Sarfati translated *La Celestina* into Hebrew in the early part of the sixteenth century. Cf. "The First Hebrew Comedy," a study in Hebrew by Umberto Cassuto in the *Kohut Memorial Volume,* pp. 121-28.

c. Abraham, son of Joseph Reuben born in Monastir, now Yugoslavia, translated into Hebrew some Spanish proverbs. Cf. I. S. Emmanuel, *op. cit.,* p. 194.

29. "Don Yehuda Abravanel compuso la *Philographia e Dialogos de Amor de Leon Hebreo,* en que mostró estremada sabiduria; es obra tan elevada, que habiéndola él compuesto en lengua Latina (sic), se halla oy traduzida en quasi

todas las principales lenguas de la Europa:...Imita perfectamente Platon, y siempre que puede lo concilía con su discípulo Aristoteles; y dizen por él lo que por nuestro Filón: aut Plato philonizat, aut Philo Platonizat." I. Aboab, *op. cit.*, p. 303. In 1937 the whole Jewish world celebrated the five hundredth anniversary of the birth of Isaac Abrabanel. Many valuable articles were published for the occasion.

30. Pierre Belon, *op. cit.* Book XII, Chapter XIV.

"Les Juifs, que ont este chassez d'Espagne et de Portugal ont si bien augmente leur judaisme en Turquie, qu'ilz ont presque traduict toutes sortes de libres en leur language hebraique, et maintenant ils ont mis impressions a Constantinople, sans aucuns poincts.

"Ilz y impriment aussi en Espaignol, Italien, Latin, Grec et Alemant: mais ilz n'impriment point en Turc, ni en Arabe: car il ne leur est pas permis."

31. Imanuel Aboab, *op. cit.*, p. 304.

32. A. Z. Idelsohn, *op cit.*, p 7.

33. Earl Jefferson Hamilton's *American Treasure and the Price Revolution in Spain, 1501-1650,* Cambridge, Mass., 1934.

34. "Les mineurs de Siderscapsa rendent une moult grande somme d'or et d'argent a l'empereur des Turcs: car ce que le grand Turc reçoit chaque mois de sa part, sans en ce comprende le gaing des ouvriers, monte a la somme de dixhuit mille ducatz par moys, quelque fois trente mille, quelque fois plus, quelque fois moins." Pierre Belon, *op. cit.,* Book I, p. 45.

35. Pierre Belon, *ibid.,* p. 46.

36. "Ils ont coustume de besongner toute la semaine commencants le Lundy et finissants le Vendredi au soir, d'autant que les Juifs ne font rien le samedy." *Ibid, supra,* p. 46.

37. *The Navigations, Peregrinations and Voyages made into Turkey by Nicholas Nicholay Daulphinois, Lord of Arfeurle, Chamberlain and Geographer in Ordinary to the King of France; continuing sundry singularities which the author hath there seen and observed...* Translated out of the French by T. Washington the Younger...Included in *A Collection of Voyages and Travels... Compiled from the curious and valuable Library of the late Earl of Oxford.* London, 1745. Box IV, Chapter XVI. Many editions of the French original published at various cities exist.

38. "Por toda Turquia tomaron los Hebreos salidos de España, las Rentas Reales de las Escolas, y comercios con que se enriquecieron mucho: y lo mismo en Africa, de muchos contratos, y negocios importantes." Imanuel Aboab, *op. cit.,* p. 306.

39. "Le plus doué de tous fut certainement ce *Joas Rodriguesz de Castel-Branco* (1510-1568) dit Amatus Lusitanus ou Habib, qui enseignait l'anatomie non seulement aux medecins, mais encore aux peintres et sculpteurs de l'Italie

en pleine Renaissance. C'est lui qui le premier explique le rôle des valvules veineuses, le premier qui entrevit la circulation du sang, le premier qui introduisit la dilation de l'urethre par des bougies metalliques, le premier aussi qui fit une resection de cotés dans la pleuresie purulente, méthodes que la chirurgie emploit encore de nos jours. Tour a tour médecin en Portugal, en Belgique, en Italie, à Raguse et à Salonique, ou il mourut victime de son devoir, il repandit la science medicale partout ou il passa....Cet illustre médecin avait fait ses études, a l'université de Salamanque. Ses cendres reposent dans le vieux cimetière Juif de Salonique.'' Saul Mézan, *De Gabirol à Abravanel. Juifs Espagnols, Promoteurs de la Renaissance,* Paris, 1936, pp. 144-5.

Amatus Lusitanus is a tremendously important personage that demands more information and evaluation which unfortunately we cannot supply here. For the medical history of Europe and of Spain and as an example of the anxiety-consumed Marrano, Amatus Lusitanus is very significant. As a doctor he was a marvelous product of the teachings he learned at Salamanca:

"In his Latin *Centuries* which ran for seven volumes, each dealing with one hundred medical cases, he discusses the history and the treatment of each individual case. At the end of the *Sixth Century* he gives his physician's oath. It speaks for itself:

"I swear by the Eternal God and by His ten most holy commandments, which were given on Mount Sinai through Moses as law-giver after the people had been freed from their bondage in Egypt, that I have never, at any time, done anything in these my treatments save what inviolate faith handed down to posterity; that I have never feigned anything, added anything or changed anything for the sake of gain; that I have always striven after this one thing, namely, that I have praised no one and censured no one merely to indulge in private passions, unless zeal for truth demanded this...

"As concerns loftiness of station, that has never been a matter of concern to me, and I have accorded the same care to the poor as to those born in exalted rank...In my methods of studying I have been so eager that no task, however difficult, could lead me away from the reading of good authors, neither the loss of private fortune, nor frequent journeys, nor yet exile, which, as befits a philosopher, I have thus borne with calm and invincible courage. And the many students which I have thus far had I have always considered my sons, and have taught them very frankly, and have urged them to strive to conduct themselves like good men.

"I have published my books on medical matters with no desire for profit: but I have had regard for this one thing, namely, that I might, in some measure provide for the health of mankind....

Given at Thessalonica, in the year of the world 5319 (1559).''

Amatus Lusitanus was born in Portugal and educated in Salamanca. He lived in many European countries and died in Salonica. Both integral Iberia and Sephardic Israel can be proud of this scrupulously honest stoic and humanitarian man of science. See for the *Oath of Amatus,* Jacob R. Marcus' *The Jew in the Medieval World. A Source Book.* Cincinnati, The Union of American Hebrew Congregations, 1938, pp. 316-319.

Amatus Lusitanus and La Celestina

"Desde antiguo se supuso personaje real a la famosa hechicera y se enlazó su recuerdo con tradiciones locales de Salamanca, donde suponían muchos que pasaba la acción del drama. Ya se consigna esta especie en uno de los escritos médicos del famoso *Amato Lusitano* (Juan Rodríguez de Castelobranco), que terminó sus estudios en aquella Universidad el año 1529. Habla en su comentario a Dioscorides de una fábrica de cola animal que habia en Salamanca, junto al puente del Tormes y no lejos de la casa de Celestina, mujer famosa de quien se hace mención en la Comedia de Calisto y Melibea: *non procui a domo Celestinae mulieris famosissimae et de quale agitur in Comoedia Calisti et Melibeae.*" Passage in M. Menéndez y Pelayo, *Origenes de la Novela.* Madrid, Casa Editorial Bailly-Bailliere, 1910, vol. III, p. XXXIX.

40. *ascama*—Hebrew term for audience approbation; *ascamot*—the plural. In the Sephardic pronunciation of words ending in *t,* there is the tendency to give the *t* the equivalent sound of the fricative *d,* as intervocalic *d* in the word *nada.*

"The name given by Spanish and Portuguese Jewish communities to the laws governing their internal administration. These laws approved and accepted as binding by the members, called in general 'yehidim,' were for the most part framed upon ancient models. They are a survival, to a certain extent, of the old internal administration of the Jewries of Spain and Portugal. Originally written in Spanish or Portuguese, they have been translated into the respective vernaculars of the countries in which these communities now exist. The *ascamot* of the English communities framed in 1664 were translated from the original Portuguese into English in the year 1819. They correspond somewhat to the 'tekanot' of the Ashkenazic communities, though the latter are more limited in their scope and more like 'decisions in council' on certain affairs of communal interest." *Jewish Encyclopedia.*

For the function of "tekanot" in the Middle Ages, cf. Israel Abrahams, *op. cit., passim.* On the inner workings of the Salonician *ascamotocracy,* cf. I. S. Emmanuel, *op. cit.*

Now we possess two very important works on the structure and significance of the Jewish Communal life in general and on the types of Sephardic Communal Units in Spain:

1) Salo Wittmayer Baron, *The Jewish Community, Its History and Structure to the American Revolution,* Philadelphia. The Jewish Publication Society of America, 1942-5702, 3 vols. (Volume III has a critical bibliography).

2) Abraham A. Newman, *The Jews in Spain,* Their social, political and cultural life during the Middle Ages. A Social-Cultural Study. Philadelphia, The Jewish Publication Society of America, 1942-5702, 3 vols.

41. For a documented study of the weaving and dyeing industry of Salonica, see I. S. Emmanuel's *Histoire de l'Industrie des Tissus des Israélites de Salonique.* Paris, 1935. The same monograph is now included in his *Histoire des Israélites de Salonique.*

42. "Que ningún obrero de ropa de Salonique, *perchero,* ni *fundidor, presador, batanero,* pueda emprestar dinero al patrón de la ropa," from an *ascama* in *Aljamiado* Spanish, reproduced by Abraham Danon in "La Communauté Juive de Salonique au XVIᵉ siècle" in *Revue des Études Juives,* Vol. 41, p. 255.

43. Joseph Nehama, *op. cit.,* Vol. IV, p. 45.

44. In 1554 the communities of Rome, Ferrara, Mantua, Romagna, Bologna, Reggio, Modena, and Venice held a Synod. Among the decrees issued was this one: "Whereas there are some who infringe the tekanah of Rabbenu Gershon, which forbids any Jew from ousting another Jew from a house rented from a Christian landlord, and whereas there are such offenders that when the landlord sells his house the Jewish tenant thereby loses his chazaka (i.e., his rights of preferential tenancy), we therefore decree that though the Christian owner sells his house, the right of the Jewish tenant to retain possession is unchanged..." Israel Abrahams, *op. cit.,* pp. 70-71 *passim.*

45. "The indispensable condition that safeguards the local *hazaka* is based upon the perfect spirit of solidarity and of social discipline, upon a sound concept of the collective interest which goes beyond the selfish interests of the individual. Far from aiming to exploit the non-Jew, it has as its aim the imposition of a barrier against the exploitation of the immigrant by the Turkish proprietor. On the other hand, it curtails competition which threatens to rob the tenant at the expense of the Turks, the only owners of the dwellings and the stores." Joseph Nehama, *op. cit.,* Vol. II, pp. 86-87.

46. Read French translation of one *ascama* on the restriction of woolen goods exploitation in Salonica, and notice the formidable mobilization of all the divine powers for the purpose of punishing those who dared disobey the rabbinical ordinance, in I. S. Emmanuel's *Histoire de l'Industrie,* etc., pp. 32-35.

47. On Joseph Nassi see Abraham Galante's "Don Joseph Nassi, Duc de Naxos, d'après de nouveaux documents" (*Conference faite à la Societé Bene-Berith le samedi 15 fevrier* 1913). Constantinople. Jacob Reznik (J. ha-Rosin):

Le Duke Joseph de Naxos (Contribution a l'Histoire Juive du XVIᵉ siècle), Paris, 1936.

48. Alice Fernand-Halphen's "Une Grande Dame Juive de la Renaissance" in *Revue de Paris,* September, 1929, pp. 148-165. "Le Cabinet des Médoilles de la Bibiothèque Nationale possède un magnifique médaillon en bronze répresentant le portrait de Doña Gracia Nasi...un médaillon de la Renaissance italienne, reproduisant le portrait d'une grande dame de l'époque et portant en exergue son nom gravé en caracters hebraique, il y a la de quoi piquer la curiosité des chercheurs." Alice Fernand-Halphen, *op. cit.,* p. 165.

49. On the Amons see Henri Gross' "La famille Juive de Hamon" in *Revue des Etudes Juives,* Vol. 56, 1908, pp. 1-26.

50. Cristóbal de Villalón's *Viaje de Turquía.* (Edicion y prólogo de Antonio G. Solalinde), Colección Universal, Madrid, 1919, Tomo II, pp. 211-12.

"En Salonique plantó nuestra gente el famoso Talmud Torah, adonde estan leyendo mas de cinco mil discípulos, con tener los Perceptores cómodos, salarios; y los discípulos pobres su vestido, calzado y mantenimiento necesario; ultra muchas Yesibot excelentísimas que ay; y treinta y seis Escuelas Generales, en que de contino se esta loando el nombre del Señor."

"...podemos dezir, que la excelente Academia de Toledo se transportó en las ciudades de Fez, Salonique, y Saphet. En ésta florecieron eminentas sabios, particularmente en la sancta Cabala." Immanuel Aboab, *op. cit,* p. 307.

Every student of Spanish literature accepted as a fact that Cristóbal de Villalón was the genuine author of *Viaje de Turquía.* Now we know better thanks to the brilliant detective work performed by Marcel Bataillon. Dr. Andrés de Laguna wrote it.

"Nous sommes beaucoup plus à l'aise pour situer le *Voyage en Turquie.* Car, si nous rejetons son attribution a Cristobal de Villalon, nous savons a quel père le restituer. Il s'âgit, ici encore d'une oeuvre qui a dormi inédite dans l'ombre de quelques bibliothèques jusqu'au seuil du siècle present. Mais d'une oeuvre aussi savoureusement espagnole que le *Crotalon* l'est peu, d'une oeuvre qui par l'agilité du dialogue, par l'ingeniosité de la fiction, par l'ouverture d'esprit et l'experience du monde dont elle témoigne, est sans contredit le chef-'oeuvre de la litterature à la fois sérieuse et divertissante que l'Espagne doit a ses humanistes erasmiens....

"De notre premier examen du pròbleme, il avait été pour nous évident que le *Voyage en Turquie* etait d'une autre plume, d'une autre essence. Ce livre postulait comme auteur un humaniste, un helleniste, certes, mais un homme instruit par la vie autant que par les bibliothèques, et doué d'un sens exceptionnel de l'humeur....

"Des recherches paralleles sur la génèse du *Voyage* et sur la vie et l'oeuvre du Docteur Laguna nous amenèrent très vite n'etait pas une relation autobiographique, mais un roman de voyage qu' amalgame ingénieusement une solide information puisée dans des livres avec les souvenirs d'une vie riche d'experience, et que l'auteur de ce roman etait bien un medecin, un grand medecin, le Docteur Laguna." Marcel Bataillon *Erasme et l'Espagne*. Recherches sur l'histoire spirituelle du XVIᵉ siècle. Paris, Librairie E. Droz, 1937, pp. 712-735.

Further documentation on the Mendez family in Turkey.

If the *Viaje de Turquía* is really a bit of fiction, the account quoted above would lose its convincing impact. But strangely enough Laguna's description of the triumphal arrival of the Mendez family is corroborated by what a German who was in Constantinople at the time wrote in his diary.

Hans Dernschivam was an agent of the powerful Fuggers, "the richest international business concern in sixteenth century Europe." He travelled in 1553-1555 at his own expense through the Balkans, European Turkey, and Asia Minor, making notes of the things that interested him.

"In 1553 an old Portuguese woman (Gracia Mendesia Nasi) came to Constantinople from Venice with her daughter and servants...The Jews are very proud of her; call her a *señora*. She lives also in luxury and extravagance; has many servants, maids also, among them two from the Netherlands. She is said to have been a Marrano and here to have become a Jewess again. She does not live at Constantinople among the Jews, but at Galata in a country home and garden for which she is said to pay a ducat a day rent.", in Jacob R. Marcus, *op cit.,* section, *"Turkish Jewry"* 1553-1555, pp. 411-417.

51. For the anti-Maimonic movement in Spain, consult Joseph Sarachek's, *Faith and Reason: The Conflict over the Rationalism of Maimonides,* Williamsport, Pa., (The Bayard Press) 1935.

52. We do not know of a better book that emphasizes the Sephardic character of the Zohar than Ariel Bension's *El Zohar en la España musulmana y cristiana* (Un estudio del Zohar, la Biblia de misticismo judaico, y del ambiente español en que ha sido revelado), Madrid, 1934. The original was written in English (*The Zohar in Moslem and Christian Spain,* London 1932) and quotations will be given from the English version. In the prologue of the Spanish translation, Miguel de Unamuno said: "Repasando el Zohar nos preguntamos si es que no viene su inspiración de la tierra y del cielo mismos españoles, del páramo leonés y castellano, de las sierras y de los esteros andaluces y levantinos. Hay en él luz de meseta hispánica y de riberas mediterráneas también hispánicas. El contenido, la materia de sus ideas—o ensueños—tiene muy poco o nada de original, como no lo tiene el de Santa Teresa, San Juan de la Cruz, Lulio y los místicos musulmanes. La originalidad está donde siempre está ella, en la expansión, en el tono, tenor y acento, en el

estilo íntimo entrañado, no en la razón—*ratio,* de *reri, hablar*—con el logos, sino en el espíritu, en el ruah en el soplo sonoro, que es sustancia de la palabra, y todo nos hace creer que aunque el rabino Moises de León lo escribiera en arameo lo sintió mas bien en romance español..." p. 12.

A thorough analysis of Jewish mysticism and the Zohar will be found in Gershom G. Scholem, *Major Trends in Jewish Mysticism* based on the Hilda Strack Lectures delivered at the Jewish Institute of Religion, New York, New York, Schocken Books, 1941 and 1946. See lectures fifth and sixth The Zohar: The Book and its Author: The Zohar: The Theosophic Doctrine of the Zohar.

53. For Joseph Caro's life, works, mysticism and legalism, see the now classic essay of Solomon Schechter, "Safed in the Sixteenth Century: a City of Legists and Mystics" in his *Studies in Judaism* (second series), Philadelphia, 1908, pp. 202-285.

"Caro, a Sephardic scholar who lived in the Ottoman Empire after the expulsion from Spain and died in the mystic community of Safed in Palestine, was one of the greatest rabbinic authorities of his generation. During his day Jewish religious unity was threatened by the welter of conflicting opinions in matters of observance, and it is not improbable that he hoped through his two chief legal works to bring about a unity in World Jewish Practice...that would hasten the advent of the Messiah." In Jacob R. Marcus *op. cit.,* p. 200.

54. Ariel Bension's *The Zohar in Moslem and Christian Spain,* London, 1932, p. 225.

55. A. Z. Idelsohn, *op. cit.,* p. 8.

56. Henry W. Bellows' *The Old World in its New Face. Impressions of Europe in 1867-1868,* volume 2, pp. 341-342.

57. Ariel Bension, *op. cit.,* pp. 227-28.

58. Solomon Schechter, *op. cit.,* p. 229.

59. Quoted by Schechter, *op. cit.,* p. 206.

60. Jacob Canaani's "The Economic Situation of Safed and the Surrounding Country in the 16th and half of the 17th Century" in *Zion* (in Hebrew) vol. 6, Jerusalem, 1934.

(For the translation of this article I am indebted to Mr. D. Slominsky, a former student of mine, now a teacher of Hebrew.)

61. This story is very well told by S. Schechter, *op. cit.,* pp. 273-75.

62. Schechter, *op. cit.*

63. For some of the melodies to which *Leha Dodi* is sung, see the often quoted work of Idelsohn. On page 9 of this book we find this poetical appreciation of this hymn; "Noch nie hat eine Dichtung sich einer solchen Verbreitung und andauernden Beliebheit zu erfreuen gehabt wie diese. Sie ist der Ausdruck der tiefsten Gefühle des jüdischen Volkes, sein Glauben und Hoffen. In ihrer Sprache sind Palastinaklänge wahr nehmbar, ihr Geist ist von der

frischen Brise Galiläischer Berge getrankt und umwolben mit dem Schleier des hellblauen Taues eines palastinischen Frühlingmorgens.''

The *Leha Dodi* is such a great contribution of Sephardic Jewry that we cannot refrain from giving a further estimate of the poem. "The Sabbath was to him (Solomon Halevi Alcabez) a living reality to be welcomed after a six days' absence with that expectant joy and impatient love with which the groom meets his bride...Catholic Israel, whose love for Bride Sabbath, and whose hope for final redemption it echoes so well, soon honoured Alcabez's poem with a prominent place in almost all its rituals; and the *Leha Dodi* is now sung all over the world on Sabbath eve, when Queen Sabbath holds her levee in the tents of Jacob." Schechter, *op. cit.,* p. 228.

Heinrich Heine caught the spirit and significance of the hymn in his poem "Prinzessin Sabbat" in *Gesammelte Werke,* Berlin, 1887, vol. II, p. 383. (The editor of this edition gives a German translation of Leha Dodi.) Alice Lucas translated it into English in *The Jewish Year,* London, 1898. p. 167 and ff.

> "Come loved Israel greet thy bride,
> Welcome the coming of Sabbath tide,
> 'Keep' and 'Remember' the Sabbath Day,
> God said on Sinai in single phrase,
> He who alone is supreme in sway,
> Endless in glory and mankind's praise,
> Come now, come, welcome the Sabbath rest..."

For the complete version of the translation by Rabbi David de Sola Pool, see *Book of Prayer,* New York, 1936, pp. 134-6.

64. A very moving analysis of Nagera's work accompanied by specimens of his poetry is given by A. Z. Idelsohn, *op. cit.,* pp. 10-13.

65. Cf. Chapter XIII (Haggounoth et Yebbamoth) Vol. II of Joseph Nehama's work.

66. For Solomon Molho and his influence on men like Joseph Caro, see Schechter's essay on Safed.

67. On the significance of the Ancona boycott, see J. Nehama, Vol. IV, and also I. S. Emmanuel's *Histoire des Israelites de Salonique,* p. 164 ff.

68. "Les marchands Juifs ont cette astuce, que guand ilz viennent en Italie, ilz portent le turban blanc, voulants, par tel signe que'on les estime Turcs; car on prend la foy d'un Turk meilleure que celle d'un Juif." Pierre Belon du Mars, *op. cit.,* Book III, chapter XIV.

69. *Monologia,* p. 309.

70. "As late as the middle of the seventeenth century, the reports which reached the Peninsula of Sabbati Zevi, the Turkish pretender who set all the Levant in a blaze, were sufficient to attract a concourse of adherents. A special watch was set at all the sea-ports to detain those who set out to join him; and a

muleteer of Toledo was punished severely for conducting suspected Judaizers clandestinely out of the country for that purpose." Cecil Roth's *A History of the Marranos,* p. 172.

"...a wave of enthusiasm ran in that fatal year 1666 through the whole of the Marrano world, where the imposter found his most steadfast supporters (i.e., in Amsterdam). In the Peninsula, as we have seen, there was a general attempt at flight to join him. A Marrano physician, who had escaped to the Levant and had been amongst the first to swear allegiance to the Pretender, received as his reward investiture to the throne of his native Portugal." Roth, *op. cit.,* p. 250.

71. "Le desir de rester dans l'orthodoxie, de maintenir une sorte de Catholicité entre eux et les Sephardim de tous les pays, le prestige aussi de tout ce qui venait, soit de Terre-Sainte, soit d'Amsterdam (la ville ou l'on imprimait la plus part des rituels, en langues espagnole et hebraique), empechaient ces negociants, ces banquiers, ces armateurs de s'isoler dans leur prosperité. Docilement ils ecoutaient et sollicitaient les avis de sages, *des hahamim,* ils les transcrivaient sur leur registre des deliberations, quand ceux qui les donnaient ne les ecrivaient pas eux-memes dans l'une des deux langues maternelles: l'hebreu et l'espagnol. Ils se soumettaient ainsi a une surveillance, a une direction morale, a une inquisition que leur garantissait à eux-memes la pureté de leurs moeurs et la conformité de leurs pratiques avec la Loi." G. Cirot, "Recherches sur les Juifs espagnols et portugais à Bordeaux," in *Bulletin Hispanique,* Vol. 99, 1907, pp. 273-4.

72. "On recevait assez fréquemment la visite de quelque envoyé, *saliah,* de Jerusalem, d'Hebron, de Saphet, ou de Thebarya chargé de faire une collecte en Europe. Ces personnages, generalement des rabbins, faisaient preceder leur nom du titre dè haham, et leur prestige était grand. La richesse et la generosité de la communauté de Bordeaux les attirait pourtant un peu trop souvent..." G. Cirot, *op. cit.,* 1906, p. 290.

Two rabbis arrived at Bordeaux in 1773 from Jerusalem. The communal organization functioning under the name of Sedaca decided to help the holy cause of Sephardic Jewry. Their minutes on the question reads: "Après avoir reconnu l'authenticité de caractere des dits deputés, et les eminents vertus dont ils nous paraissent doués, nous nous sommes efforcés dans cette occasion pour leur donner des preuves de notre sensibilité a leurs malheurs et de notre generosité, en deliberant unaniment qu'il sera payé par notre sendic la somme de quinze cens livres que nous allouons à Jerusalem, et de plus deux cens livres pour tenir lieu aux deputés de leurs frais de voyages et nourriture depuis leur arrivée jusqu'a leur depart, sous clause expresse qu'ils ne demanderont rien a un des particuliers de la nation sous aucun pretexte et que la presente deliberation sera transcritte sur le registre dont ils sont porteurs, lequel nous sera representé toutes les fois qu'ils nous deputeront des envoyés ce qui ne sera que tous les dix ans a peine de n'avoir égard aux députations prematurées." Apud G. Cirot, vol VIII (1906), p. 291.

Smyrna Jewry received in 1775 from Bordeaux a thousand *livres* to help the victims of a conflagration. The Sephardim in Bosnia at another time were given 200 *livres* by the same community.

73. David de Sola Pool's "Early Relations between Palestine and American Jewry" in *The Brandeis Avukah Annual of 1932,* Boston, 1932, pp. 536-548.

74. Quoted by Dr. Pool in the above-mentioned essay, p. 546.

75. On Carigal, see *The Literary Diary of Ezra Stiles* (President of Yale College) (Edited...by Franklin B. Dexter) New York, 1901, vol. I, pp. 362-3; 367-8; 360-1; 386-9; 398-400; Portrait of Carigal, vol. III, p. 94.

For further accounts of *shelihim* or messengers, cf. chapter VII of Morris A. Gutstein's *The Story of the Jews of Newport: Two and a Half Centuries of Judaism, 1658-1908,* New York, 1936.

Lee M. Friedman, *Rabbi H. Isaac Carigal.* His Newport Sermon and his Yale Portrait. Boston, Privately Printed, 1940.

(A Sermon preached at the Synagogue, in Newport Rhode Island, called *"The Salvation of Israel."* On the day of the Pentecost, or Feast of Weeks, the sixth day of the month *Sivan,* The Year of the Creation, 5533: or, May 28, 1773. Being the anniversary of giving the Law at Mount Sinai.

By the venerable Hacham, the learned Rabbi, Haim Isaac Karigal, of the city of Hebron near Jerusalem, in the Holy Land. Newport, Rhode-Island: Printed and Sold by S. Southwick, in Queen street, 1773.)

76. M. A. Gutstein, *op. cit., pp.* 125-129.

77. "Il faut en conclure que l'espagnol était la langue de ces *schelihim,* et que les Congregations de Jerusalem, Hebron, Thebarya, et Saphet, auxquelles celle de Bordeaux reservait ainsi un part de ses aumones, etaient originaires d'Espagne." G. Cirot, *op. cit.,* (1906) p. 293.

78. Fidel Fita's "El judío errante de Illescas (1484-1514)" in *Boletín de la Real Academia de la Historia,* vol. VI, 1885, pp. 130-140.

79. Fidel Fita, *op. cit.,* p. 134.

80. *Retrato de la Lozana Andaluza.* En lenguaje español muy clarísimo, compuesto en Roma. El cual retrato demuestra lo que en Roma pasaba, y contiene muchas más cosas que la Celestina. (*Colección de Libros Españoles Raros o Curiosos.* Tomo primero, Madrid, 1871.)

What precedes the conversation quoted in our text is very interesting for many reasons.

"Como entraron a la judería y veen las sinogas, y como viene Trigo, judío a ponerle casa."

Lozana—Aqui bien huele, convite se debe hacer, por mi vida, que huele a proquera asada.

Rampen—No veis que todos estos son judíos, y es mañana de sábado que hacen el adefina? Mira los braseros y las ollas encima.

Lozana—Sí, por nuestra vida, ellos son sabios en guisar a carbón, que no hay tal como lo que se cocina a fuego de carbon y en olla de tierra;...

81. *Lozana Andaluza,* pp. 76-77.

82. *Viaje de Turquía,* vol. I, pp. 127-129.

83. Quoted by R. Menéndez Pidal in "Catálogo del Romancero judío-español" in *Cultura Española,* section II, pp. 1050-55.

Captain Domingo de Toral remarked on the contacts between the Sephardic Jews of Aleppo and Western Europe: "Hay en esta ciudad (de Alepo) mas de ochocientas casas de judíos...tienen su barrio aparte...la lengua comun suya y casera y entre ellos es Castellana, la cual conservan desde que fueron echados de España...sus hijos envian a Europa, a Flandes y *España* y Italia, y Inglaterra y las *islas,* y asi no se hablará con ninguno que sea de moderada consideracion, que no traya estado en estas partes muchos años...y en siendo de mayor edad se retiran a Alepo y a otras partes donde tienen sus casas."

84. Imanuel Aboab, *op. cit.,* p. 308.

V

Cultural Erosion

The two types of Sephardic communities that emerged into final shape in the seventeenth century went through two distinct stages of development. Western Sephardic Jewry, whether in the islands of the Antilles or on the American continent, or again in England, France, Holland, Portugal, Italy, Germany, went through periods of flourishing existence when the Peninsular inheritance evolved in terms of religion and culture. As we reach the eighteenth and early nineteenth century, we find a gradual shrinkage and final disappearance of the linguistic equipment of the Sephardic Jews of Marranic experience. Spanish and Portuguese having ceased to be the languages of empires in ascendancy, the Marranos, through the various experiences common to their fellows, such as the new ideas of the Encyclopedists, the new literature of the Romantic period, the new political ideologies and practices, the new interpretation of nationalism, were no longer prone to preserve as a domestic and communal instrument of communication and creation the languages of their Peninsular forebears. Influenced by the new economy and the prevailing opinions their religious fervor weakened considerably. Atheism, deism, and the various forms of Christianity attracted them to different and new doctrines and modes of life. These Western Sephardics lost their Hispanic heritage but gained other advantages, if not superior, at least for contemporary purposes, of great validity. On the whole the Jewish religion was the only loser. The processes of loss and gain among the Marranic communities do not concern us here. Our chief concern is with the African and East Mediterranean Sephardic Jews who for over a period of three hundred years after their golden era in the sixteenth century, continued conserving certain precious, most precious folkloric items of the Peninsular soil, such as the *romances, muwassahas* and *zéjeles.*

In recent times the application of biologic and geologic concepts to history and cultural patterns has been fruitful. Many philosophers have been dubious of the conclusions drawn from the bio-geologic hypothesis. Since we are not defending the method as the only instrument of discovery and analysis, we do not feel constrained to present a brief in its favor. We are satisfied with the concept because it enables us, in a metaphorical sense, to explain succinctly the three hundred years of history of the Levantine Jews. Organically speaking, the Sephardic communities were able for a century or more to develop in a foreign soil the healthy products of their Peninsular culture. Due to their incomplete detachment, to the economic power enjoyed in an Empire reaching its zenith, and to their still vigorous traditions, they could create and maintain a fine form of Hispano-Hebraic culture. Sephardic Jewry reached its plenitude. (Biological terms are convenient here.) Thereafter the stages of loss, degradation, and decay took place. Processes of depletion set in, and there were no counter movements to reinvigorate the disintegrating organism. Behind the metaphor there are certain positive facts. Anticipating at the moment the complete collapse of both types of Sephardic communities, we would here refer to the Conference of Sephardic Communities held in London, May 26, 27, and 28, 1935. One of the delegates confessed the deplorable decadence of Hebraic learning among the Sephardim all over the world.

> By the grace of God we have in our ranks doctors, lawyers, engineers, architects, professors, historians, scholars, philosophers, etc., yet as concerns Jewish culture and rabbinical culture in the highest sense of the term our poverty is pitiful.

The former chief rabbi of Turkey, Hayim Nahum, for many years spiritual head of Sephardic Judaism in Cairo, Egypt, emphasized the absence of seminaries for the training of Sephardic rabbis:

> Non seulement le nombre des Seminaires qui existaient jusque vers la fin du siècle dernier, a progressivement diminué, mais les études rabbiniques ont considérablement baissé de niveau comme aussi les aspirants au Rabbinat se font de plus en plus rares. Les études juives qui réunissaient un grand nombres d'adeptes au XIXe siécle sont, aujourd'hui, délaisées et l'intérêt pour notre patrimoine religieux et spirituel risque de disparaître dans quelques années.

Another eminent Sephardic scholar lamented the lack of creative investigations in the glorious Spanish past among Hispanic Jews who have left the task to their Ashkenazic brethren:

> If valuable research has been carried out by the Russian and German Jewish scholars in that well-known part of our rich Sephardic literature produced in the "Golden Age of Judaism" cannot we, the descendants of those Sephardim, at least equal the achievements of our Ashkenazi brothers?

Significantly enough the Sephardim awakened to the danger threatening their patrimony by planning the means that would restore unity to the Western and Oriental communities on the basis of the religion common to all. Their efforts and the results are matters of the future. Having pointed out as graphically as possible the acknowledged decadence on the part of the Sephardim themselves, we can now call attention to the various stages through which that culture, rich in actuality and possibilities, passed.

Characterizing the outstanding events of Hispano-African, Levantine Jewry, we see the pseudo-Messianic movement of Shabbetay Seví as the all-disturbing factor in the seventeenth century; the composition and publishing of the *Meam Loez* or the so-called Popular Encyclopedia of Oriental Sephardism, as the redeeming feature in the eighteenth century; and in the last century the erosive processes having debilitated the culture of the Mediterranean Sephardim of the rich loam and salts making life bearable, painful attempts were made to resoil and refertilize the whole terrain. In more precise terms, the nineteenth century saw the importation of Western ideals and a revival of economic well-being. Finally the scantily reawakened Sephardic folk, at the beginning of the present century, prompted by new hope and a new promise in the lands of the West, left by the thousands their homes in Turkey, Greece, Bosnia, Bulgaria, Morocco, for France, the United States, Palestine, and Hispano America. In a period of less than twenty years, about 60,000 Hispano-Levantines settled in the United States.

Prelude to Sabbatayism

By the end of the sixteenth century many of the problems that confronted the Iberic immigrants had been tackled and solved. With the establishment of the communities and the concomitant agencies for education, religion, social exigencies, political demands, and economic needs, order and stability were conferred upon the lives of the banished. To the modus vivendi a challenge was to come with the non-Sephardic Jews. Through example, precept, numbers, they were to a great degree able to absorb their brethren of differing traditions. Calamities, such as conflagrations, earthquakes, plagues and the collective responsibility towards the Turkish Government in matters of taxation, made intracommunal cooperation a material and moral necessity. There were still other obligations incumbent upon all, such as the ransoming of Jewish slaves, the creation of means for self defense against persecution, and the maintenance of the line of continuity in Palestine through the support of institutions. The chief obstacle encountered however was the recalcitrant character of the Iberic Jew, which refused for a long time to submit to discipline. Since the traits that made for separation in the sixteenth century were in evidence again in the twentieth century among the Sephardim who migrated to New York, it is not out of place here to quote the words of Joseph Nehama on the character of the Iberic Jew. We shall have occasion to refer to a report prepared by an Ashkenazic social worker on the diminutive units of Sephardic Jews in New York, wherein we find an analysis that remarkably coincides with that of Nehama. In an empirical fashion this social worker arrived at conclusions resembling on the whole those of Sephardic Jews who have given thought to the dispersive tendencies in their character. If we find the same spiritual mechanism functioning in twentieth-century America as in sixteenth-century Salonica, it means that aside from similar sociological situations, the innate tendencies of Sephardic Jews are at the bottom of their centrifugal behavior.

In the enthusiasm of their reunions, in the atmosphere of reconciliation and fraternity which were generated in them, often they succeeded in conjuring away the imminent disruptions. But the fiscal interests, the struggles to exert influence, the questions concerning *cavod,* i.e., the search for honorable distinctions, the rubbing of people's sensibilities the wrong way, often had the upper hand over the appeals to unity. The spirit of clannishness conquered. On this score the Sephardic Jew for a long time remained Castilian, ready to break loose, chafing under any yoke. *Esta es Castilla que face los homes y los gasta,* affirms an adage of the lost fatherland, and this adage conserved all its verity in this place (Salonica). Castile undoubtedly had tempered the character of her

children, but she had imbued them with an excessively strong instinct of
independence, at the same time that she nourished their inventive minds.
It was difficult for those proud Castilians, Catalonians, Aragonese, to
give themselves up as beaten. They found the way to overcome their obstacles. New temples must not be built, said their laws. What of that!
They went ahead and established private oratories or chapels where they
and their friends came together...[1]

A Sephardic scholar, Dr. Saül Mézan, who has been thinking on matters pertaining to Sephardism, believes the decadence of the Peninsular
pattern started as soon as his ancestors left Spain. Had he delved more
deeply into the sixteenth century he would have discovered a flourishing
civilized life all over the Sephardic world. What he says for the period
subsequent to the Sabbatayic movement is very true however.

L'orage de 1492 vient détruire la symbiose heureuse des Juifs, Chrétiens,
et musulmans...The new environment *"c'était un abri pour le corps,
mais une abîme pour l'esprit."*...ils se trouvèrent subitement trans-
portés dans un autre milieu qui leur était tout à fait étranger, qui n'avait
rien de commun avec un milieu proprement dit...Ils se trouvaient, en ef-
fet, parmi des peuples inconnus et presque barbares, avec lesquels il
n'avaient et ne pouvaient avoir aucun point de contact spirituel...*La
décadence, donc, commença avec l'établissement des Sefardis en Orient,*
et s'il est vrai que les colons de Salonique et ceux de Constantinople
étaient en relations de plus en plus rares, d'ailleurs, avec les Marranes
d'Espagne et de Portugal (v. Menéndez Pidal), et que ces relations ont in-
fluencé en quelque sort leur culture en général, et leurs folklore en particular, il n'est pas moins vrai que cette influence n'était perceptible que
dans les grands ports maritimes et qu'elle était presque nulle à l'intérieur
du pays. Quoi qu'il en soit elle était incapable d'enrayer la marche rapide
de la décadence judéo-espagnole.[2]

Dr. Mézan's statements contain two or three valuable notions. The
idea of *symbiosis,* another biological concept, suggests one of the processes of cultural nurture. The incapacity to create a new *symbiotic* relationship by the Oriental Sephardic Jew explains why his culture for over
three hundred years went on depleting itself. Astonishing as it may
seem, the statement is yet an irrecusable fact, after four hundred years
of residence in Turkey, the majority of Jews could not read or write
Turkish.[3] In Spain they wrote Spanish in Hebrew characters, yet in their
new milieu they did not deign to transcribe Turkish in rashi symbols.

For one thing they knew very little Turkish and for another thing Turkish did not touch their inner being. The Peninsular Jew had lived for centuries with Mussulmans, learning a good deal from them. As a matter of fact, the Islamic world had been a more congenial place for a Jew than a Catholic milieu during certain critical periods of history. Yet in Turkey he was incapable of profiting from the Turanian mode of existence. Admittedly the Turkish culture was of a lower level than that brought by the Peninsular Jew. Training in the professions, for example, which had been a blessing in the West, was no longer possible for the Peninsular Jew. In *Viaje de Turquía* there is a burlesque story confirming the sweeping generalizations of Dr. Mézan regarding the irreparable decadence at work as soon as the uprooted Jews reached their new milieu. Medicine, scientifically and empirically, had been cultivated in Spain by the Jews for centuries. Turkey did not offer any medical centers and the medieval Jew who had brought the primary notions of the art of healing from Spain could not renovate them. The Marranos were a class by themselves. Their position gave them access to the best medical schools of Spain, France, Italy. The medieval Jew had to be content with empirical notions.

> Tras todo esto vino un médico judío de quien no rezaba la Iglesia, que se llamaba *él licenciado* y prometió si se le dejaban yer que le sanaría. El Bajá, por ser cosa de medicina, cuando vino remitiómelo a mi rogándome que si yo viese que era cosa que le podría hacer provecho por envidia no lo dejase. Yo se lo prometí, cuando vino el señor licenciado comenzó de hablar de tal manera que ponía asco a los que lo entendían. Yo le dije: 'Señor, ¿en cuántos días le pensáis dar sano?' Dijo que con la ayuda del *Dio* en tres. Repliqué si por via de medicina, o por otra. El dice que no, sino de medicina; porque aquella era trópico y le habían de sacar, que era como un gato, y otros dos mil disparates; a lo cual yo le dije: '*Señor el grado de licenciado que tenéis, ¿hubistele por letras o por herencia?' Dijo tan simplemente: No señor, sino mi agüelo estudió en Salamanca y hízose licenciado, y como nos echaron d'España, vinose aca, y mi padre fué médico que estudió en sus libros y llamose ansi licenciado, y también me lo llamo yo: '¿Pues a esa cuenta también vuestros hijos después de vos muerto se lo llamaran?' Dice: Ya señor, los llaman licenciaditos.*

Language and Decadence

The sarcastic and witty author of *Viaje de Turquía* who supposedly lived in the middle of the sixteenth century in Constantinople as a slave for a few years would not have spared the Jews, had their Spanish been outlandish and ridiculously archaic. From negative evidence, then, the Spanish spoken in Constantinople was sufficiently pure to pass unobserved. But this state of the language did not last long after the sixteenth century. The theocratic structure of the Sephardic communities in Morocco, Egypt, Palestine, and Turkey must not be forgotten. One inevitable consequence in the *ascamotocracies* was the triumph of Hebrew over the Hispanic vernacular. The Marranos in Leghorn and Amsterdam founded in the seventeenth century literary academies on the model of those of Madrid, Lisbon, Coimbra. In those academies Spanish and Renaissance culture went together. On the other hand, when literary circles were started in Constantinople and Salonica, Hebrew was the language for poetical compositions.[4] Erudite and poetic creations were cast in the Hebrew language; Talmudic, Biblical and medieval modalities of Hebrew were exclusively cultivated. When a scholar of the first rank wrote on practical ethics, he had to append a glossary of Castilian terms which he feared would be unfamiliar to his readers, but he defined them in Hebrew instead of in Spanish.[5] The prestige enjoyed by Hebrew worked irreparable harm because it perpetuated a mandarin class. The ordinary Sephardic Jew was incapable of following the Hebrew sermons or books. Pedantry in the West manifested itself in the excessive injection of Latin words and expressions in works supposedly composed in the familiar vernacular of the people. In similar fashion, Sephardic pedantry employed a superabundance of Hebrew words in the Spanish spoken by the masses. This preference of Hebrew over Spanish caused the neglect of the everyday speech. To a certain extent, access to the Bible, the Zohar, the Talmud, the medieval treatises, made for continuity with the old, but that fund of knowledge exhausted itself. A very obvious truth is that the books of old are a living source if the people who read them bring to them ideas with which to interpret them. Nothing is less profitable than a study of ancient authors with discredited ideas. The rabbis of the Orient were not in a position to receive the extraordinary contributions of Renaissance Europe. The few who received echoes of that effervescence had to contend with the impermeability of the closed theocracies.

Among the direct or contributory causes of the impoverishment of the Spanish language in the Orient is the exclusive use of the Hebrew alphabet in its various forms for the transcription of Spanish. Printed works appeared in the square Hebrew type or in the Rashi cut. The alphabet used for the cursive writing of Judeo-Spanish differs a good deal from that used by the Ashkenazic Jew for writing Yiddish. Students of Spanish civilization know of an *aljamiada* literature; that is, Spanish compositions transcribed in Arabic or Hebrew letters. In Spain proper this practice was harmless. As is known, Arabic has no "p" sound, yet there must have been a large number of Moriscoes who could articulate that sound. Outside Spain the new generations would have had no motive for trying to learn Spanish with "p" sounds. Among the Jews, the Hebrew alphabet made no provision for the distinction between single *r* and double *rr* or for the distinction between Spanish *i* and *e,* and so forth. Children who learned *aljamiado* Spanish in Turkey, if they came of non-Sephardic or of non-Castilian homes, could not easily be corrected.[6] These distortions of pronunciation were not altogether impossible of correction, but the Jews had no access to Spanish works written in Latin characters.

La masse connaît de moins la graphic latine, privilège des lettres, pour qui, seuls, le Castillan imprimé en Espagne reste accessible. *Aucun ouvrage en caractères latins n'est jamais livré aux presses.* Et c'est là un vrai malheur. A la fin du seizième siècle, les conséquences n'en sont pas encore nettement visibles, car l'avant-garde de la génération d'alors continue d'être de haute culture; elle nourrit fortement son esprit, et constamment le régénère dans le commerce des maîtres de la pensée qui, dans toute la chrétienté, s'affirment, à cette époque, avec une indépendance audacieuse et une prodigieuse autorité. *Dans le peuple et parmi les lettres moyens, on rompt cependant presque toute attachement avec la littérature de la mèrepatrie, qui juste a ce moment, prend un merveilleux essor.*

"Ainsi l'écriture juive, véhicule de science et de vie de l'âme pendant tant de siècles, quand les Sefardis étaient en commerce étroit avec les arabes et les castillans, avec tout le monde exterieur et pouraient verser dans leurs oeuvres le suc de la pensée et du savoir de l'élite de l'humanité, l'écriture juive, maintenant que les Sefardis sont jetés sur l'îlot balkanique salonicien, met autour du peuple une haie sévère. Elle fait bonne garde autour des cerveaux et en éloigne tout ce qui ne concorde pas strictement avec la tradition: Ce peuple parle castillan presque latin, et le castillan lui est lettre morte dès qu'il s'exprime entre les pages d'un livre qui vient de la mère-patrie. On peut dire, sans exagérer, que l'écriture rabbinique adoptée pour la transcription de l'espagnol est une cause éssentielle de l'abaissement de la communauté sefardite. Elle a orientalisé et fossalisé ce rameau d'un peuple qu'avait été jusque là fortement occidentalisé.''[7]

The Hebraic alphabet dessicated and sterilized the Sephardic field of thought. Harsh as this verdict sounds, it is nevertheless the summation of a melancholy fact. Had there been a realization on the part of Sephardic leaders of the inseparable nature of their religion with the Spanish language, they would have tried to keep in touch with the ever-evolving tongue of Spain. Lack of thought on their part contributed in converting Spanish into a jargon mixed with elements foreign to the genius of the Spanish language. Not even in the nineteenth century, as we shall observe later, did the leaders become aware of the need of either preserving a cultivated vernacular other than Spanish or rejuvenating the adulterated dialects spoken in their Levantine communities. Historical events have their own way of supervening in the lives of men. A priori projections into the past are entertaining but they do not alter what actually occurred. With a slender vocabulary, a faulty syntax, a rough hewn style, and the aid of foreign words and phrases, the Sephardic Jew wrote Spanish books in Hebrew characters.

Los libros que fueron escritos en la lengua judeo-española, judesmo, o ladino son muchos. Esta sección de la literatura judía es demasiadamente rica y grande más que las otras secciones no hebreas. Todavía en estando los gidios en España ya habían escrito libros en sus lenguas. Y los emigrados a Italia y a Holanda escribieron libros diferentes en un español muy claro sin mezclar palabras estrañeras y es por esto que el trazlado de los escritos santos que fuéron estampados aínda estaban demasíadamente claros y limpios por lo que fué inmediatamente después de la expulsión de la peninsula ibérica. Este lenguaje es fuerte (difícil) para los *elevos* (discípulos) para comprenderlo y los maestros son obligados de explicar las palabras españolas que no se usan más en la habla de las masas... *También en Turquía composaron munchas composiciones en ladino y muchas de ellas se perdieron por la falta de bibliotecas públicas en el oriente.* El viajero francés Nicolas de Nicolay, que estuvo en Constantinopla en el año de 1551 escribe que los gidios estampaban libros en diferentes linguas y también en español. Rebí Yacob ben Habib en su Introducción a su libro Enn Yaacob (El ojo de

Jacobo) dice que encontró munchos libros en español, y entre los libros antiguos se topan el libro *Naar Pison* (El Río Pesón) escrito por Rebí Yaacob Aboab estampado en Constantinopla en 1538. El libro *Ann Agat Ahayim* (Regimiento de la vida) que lo compuso Rebí Mosé Almosninos, estampado en la impremiría Yabetz de Salónica en 1564 y a la fin de su libro hizo una lista de las palabras la mas fuertes (difíciles) y las trasladó al hebreo. El la llamó a la lengua española "romantí" (sic) (Romance) y se cree que quijo (quiso) decir roman o sea latino.[8]

As long as memories retained their vigor; as long as the Marranos embodied themselves in the medieval Hispanic communities; as long as Spaniards for one reason or another entered the midst of Sephardic Jews, just so long the Spanish language was slow in deteriorating. But as people of other language habits learned the rapidly corroded Spanish, there was no stopping that linguistic wear and tear. Spanish enjoyed great prestige in the Orient not only among the non-Peninsular Jews but also among the neighboring Gentiles. At Salonica it was conceivable for Greeks and Turks who dealt with Jews of that town to employ Spanish for social purposes. There is, moreover, a unique case of a highly cultivated English merchant who, in the seventeenth century, found it necessary to learn Levantine Spanish for conducting business. On his return trip to England, his vessel stopped at Cadiz. Confident of his knowledge of Balkanized Spanish, he felt at ease on Spanish soil. This is a delicious bit of irony!

> Our merchant was not ill qualified to travel in this country and to converse in the great trading towns; for he spoke *Giffoot* very fluently, which is corrupt Spanish. But because the Jews write it in Hebrew characters (which he also could) it is called Giffoot, or the language which the Jews speak; so having this dialect at command, he was his own interpreter. I suppose they did not stay long at Cadiz; for as soon as the ships were come about, they went aboard, and pursued their voyages...[9]

Pseudo-Messianism

Plays, novels, short stories, and other sorts of books have been written in many languages on the strange Spanish-Jewish false prophet who stirred and agitated seventeenth century Jewry. Shabbetay Seví ben Mordehay has been reviled, laughed at, misunderstood, by the Jews after his humiliating failures, and worshipped by a small sect who found refuge in Islam. As a historical phenomenon, his messianism is understandable as an outgrowth of the millennial search of Israel for her Saviour. The popularization of the Zohar through the printing press reaffirmed the messianic aspirations. Hebraic mysticism moved at first within orthodox Judaism, with emphasis on individual purification within the demands of the community. Purification of body and soul suggested the idea of spiritual freedom. Spiritual freedom, however, was associated in the minds of some with the final redemption through Israel's salvation. On and off there had been unstable Jews responding to the Messianic call. Their failures never for long deterred others with the same goal and ambition. The sixteenth century had seen the Ethiopian Reubeni and the Portuguese Salomon Molho come to sad deaths. Prophets learn not from experience; they wish to transcend it. Some have wished to explain the meteoric messianism of the Smyrna Sephardic in terms of economic distress and political instability. But the Jews of Turkey had not suffered too much. It is true that the Chmielnicki massacres of Polish Jews had saddened the entire Jewish world. The Marranos were conditioned for messianic experiences because they had refused to comply with the Catholic tenet for the arrival of the messiah, their contention being like the Jews' that the Messiah had not yet come. He was still expected. Zoharic predictions, Jewish degradations, millenial aspirations, apocalyptic calculations, and special local circumstances contributed to the appearance of Shabbetay Seví in the seventeenth century. "This stange man produced such a disorder, such a stirring in the religious beliefs not only among his coreligionists in the Ottoman Empire but also among the Jews of all Europe, so that the disturbances caused by Shabbetay had repercussions for almost a century and a half after his death."

Sabbetay Seví was born in 1627. His father was a poultry dealer who made lots of money as the agent of an English merchant. Through contact with a Protestant from England, this Smyrna Jew heard stories about the coming of the Messiah. Shabbetay as a boy heard in turn the echoes of the predictions while studying the Kabbala. Soon a predisposition developed in him to entertain the idea of the Messiah personally. By nature he was a lover of solitude. Even in childhood he shunned the companionship of his playmates. Like all neophytes of the occult, he went through the ascetic phase.

Believing through the example of his contemporaries that in order to be initiated in all the mysteries of this science (Kabbala) an ascetic life was necessary, he got into the habit of fasting often, and of bathing in the cold waves of the sea, in summer as in winter, day and night. Another characteristic of his youth was his aversion to marriage. Even though his parents married him off, in accordance with oriental custom, early in his youth, he abstained from all marital relations and finally repudiated his wife.

By the time he was twenty he had young disciples who believed in him. His reserve, his charming personality, his preoccupations, and his economic independence contributed to his local success. These personal talismans enabled him to conquer in Jerusalem, Cairo, Salonica, and Abydos.

His hair and beard were magnificently black, in contrast with the whiteness of his skin. Endowed with a silver tongue, his speech had a musical quality to it; he was besides unusual in his power of song; this is a detail worthy of note, for his beautiful voice had a great share in the bewitchment that this founder of the new mystical sect produced among his followers.

Jewish communities have always been afraid of the individuals who bring radical innovations into religion. Sad experiences in the past have made the rabbis apprehensive. Sephardic Smyrna excommunicated Shabbetay Seví when he was hardly twenty. For fifteen years Shabbetay travelled within the Turkish Empire. At Constantinople he found a rabbi who showed him an apocryphal book with the name of the messiah to come, and strangely enough his name was like that in the apocryphal book. For the Messiah to be a reality he had to be in Jerusalem. And Shabbetay soon found himself in the national home of Israel. "From the first moment of his arrival, Shabbetay kept quiet, fearing to cause any scandal. He was satisfied to fast often, to sleep as cautiously as he could on the tombs of the Jewish holy men, with the idea in view of assimilating their prophetic spirit, and he would shed bitter tears while praying by candlelight. Shabbetay measured the length and breadth of his room, wrapped in a deep meditation. Sometimes he was found singing *Spanish ballads of love,* but of a mystic love. He was very fond, says a chronicle, of a certain *romance,* the heroine of which was the daughter of a king, whose lips were red like coral, and whose flesh rivalled the whiteness of milk when she got out of her bath. To win popular favor, Shabbetay employed a very clever means, in spite of his simplicity. He always provisioned himself with bonbons, which he generously distributed among the children he found on his way. They in turn satisfied him with the touching title of *Padre Santo,* as soon as they saw him coming from a distance.''

The decisive moment in his life came when he was chosen *Shalliah* by the community of Jerusalem which was experiencing hard times. Raphael Joseph of Aleppo was the mint inspector of Cairo. A student of the Zohar, an ascetic by inclination, a man of great piety, this rich Jew was a blessing to his community. Shabbetay had met him in Egypt before going to Palestine. It was to the Aleppo Jew he was sent for funds. Shabbetay had no difficulty in procuring money for the poor. His material success rebounded in favor of his messianic adventures. While in Egypt he married a Jewess of Polish origin who as a child had been reared in a Catholic convent. After running away from the convent she had been sent secretly to Amsterdam and from there she had gone on her own initiative to Leghorn where as a whore she wished to experience the dregs of sensuality and degradation in order to become fit to be the bride of the messiah. Sarah and Shabbetay, one with the witchcraft of her sensuality and the other with the siren-song of mysticism, succeeded in upsetting the life of their coreligionists. Forced out of Jerusalem, he soon found allies in disciples who believed in him and who wished to exploit him for their own ends. The Messiah's return to his native city caused a mass hysteria unparalleled in Sephardic history.

The Smyrna community felt proud of having given birth to the Savior of Israel. Everyone in the town was soon overcome by the divine intoxication: in fact, one could see men, women, young girls, and even children fall down in ecstasy, and new Pythonesses prophesied the divine mission of Shabbetay. The convinced partisans tortured themselves in many ways: they fasted during the day; they devoted their nights to singing pious litanies; they bathed in cold water or buried themselves up to the waist in snow, in holes dug in the ground, remaining until they were frozen. The popular madness did not stop there. Under the pretext of hastening the hour of deliverance, in order to force the Heavens to send down the last souls on reserve, many Jews from Smyrna, especially from Salonica and from other cities, hurriedly married off their children scarcely twelve years of age; those to be born of these unions would deplete considerably the reservoir of souls. In her favor Salonica could point to seven hundred marriages of adolescents who had hardly reached the age of puberty. To be impartial we must say that the agitation produced by Shabbetay was partly due to his wife Sarah, who by her wanton beauty excited the sensibility of the young. In the frequent processions Seví made across the city—for he had a special weakness for this type of ceremony—people saw something unseen before in the Orient: men and women participating simultaneously in this religious masquerade: people who were strangers to each other going into the same frenzy, dancing, singing, and embracing each other. This promiscuity gave rest to many scandals. When the Messiah crossed the city, the crowds gathered around him singing Psalm 118: 'The right hand of the Lord is exalted: the right hand of the Lord doeth valiantly!'

The abracadabric year 1666 saw the climax and comic dénouement of this melodrama. The hostility of those rabbis who refused to be mesmerized by the hallucination, the opposition of the governmental authorities of Smyrna, together with the desires of Shabbetay and his followers to hasten the day of reckoning, made the Messiah go to Constantinople. The Turkish authorities handled this disturber of the peace cautiously. Imprisoned at Abydos, Shabbetay through bribes converted his jail in the Dardanelles into a shrine. A Polish Jew who also maintained he was the Messiah, spitefully denounced Shabbetay to the Turkish government as a conspirator. Summoned before the Sultan, Mohammed IV, he could not withstand the tests of invulnerability to which he was to be subjected: to save his life he recanted and accepted Islam. The Messiah turned out to be a fraud. From his exalted promises he fell ignominiously to being a doorkeeper of one of the palaces. Compelled to take a second wife he was initiated into the religion of Mohammed, without renouncing Sarah the enchantress. Thousands of his followers became converted likewise. The loves and dreams of his childhood, however, never abandoned him. Stealthily he attended services at the synagogues. The Turkish authorities were unwilling to tolerate this backsliding, and so to finish him they exiled Shabbetay to Albania where he died at the age of fifty.

His sisters and brothers sustained the small community of converts who became crypto-Jews within Islam. For over two hundred and fifty years these followers of Shabbetay have lived apart from the Jewish community, yet without identifying themselves entirely with the Turkish world. The followers of the Smyrna Sephardic lived, up to the time of the Greek occupation of Macedonia, in Salonica. Now practically all of them have transferred their businesses and residences to Istanbul. About their customs very little is known. They are so secretive that all attempts at penetrating their mores have failed. The late scholar, Abraham Danon, by accident got possession of the articles of faith to which they subscribe. It is important for our purpose to know that this "catechism" was redacted in Judeo-Spanish. Theodore Bent, who wrote an article on this sect of Crypto-Jews within Islam, in 1888, estimated them to be about eight thousand. He learned before Danon that these Islamic converts (Dünmehs) read their prayers in Judeo-Spanish... "a *paytan,* for so they call their officiating priest, presides, reads their services in Judeo-Spanish."

The Maaminim, as they are also called, are an ever-present reminder of the messianic agitations within the Sephardic world. For students of Peninsular culture they illustrate the permutations undergone by the Spanish language. In their case it is seen how, in spite of conversion into Mohammedanism, the Spanish language continued to exercise its power even when it was no longer the indispensable instrument of communication for a people that soon assimilated the language and customs of the new country. As Turks the Maaminim learned Turkish—something the Jews in Turkey did not do for centuries. Therefore Judeo-Spanish could not serve them as their only language. But Spanish was hallowed with so many memories that it persisted in unifying this remnant of a remnant that is Israel. *Judeo-Spanish, in lieu of Hebrew, became the holy language of these Dünmehs.* We cannot forget the Maaminim. Their Messiah sang *romances* and they in their way have been reverential toward the Spanish language.[10]

Economic Background of the Folk Encyclopedia

In the long run the Sabbatayic movement was detrimental to the best economic interests of the Sephardic Jews in the Orient. The hysterical agitation caused the neglect of their material interests. While they were caught in the whirlwind of messianism, their Greek and Armenian competitors began to encroach upon their domain. European commerce was making further inroads into the native economy. Products of Western Europe began to dislodge the handicrafts of Turkish inhabitants. A slow decline in economic power had other causes, too. The Ottoman Empire was no longer able to control the Mediterranean Sea. Loss of territory and prestige were translated into a less brilliant mode of existence. If the masses of the Jews were the first to suffer from the unfavorable conditions, the upper strata succeeded for a longer period to enjoy the benefits of certain commercial enterprises. The burden of communal taxation was shifted to those able to pay. As in Spain, so in *Sepharad ha-Ghedolá*, the proud mendicant who believed in the responsibility of his more fortunate brethren, multiplied in alarming numbers.

> Some there may be accounted rich, if the very high taxes, imposed and paid for maintaining the poor, did not almost reduce them to the same pass. For at least one-tenth of their income goes of course that way; and moreover their beggarly Jews extort from them great sums which they demand as charity, saying, 'You are bound to relieve the poor. I am poor; give me relief.' It is a proverb that Jews beg *con bastón en mano,* that is, with a stick in their hand: and in good earnest the rich men are forced to comply and part with a good deal upon such kind of compulsion.[11]

The Capuchin monk, Michel Fèbre, and Sir Dudley North, who were in Turkey during the seventeenth century, reported the rôle played by the Jew in international trade. Even when conditions were becoming critical they still were the intermediaries between the foreign merchants and the native business men.

> Ils sont si adroits et si industrieux qu'ils se rendent nécessaires a tout le monde: il ne se trouvera pas une famille considèrable entre les Turcs et les marchands étrangers où il n'y ait un Juif à son service, soit pour estimer les marchandises, et en connaître la bonté, soit pour servir d'interprète au pour donner avis de tant ce qui se passe. Ils savent dire à point nommé et en detail tout ce qu'il y a dans la ville, chez qui chaque chose se trouve, son prix, sa qualité et quantité, si elle est à vendre ou a échanger, si bien qu'on ne peut prendre que d'eux les lumières pour le commerce. Les autres nations orientales comme les Grecs, les Arméniens, etc., n'ont pas ce talent et ne savaient arriver à leur adresse: ce qui oblige les négociants de se servir d'eux, quelque aversion qu'on leur porte.[12]

The not too benevolent monk (so far as the Jews were concerned) was shocked to learn that the solidarity among them was so great that in the business world trade-union practices, so to speak, prevailed. For example, commercial agents once engaged by foreign firms were protected by the Jewish community from being dislodged by competitors. Public opinion opposed anyone taking his brother's place. Under pain of being excommunicated, he kept his hands off his neighbor's business. The source of one's livelihood was considered a sacred right protected by the *ascamotacracy*, just as the Sephardic Jew at Salonica enjoyed the right of tenancy in the store or house he occupied. The foreign merchant coming from a deliquesent society could not comprehend the religious significance attached to this protection of a man's livelihood. To the foreigner this practice was a form of tyranny since the merchant could not get rid of his agent for any reasons good or bad. Here is another statement about the same medieval custom:

> When a fresh merchant or factor comes to Constantinople, the first Jew that catches a word with him makes him his own, his peculiar property, calling him his merchant; and so he must be as long as he stays, and from this time, no other Jew will interpose to deprive him of his purchase, but as soon rob a house as do it. And thus, by compact a custom among themselves this sacred rule of right is established...
>
> On the other side, the merchant can no more shake off his Jew than his skin. He sticks like a burr, and whether well used or ill used, will be at every turn with him; and no remedy...
>
> It is not a little convenience that is had by these appropriated Jews; for they serve in the quality of universal brokers, as well for small as great things. Their trade is running up and down, and through the city, like so many of Job's devils, perpetually breaking after one thing or other, according as they are employed. If the merchant wants anything, be it never so inconsiderable, let him tell his Jew of it, and, if it be above ground, he will find it. This is accounted a common advantage; for there are multitudes of people that have need of each other and want means to come together, which office the Jews perform admirably.[13]

Lady Mary Wortley Montague, who visited Adrianople in 1716-1717, was also impressed by the apparent prosperity of the Jews of that city. She could not have had of course a standard of comparison between the condition she noticed and those that preceded. As a tourist, dressed in Turkish clothes, she could observe that the Jews of Adrianople held important positions in the economic life of the auxiliary capital of Turkey.

I observed most of the rich tradesmen were Jews. That people are in incredible power in this country. They have many privileges above all the natural Turks themselves, and have formed a very considerable commonwealth here, being judged by their own laws. They have drawn the whole trade of the empire in their hands, partly by the idle temper and want of industry in the Turks. Every pasha has his Jew who is his *homme d'affaires;* he is let into all his secrets and does all his business. No bargain is made, no bribe received, no merchandise disposed of but what passes through their hands. They are the physician, the stewards, and the interpreters of all the great men. You may judge how advantageous this is to a people who never fail to make use of the smallest advantages. They have found the secret of making themselves so necessary that they are certain of the protection of the court, whatever ministry is in power.[14]

Discounting these sweeping statements, overlooking the inaccuracies and inadequacies in these superficial observations, we see one thing remains true. In the early eighteenth century, small numbers of the Jews were in power, in commerce and the professions. The autonomous life of the Jews within a commonwealth of their own attracted the attention of monk, diplomat, romantic lady, merchant coming from abroad. Either lack of curiosity or preparation must have made them remain ignorant of that mysterious world that kept the Jews together. A clever English merchant could go as far as to learn how to speak what he called *Giffoot,* an opprobrious term for the Spanish of the Sephardim. But even he could not understand the forces giving them cohesion. The eighteenth century Sephardic communities were not touched by the doctrines blowing across Western Europe. If the new did not penetrate, the old was struggling to perpetuate itself. A new lease of life was bestowed upon the speech of the masses through the publication of the *Meam Loez.* The Zohar had brought a calamity in the form of Sabbatayic messianism. Fear gripped the communities that made them look askance at that cryptic book. What was to take its place? Reabsorption into orthodox Judaism was the answer. Yet the Hebrew language was a formidable obstacle that the masses could not overcome. Judaism could only be reinvigorated through the Spanish language as spoken by the pure descendants as well as by the Sephardized Jews. It was a stroke of genius that made Rabbi Jacob ben Mahir Hulí publish the first volume, in 1730, of this great popular work, designated under the strange title of *Meam Loez.* Before explaining the character of this popular encyclopedia of Oriental Sephardism, let us transcribe verbatim the account of Mr. Albert Levy, editor of the now defunct Judeo-Spanish weekly, *La Vara,* that was published in New York City. In a Sephardic restaurant on Allen Street, Mr. Levy very vividly recollected the function of the *Meam Loez* in Salonica where he was born and brought up in the popular tradition of his people.

> Sabat la tadre, después de los servicios del *arvit* (oración de la tadre) los *fideles* se rendían en sus casas después de la *Avdalá* (oracíon de santificacíon, o sea bendicíon sobre la divisoria entre la terminación   del Sabat y el principio de los días de entre semana) y después de cantar el famoso canto de *Amavdil* (que quiere decir, El que aparta) de:
> > Buenas semanas veo venir,
> > las salgamos a recibir,
> > para que nos deše el Dio vivir
> > a nos y a todo Istrael.
> > Venid todos y nos aguntemos
> > y a su nombre bendizeremos
> > y de él demandaremos
> > la rehmisión (rendención) de Istrael; etc.
>
> se ayuntaban en grupos en una casa donde los vezinos de abaso, de arriba, denmedio y de los entornos participaban a la lectura del *Meam Loez.* Hombres y mujeres de todas las edades escuchaban con una atención religiosa a uno de la compañia, el cual en alta voz *meldaba* unas cuantas páginas tocante a la porción del Pentateuco de la semana.
>
> A la fin de la lectura recitaban el *Kaddis* de Rabanán (la santificacìon de los sabios) y espartían *belgamones,* una sorta de dulçura a todos los asistentes. Luego después empeçaban a jugar a los *filganes* y se continuaba hasta una hora avançada en la noche, retirándose, en *suétandose* unos con otros diziendo:
> > semanada buena *y betof talén* (con bueno que durmas) y la repuesta que se daban era:
> > *takitz berrahamim tovim!* (que te despiertes con las piadades buenas.)[15]

Mr. Albert Levy was in his late thirties: he describes the customs prevailing up to the first decade of the twentieth century. The *Meam Loez* was a living force for two centuries all over the Oriental Sephardic world. The Salonican scholar Michaël Molho, author of the "Contribución a la historia de Salonica" composed in Judeo-Spanish, wrote a very fine appreciative essay on this Sephardic work. As far as we know, he is the first to have treated this subject in a modern language. Upon request he sent a study for our approval and future publication in a magazine on Sephardic culture which the Instituto de las Españas intended to establish. The knowledge and quotations given below came originally from this unedited article: *Le Meam Loez: Encyclopédie Populaire du Sefaradism Oriental.*[16]

When Israel went out of Egypt, the house of Jacob, from a people of strange language. The italicized words in this first verse of Psalm 114 in the original Hebrew gave the title to the work we are to analyze. Commentators and scholars in the Middle Ages took the expression to mean—the vernacular of the Jews. In France, for example, *Meam Loez* meant for Rashi, the people who spoke French and not Hebrew. The Judeo-Spanish translation of the Psalmic words were *Pueblo aladinán,* that is to say, people without Hebraic culture. The *Meam Loez* aimed at instructing and entertaining the masses in Jewish lore by putting at their disposal the incalculably rich treasures of Bible, Zohar, Talmud, and Rabbinical literature of all branches.

> Redacted in ladino, in Judeo-Spanish, in a style without pretensions, simple and accessible to the large public, it puts at the disposal of all those lacking the Hebraic tradition what constitutes the vast Jewish literature of all times, comprehending so much that it is instructive and attractive. It forms a real encyclopedia for the use of persons without culture and incapable of acquiring by themselves all that a Jew must know about Israel's past, its beliefs, its traditions, its legends, its moral principles, its laws, its philanthropic regulations regarding poverty, hygiene,...

As is well known every Sabbath the Jews read at the synagogue a section of the Pentateuch, not haphazardly. The whole of the Pentateuch is read from beginning to end on successive Sabbaths, during a year. Round each verse, chapter, episode, book, have arisen commentaries, exegetical, philosophical, mystical and historical. Rabbi Hulí's idea was to compile round the Pentateuchal selection of the week the diverse materials from numerous works that had anything to bear upon the selection. He was able to finish the book dealing with Genesis. No other work aiming to instruct the masses previous to the first volume of the *Meam Loez* had met with any popular success. Flattered and encouraged by the instantaneous enthusiastic reception given his work,

Rabbi Hulí did not get beyond half of the book of Exodus. The first edition of one thousand volumes, though very expensive, sold very quickly. Something new had been offered the Sephardic masses and with alacrity they responded to the magic of the work.

> The Meam Loez is varied, rich, profound in its contents. It deals with the institutions of Judaism, of its ceremonies, its rites, its ethics, its philosophy, its prophylactic rules, its history, its comment upon the prescriptions of the Law, clarifies them by surrounding them with a profusion of details borrowed from all the commentators. This heap of notions is strung together with the golden thread of anecdotes, legends, and historical accounts and folklore. Nothing of affectation, gravity, pretentiousness. A stream of naturalness crosses its pages which have throughout the tone of a familiar chat, of an amusing story. No apparent didacticism or erudite mannerisms. It is a friend that leads by the hand, teaches you, amuses you, invites you to laugh and at times excites you emotionally and makes you cry. It enthralls and holds the attention of the least curious among its readers or listeners.

Upon Hulí's death the work was continued by Rabbi Isaac ben Moses Magriso, who finished what had been started by the originator of the idea in 1764. Thereafter seven more authors tried to contribute one or more volumes to the series, hoping thereby to bring to a close the encyclopedic undertaking. The other authors were: Isaac Argüeti, who finished the work on Deuteronomy; Menahem Mitrani of Adrianople printed in 1851 and 1870 volumes one and two on the book of Joshua; in 1890 Isaac Judah Aba presented to the public the commentaries on Isaiah II; Nessim Moses Abad, 1898 came out with his work on Ecclesiastes; Hayim Isaac Sciaky, the last to add to the series, worked on the Song of Songs. The disastrous fire of 1917 in Salonica destroyed among other things the finished manuscript of Isaac Perahia's volume on Jeremiah for the *Meam Loez* series. There are twenty-four books in the Bible; only eleven of these have *Meam Loez* equivalents, but the *Meam Loez* series comprises fifteen volumes because more than one volume was dedicated to some of the books. The commentaries on the books of Genesis and Exodus have been the most popular. The golden days of the race as told in those books have exercised an irresistible literary witchcraft over Jews, Christians and Mohammedans. Hulí's work on Genesis was published and reprinted in Constantinople in 1730, 1748, and 1823; in Leghorn in 1822; in Smyrna in 1864; in

Salonica in 1798 and in 1897. Exodus has two volumes in the series published in Constantinople in 1733, 1746, 1753, 1763; in Salonica in 1799, 1803, 1865; in Leghorn in 1823; in Jerusalem in 1884, 1886; in Smyrna in 1859, 1864, 1865. The dates and places of publication of the *Meam Loez* show how the printing press unified the Sephardic world. Besides there being Sephardic Jews in Leghorn, Smyrna, Jerusalem, Salonica, and Constantinople, where the *Meam Loez* was printed, we infer from these figures the popularity of the work which served to maintain the Spanish language notwithstanding all the factors that worked against its preservation. Those who did not own the expensive volumes joined reading groups, such as the one described by Albert Levy, where they heard week after week the enchanting pages of the *Meam Loez* in the unadorned language of every day.

> The authors of the Meam Loez deliberately repudiated all forms of a flowery and elaborate language. They went ahead, *currente calamo,* their pens cheerfully trotting along, bridle loose, as it were, without worrying about elegance, selectivity, not even about order or syntax. They expressed themselves in the commonest language of their day, with the words known to everybody. Each one of them spoke like the people of his day. And we can see in the fifteen volumes of this work, precious specimens of the Judeo-Spanish dialect of the Orient during two centuries; we can follow across the pages of these venerable books the evolutionary chain of this curious Hispanic inheritance, with its progressive corruption. Nothing resembling those erudite expressions, those incomprehensible, oversubtle constructions, those literary allusions, those accumulations of rare words so much loved by more than one Oriental rabbi. The successive authors of the *Meam Loez* know how to employ an abundant language, clear, fluid, and very Latin, due to the transparency of the intimate and logical structure of its ideas. They succeeded in expressing the most abstruse notions in a vivid, direct, and vigorous style. They used many Hebrew words, but only those everybody understands, which have acquired the right of citizenship in the common tongue. And if in the course of their exposition they felt the least doubt about the clarity of their language, they did not hesitate to have recourse to examples, to common images, to paraphrasing, and they did not leave off a subject unless they had the full certainty that they had made themselves understood.

The *Meam Loez,* the *Meldado,* and the newspapers in the nineteenth century were the institutions that helped preserve the dialects of the

Judeo-Spanish communities. On account of the gregarious character of Jewish life, the Sephardim heard the Spanish of the *Meam Loez* in groups, and at the cafés the newspapers of Vienna, Salonica, Smyrna, Constantinople were read aloud. A great school for the spoken word has been the domestic gatherings held for the purpose of celebrating the anniversary of the deceased.

The Meldado

Under a variety of names we see designated the Jewish custom of holding domestic commemoration for the dead among the Sephardim. The name most familiar to us is *meldado,* meaning literally that which is read. Meldar, for *leer,* as the word preferred by the Spanish Jews even in Spain during the Middle Ages, has been given a number of etymologies.[17] Whatever its origin, the word meant to read, and some derivatives are *meldar* as the substantive for an elementary school where Jewish subjects are taught exclusively. "Allí en el meldar vide cosas que me dexaron el más penible recuerdo en el corazón." The *meldado* is what the Yiddish-speaking Jews call "Jahrzeit." Particularly, during the first years after the death of a close relative is the anniversary of that event religiously observed. Usually after sunset, in the home of the deceased, a table covered with a paisley shawl, lighted candle, Hebrew books, would serve as the symbol that a *meldado* was being observed. As is known, Jewish ritual demands at least ten people, ten male adults, present for the celebration of any consecrated event, as a circumcision, a public prayer, a wedding, etc. Since the *meldado* had many attractions in the homes of the well-to-do, many times the number ten would congregate to honor the dead. First, the evening prayer was pronounced in unison at times, at other moments the haham or rabbi would sing alone. At the close of the prayer, the male survivors of the deceased recited the appropriate benediction on behalf of the dead. By the time the ceremony of prayer was over, the surrounding corridors of the house would be filled with women, old women, married women, the women related to the family, and some poor women who joined the celebration for warmth, some biscuits, and some money. In the room where men congregated, the rabbi would tell legends, stories in connection with some venerable passage of Holy Scripture.

These gatherings throughout the year in different Jewish homes at various intervals, sometimes many celebrations honoring the dead held simultaneously, constituted one of the fundamental Sephardic institutions making for the preservation of Jewish life and Sephardic customs and the Spanish language. The *meldar* perpetuated the traditions among the children. The Spanish used was of the archaic type employed in the Ladino versions of Holy Scriptures. The synagogue likewise was a continuation of the liturgical atmosphere of the school. Whatever Spanish was employed in the services went back to the thirteenth or fourteenth century. But at the gatherings held for commemorating the dead, the Spanish used was that of everyday conversation. It was expected of the rabbi to give an edifying talk based on Jewish lore. By the time he began his discourse in an informal manner, the women and children in the house would approach the open door of the room where the lighted candles on the paisley shawl glowed and the men who had said the evening prayers were ready to listen to the stories prepared by the rabbi for the occasion. The language used by the rabbi saved the Spanish language from more rapid deterioration than it was bound to suffer in a foreign environment.

By the time the rabbi finished with his stories, all had relaxed, their troubles were forgotten, and their feeling of solidarity through religious practice and language participation was strengthened. After the talk, everybody was served Turkish coffee with *biscochos,* biscuits prepared ad hoc for the *meldado.* A sesame confection invariably accompanied the coffee. In many homes Turkish halvah took the place of sweet confections. The Sephardic Jew is a very domestic man. Provision was always made for the men to take biscuits and meldado-sweets to their wives. Satisfied in many ways, the guests left the house where the *meldado* had been entertained and edified by the rabbi, they had talked with their acquaintances, and they had drunk aromatic coffee and eaten good biscuits. The beadle of the synagogue who had invited the guests by word of mouth, the rabbi, the smaller fry in the rabbinical world, the mendicants who were present, in addition to the common benefits, received money as charity from the master of the House. Piety without charity was inconceivable in Israel.

NOTES

1. Joseph Nehama, *op. cit.*, III, pp. 94-95.

2. Saül Mézan, *Les Juifs Espagnols en Bulgarie,* Sofia, Éditions d'Essai, 1925, pp. 33-34.

3. Conditions in Turkey changed radically with the leadership of Kemal Attatürk. His Westernization of his Turkey, change of head gear and outer garments for men and women, the abandoning of the Arabic script for writing Turkish and its substitution by the Latin alphabet with modifications, the suppression and subordination of foreign elements considered as wards of the great Powers, compulsory education laws, military conscription for all, Mussulman, Jew and Christian—these and several other innovations transformed the lives of the Turkish Jews from the late twenties to the present time.

4. "La communauté de Salonique comptait au XVIe et au commencement du XVII siècle un nombre important de poétes, dont les écrits ne nous sont d'ailleurs que rarement parvenu... Le gout de la poésie était alors si developpé à Salonique que certaines familles, comme un siècle plus tard en France, entretenaient des salons fréquentés par les Poètes et oú l'on s'adonnait à des tournois poétiques. Le chef des familles qui comptait également parmi les poètes dirigeait ce salon, arbitrait les concours. Une de ces familles fut celle de Ben Jahia." Among the poets who distinguished themselves, all wrote in Hebrew. Compare this state of affairs with the Portuguese Spanish writing of the dramatists, commentators and poets of Amsterdam... I.S. Emmanuel, *op. cit.,* pp. 191-200.

5. This was the case of Almosnino's *Regimiento de la Vida.* "Ce livre fut écrit en bon espagnol et imprimé en caractères hébreux... En fin à titre de conclusion, Almosnino donne l'explication par ordre alphabétique des mots espagnols difficiles. Ce livre fut transcrit et imprimé en caractères latins par Samuel Mendes de Sola, J. S. Gabay et Y. Piza à Amsterdam en 1729." I. S. Emmanuel, *op. cit., p.* 181.

6. Professor Ignacio Gonzàlez Llubera of Queen's University of Belfast is an assiduous student of Judeo-Spanish literature written or printed in Hebrew characters. His edition of *Coplas de Yoçef* most carefully tries to reproduce the aljamiado text in transliteration, always reproducing the equivalent consonants and ambiguous vowels. For example: "Esaw desta[h] manera[h]. Luego obo fablado;" the small *h* is to indicate the Hebrew letter; and then the *vav* or vaw of *obo* could be also read *hubo.* Take again first a transliteration of a sentence from Almosnino and compare the Latin "charactered" of a sentence as it appeared in the Amsterdam edition referred to above.

"Y en cuanto (a) la primera (virtud) que es la fortaleza, es de saber que se divide en tres *maneras y* especies diferentes y por *megor* dezir se toma en tres modos, que son un modo *largo* y estrecho y más estrecho."

"En cuanto *a* la primera virtud, que es la Fortaleza, *has de saber* que se divide en *tres suertes* y especies diferentes, o por mejor dezir, se toma en modo *lacto, estricto* y más estricto."

Any student of the Spanish language notices at first sight an improvement in the Amsterdam version: we have the preposition *a* replaced, *lato* and *estricto* are preferred to *largo y estrecho*. *Largo* and *estrecho* are good permanent words of the language but are not suitable for intellectual discourse. We need not stress the point any further; there was not in the Orient any means to stop the impoverishment of the Spanish language.

7. Joseph Nehama, *op. cit.,*: *L'Age d'Or du Sefardisme Salonicien* (1536-1593) Deuxième·fascicule; Paris, Librairie Durlacher and Salonique, Librairie Molho, 1936, p. 206.

8. Only the student of Spanish can savour this archaic Spanish perverted by Gallicisms and feel a sense of embarrassment before its clumsy expression.

9. Roger North, *The Lives of the Right Hon. Francis North. . .of the Hon. and Rev. Dr. John North,* London, 1826, Vol. III, p. 93.

The merchant in question was Sir Dudley North (1641-1691).

The word *Giffoot* that North uses for Judeo-Spanish is an approximation of the Turkish word *Chifút,* a derogatory and vituperative designation for Jew.

Also cf. Michel Fèbre, "Théâtre de la Turquie" (middle of the XVIIth century) in *Revue des Études Juives,* XX, p. 97.

Cf. Alfred C. Wood, *A History of the Levant Company,* Oxford, 1935, pp. 214-215.

"The business done was purely wholesale and it was dominated by the Jews who then controlled most of the trade of the Levant. They farmed the taxes for the Turks, especially the customs, they were the bankers to whom the Franks had recourse when they had to borrow to pay an *avenia,* and it was with the Jew middle-man, not with the Turkish customer that the English merchant usually conducted his trade."

10. On this false messiah there is not as yet a definitive work. Not even the brain of a popular novelist could have conceived of a character so strange and fascinating in his flight of imagination as this Smyrna Sephardic Jew of the seventeenth century. The quotations dealing with Shabbatay Seví (1629-1679) have been translated from the French text of Moïse Franco's *Essaí sur l'Histoire des Israélites de l'Empire Ottoman, depuis les Origines jusqu'a nos jours,* Paris, 1897, pp. 94-114...Abraham Galante, born in Smyrna, summarizes his findings on his fellow townsman in *Nouveaux documents sur Sabbetaï Sevi, organisations et us et coutumes de ses adepts...* cf. *Histoire des Juifs d'Anatolie,* Istanbul [Imprimerie M. Babok], 1937, Vol. 1, Chapter

XXXI, pp. 236-256... Moses Bensabat Amzalak, *Shabbetaì Seví:* Una Carta em Portugués de secolo XVII en que se testemunharn factos relativos a sua vida. Lisbon, 1926... Abraham Danon (1857-1925) was one of the few Sephardic scholars who contributed a great deal of new information, on the Smyrna messiah and his sect:

a) "Influencia de Sabatai Cevi" in *El Progreso* (a magazine redacted in Hebrew, Judeo-Spanish and Turkish) published in Adrianople, 1888-89, pp. 269, 300, 315, 331.

b) "Documents et Traditions sur Sabatai Cevi et sa Secte" in *Revue des Études Juives,* XXXVII, 1898, p. 103 ff.

c) *Une Secte Judéo-Musulmane en Turquie,* Paris, 1898, 20 pages.

d) "Amulettes Sabatiennes," in *Journal Asiatique,* 10e Série, Vol. XV, 1910, p. 331 ff.

e) *Études Sabatiennes,* Paris, Durlacher, 1910, 48 pages....

The Mohammedan Crypto-Jews of Turkey

They are the followers of S. Seví and are known as the *donmehs* or *Maaminim.* "The Donmehs of Salonica are the descendants of those adherents of the pseudo-Messiah, Sabatai Seví, who followed him into apostasy; and while ostensibly conforming Moslems, they practice a Messianic Judaism in their homes." Cecil Roth, *op. cit.,* pp. 5-6.

11. Sir Dudley North's remarks on the Jewish beggars is a penetrating observation. How very like the *mendigos* of Spain! cf. Roger North, *op. cit.,* Vol. III, pp. 51-54.

12. See Note 9.

13. See Notes 9 and 11.

14. *The Letters and Works of Lady Mary Wortley Montague.* Edited by her great grandson, Lord Wharncliffe, London, 1837, 3 vols., see Vol. I, pp. 410-411.

15. *Arvit, av'dalá, amavdil, kaddis, betof, talén, takitz, berahamim, tovim,* are Hebrew words whose meanings are given in the text. *Fideles, una sorta de, suetarse,* are Hispanized-French words. *Berganìon* or *belganion* probably of Turkish origin.

16. When Rabbi Molho learned that his essay was not published he had it printed in his native city. See Michael Molho, *Le Meam-Loez. Encyclopédie populaire du séphardisme levantin.* Thessalonique, 1945. In the Avant-Propos we read: "Sur la demande de Mr. M. J. Benardete, directeur de *Estudios Sefardies* a' l'Université de Columbia de New York, J'ai dirigé en 1936 une étude sur le *Meam Loez.*"

17. The author remembers from his childhood days this little song where

Meldar means school, and *meldar* to read, to study. *Torá* and *malah* are Hebrew words for the Law and angel:

> La *Torá* la *Torá*
> El hijico la dirá
> Con el pan y el queso.
> Indose para el Meldar
> Encontróse con un *malah*.
> —Ande vas hijo del Dio.
> —A meldar la ley del Dio
> —Vidas que te de el Dio
> A ti y a tu padre
> Y a todos los gidios.

VI

Decadence and Regeneration

An American thus described the Sephardic Jews of Constantinople in 1835:

> I think it will hardly be denied that the Jewish nation in Turkey is in a complete state of indigence, as is sufficiently proved by the mean and vile employments to which individuals devote themselves... There is no appearance of comfort, no appearance of competency among them; everything, where sight and smell are concerned, among them is extremely disgusting, and passing through their quarters, the sounds that assail the ears prove that they are a querulous race, destitute of domestic peace and comfort... The Jews in their isolated state constitute a society regulated by a government formed by a mixture of aristocracy and theocracy; but the latter prevails, and the ancient maxims of the Mosaic laws have so greatly extended their influence over the oligarchy that we are somewhat surprised to find in appearance a well regulated republic in the midst of arbitrary power and anarchy.[1]

Whoever in the last century reported on the Peninsular Jews living in Turkey, whether Gentiles or Jews, gave a very dismal picture of their material and spiritual conditions.

The political frame in which they moved must be explained for an understanding of how the Sephardic unity of many centuries broke down through the dismemberment of the Turkish Empire. Social pressure in response to the nationalistic policies of Kemalist Turkey today discourages the Sephardic Jews from speaking Spanish and also from printing Spanish in their newspapers. This triumph of occidental nationalism à outrance was the victory won through bloody sacrifices. Needless to say, a smaller Turkey has meant a new type of Jewish culture.[2]

Before reaching this development, the Sephardim witnessed the following stages in the history of their world, being both beneficiaries and victims. Like the rest of Europe, Turkey suffered economic transformations. Machine-made products were imported in large quantities. Large investments of foreign capital built up railroads, power houses, monopolies. Foreign imperialistic designs aimed at emasculating Turkey. Fortunately for her the failure, on the part of the great powers, to come to an agreement prolonged her valetudinarian condition. Through foreign meddling Turkey lost much of her European territory. Out of her losses new countries were created: Greece, Bulgaria, Montenegro, Serbia, Rumania. Rivalries between England and Russia and the other Powers at the expense of Turkey precipitated many wars: the Crimean War, the Russo-Turkish War, and the Balkanic Wars, the Italo-Turkish War, the World War, and the Graeco-Turkish War. Kemal Pasha in the twenties of this century rescued Turkey from oblivion by inflicting a crushing defeat upon Greece in Asia Minor. Contrary to prejudiced accounts of Turkey in the nineteenth century, there were indeed various attempts at a rehabilitation of Turkey: the destruction of the tyrannical Janissaries, the introduction of constitutional reforms under Abdul Medjid and Abdul Aziz, and the elimination of the bloody Abdul Hamid by the Young Turks. Finally through the nationalistic policies of Kemal Pasha, Turkey acquired a healthy government.

The slow westernization of Turkey and the Balkan countries had tremendous effects upon the Sephardic Jews. The breaking-up of the Turkish Empire was responsible in many ways for the further deterioration of the Spanish language they spoke. Before the nineteenth century the Jews of Sophia (Bulgaria), Severin (Rumania), Sarajevo and Monastir (Yugoslavia), Salonica (Greece), Adrianople (Turkey), had no need to know the languages of those territories before they emerged as new countries, since the Judeo-Spanish dialects served for practically all their necessities and emergencies. With the new political conditions they were slowly bound to acquire a good working knowledge of the respective languages. The creation of the nationalities is the chief cause for the complete decline of Judeo-Spanish. Wretchedness in matters economic, obscurantism in matters religious, and a depleted repertory in matters cultural, characterized the Sephardim of the nineteenth century. That century, as elsewhere, brought to Turkey and the Balkans, to Egypt and

Morocco, the benefits and injuries of modern civilized life. Outside the new influences coming through commerce and industry, there were two channels through which regeneration came. These were the Protestant and Catholic missions, on one side, and the schools and shops of the Alliance Israélite Universelle. To these forces for the widening of spiritual horizons must be added the creation of a Sephardic press, the inevitable contacts with the indigenous cultures of the new nations, the initiation into the borderline of French, Italian, German, and English modes of being.

Among the causes accounting for the decadence of Sephardic life in the nineteenth century must be included the loss of economic wellbeing. More alert than the Sephardim, the Greeks and the Armenians succeeded in occupying coveted government positions. The Armenians outrivalled the Jews to such an extent that very powerful Sephardim were strangled at the behest of the former after the destruction of the Janissaries with whom they had been too closely associated for their own good. Among the victims was Behar Carmona who was betrayed by the Armenian, Cazaz Autún. The Jews of Constantinople considered Carmona's death a national calamity. A long poem was written and sung like an elegy:

> Ajuntemos mis hermanos
> A cantar esta endecha
> Porque nos cortó las manos
> El Dio en esta echa.
> Todo el mundo lo lloraron
> Porque era muy amado,
> De los ojos me lo quitaron
> Sin culpa y sin pecado.
> Lloremos y endechemos
> Por el mal que mos vino
> Si mil años viveremos
> No mos sale del tino.

The Sephardim lost practically all traces of the learned professions. Medicine, which had been a favorite field of research and practice among them, degenerated into an amalgam of empirical notions and oriental magic. Whereas some Greeks and Armenians were entering the field of Islamic jurisprudence, the Jews were content with the rabbinical courts. The newer professions of engineering, architecture, industrial management were entirely strange pursuits to them. If the upper classes were ignorant, it goes without saying that the lower were worse. Salonica by the first quarter of the nineteenth century had lost her weaving industry as a result of European competition. Fewer and fewer men had an enlightened training in the trades. Here is what a scholar said about the Jews of Constantinople:

> The Jewish community had fallen from its ancient glory. When the Jews of Spain, banished from their country, came to establish themselves in large numbers in Turkey, they obtained high positions at the Sublime Porte, and their descendants occupied for a long time an important place in the State. Little by little they were deposed by the Greeks and Armenians. The latter pushed themselves slowly to the high positions in the Administration and monopolized commerce while the Jews day by day became poorer and more wretched. This decadence was derived in great part from their low intellectual status and from the absence of an authority recognized by all which might have imposed proper measures for the raising of the intellectual status of the Israelites.[3]

Materially the Jews were unable to escape the limitations of their low environment. As soon as they established themselves in the Orient, they were exposed to uncontrollable forces of destruction. Lack of a concerted policy to eliminate the causes of calamities, such as fires and plagues, played havoc upon the Jewish population. The sweeping fires of Salonica, for example, in the sixteenth century practically destroyed forever the few libraries of the Sephardic savants. Periodically these wholesale fires weakened the stamina of the Jews. And for centuries there was no remedy in sight. No wonder the sense of hopeless fatality crept into the very marrow of the orientalized Sephardim. The Janissaries everywhere in Turkey exploited the pusillanimous Sephardim by blackmail and when that did not give results they set fire to the Jewish sections in order to sack their homes. Abjection touched bottom when the Sephardim no longer stood for their rights. Little children, Christian or Mussulman, could mock grown up Jews by threatening them with a shotgun or a knife.

> The city of Salonica has seen many public disasters. It has suffered a thousand calamities: plagues, cholera, and other contagious diseases; severe earthquakes, wars, violent explosions of gunpowder deposits and

ammunitions; sea storms, tornadoes, frightful wind storms, devastating rains; disastrous hailstorms; spoliations, spectacular thefts, cruel assassinations, military uprisings, and Janissary tyranny. In brief, everything calamitous has befallen her at one time or another.

Of all these catastrophes, of all these frightful happenings, the most destructive and overwhelming, the most frequent also, has always been the epidemic of fires. And what fires! They swept away everything in their path, and over night they left whole families ruined and in despair; throwing whole families over night from their rich positions into dire poverty. It was not only Salonica but all the large cities in the East found themselves exposed to such destruction. There is no miracle or mystery in that course of events. The reason for those misfortunes is quite clear and evident. The cities in our world, especially those that had large populations, were almost all of them badly laid out. Aside from this general defect, the houses were all built of inflammable materials, such as loosely nailed boards and reeds. The narrow streets were very twisting and winding. There were no gutters for water, no order, no system in anything. Filth accumulated in every section of the city, and these were microbe-breeding places in the summer and deposits of mud and sewage in the winter.

A factor recognized by all students of Sephardic history as responsible for the moral and spiritual backruptcy of the Hispano-Levantine communities was undoubtedly the theocratic opposition to progressive innovations introduced from abroad. Religiously the accretions accumulated in the realm of belief and customs were inimical to the good life which the rabbinical authorities were supposed to promote. Superstitions possessed everybody and there was no counteracting force of reason to check their paralysing effects. To the student of folklore, superstitions are so many specimens of human phenomena; but to the leaders of a people superstitions are terrible obstacles for the regeneration of their own kith and kin.

Without any distinction of rank or age, all the inhabitants of Salonica, men and women, Jews and non-Jews, believed in the existence of evildoers (Sheddim) who were also called "those who are better than we," or "those from below." Thousands of people swore that they had suffered the tricks and queer and ugly deeds of these phantoms; others affirmed having established their presence and heard their voices; still others went so far as to say they had seen and touched them. According to these weak minded people, the evil spirits assumed a thousand and one forms, of persons, of animals, of house objects, such as pieces of furniture, kitchen utensils, and other things. Often "those who are better than we" appeared as made partly of man, partly of animal, or partly of an object. Evil spirits in the form of an animal, had the voice of a man; others in the form of a man had a camel's head or a cow's head; they crowed like roosters, walked on duck feet, rowed in paper vessels, flew without wings. Water pitchers danced; washing vessels went for a walk; pails laughed; lamps opened their mouths; brooms gnashed their teeth; beetles wept heart-breakingly. In short, it is hardly possible to imagine the downright foolishness that a large portion of the population permitted to pass their mouths in all seriousness as if they were saying something as holy as the ten commandments.

As to the clothes of "those who are better than we" it was a phantasmagoric concoction; cotton hair, wire shoes, flannel arms, flying sheets, fur belts, plush hats, writing equipment in the belt made of ice, spectacles of fire, flaming walking sticks, and everything in a thousand and one colors.

Whole families believed themselves assaulted by "those from below." They abandoned their houses and went to live in sections of the city far from their old abode without saying a word to anyone. Fearing lest the Sheddim would learn of their new quarters, they kept their experience to themselves. Others believed that the evil spirit or the devil possessed them. They fasted twenty-one days in succession, and at times took a physic to rid their bodies of the evil spirit.[4]

The whole history of the superstitions entertained by the Sephardim is by no means exhausted in this vivid account by Saadi Levy. Amulets against evil spirits and sicknesses were worn by children and adults. Recourse was often had to Mohammedan women and dervishes for all kinds of illnesses. Maimonidean rationalism would have blown the whole sub- and super-structure of superstitions into nothing, but the "Guide to the Perplexed" had no influence. Elementary virtues and religious practices preserved the people from complete submersion into a necromantic abyss. Great love for the holy law exaggerated the reverence toward the printed word when the ability to master it had disappeared from among the majority or had been confined to the very few who in turn were not exceptionally enlightened.

Whenever there were collections of books, you found *ghenizas;* especially in the religious schools (meldares), in the synagogues, in the colleges (Yeshivoth) and above all in the printing shops. Everything that had any printing on it was deemed holy by the people who were fanatic, considering it as an article of the Law. The word "Law" meant religion, and no one dared touch it without fear and trepidation. When any one saw a piece of printed paper on the street, he picked it up, kissed it, and looked for an elevated place where to put it. No one dared trample upon the "Law." If he happened to be near a meldar or a synagogue, he took the paper right away to the ghenizá.[5]

Naturally this taboo around the chief totem of Israel, its Law, engendered intolerance and even violence. Organized intolerance was centered in the rabbinical circles. The fulminating weapon of *herem,* or excommunication, was incautiously exercised against the real bene-factors of the community. The Sephardic *ascamatocracies* had an economic basis. Meat slaughtered in the ritual tradition, the so called Kosher meat, was a monopoly bought for a certain sum by Jewish but-chers. Many times the privilege was bought for a ridiculous sum and the income was many times the amount paid. Each pound of meat was sold at a higher price because community revenue was raised that way. Bonds of interest were established between the communal officers and the monopolists. Administrative abuses and other irregularities could not be corrected. When foreign agencies began to work on behalf of the Sephardim, no distinctions were made between the Jewish agencies and the Christian ones. Instinctively, the masses realized their mode of exis-tence was being submitted to radical change. The rabbinical authorities dimly too were aware that the many-century closed world was being destroyed. Wrath, violence, blind defense, were the many weapons they tried, rabbis and people, in order to counteract progressive movements. Liberals, usually, feel a sense of superiority when they meet opposition to their good intentions. Their program of regeneration is often defec-tive. As we shall see, the emancipated Jews were not very clear as to the things to be destroyed and the things to be preserved. Incomprehension on the part of the progressives does not excuse the indefensible position taken by the orthodox conservatives. Malfeasance, crookedness, finan-cial and moral procedures in the running of the community, deplorable unhygienic conditions in the *meldares,* the uncontrolled superstitions—these defects condemned the conservatives. An episode in the life of the Sephardim in Constantinople, in the field of progressivism versus fanaticism will illustrate the critical status in the nineteenth century:

There was at that time (1862) at Constantinople a party of fanatical rabbis absolutely opposed to all attempts at progress. The leaders of this clique were among others Rabbi Izhak Acrish and a certain person named Camhí. By their fanatical sermons and by the menace of excommunication, a terrible weapon that never missed its goal, these lunatics excited the mob spirit of the lower classes against the benefactor of the community. Besides, under the threat of anathema, all the parents had to withdraw their children from school where, according to the rabbis, the propaganda of Christianity was carried on. The fanatical faction did not however feel satisfied. Rabbi Acrish in person had the audacity to appear before Count Camondo and to excommunicate him by reciting before him the consecrated formula. Astonished by this unexpected boldness, the Count was not able to say a word in defense. But by the next morning he succeeded by order of the Chief Rabbi to send Rabbi Izhak Acrish to prison. According to the accounts of actual witnesses, it was in the prison of Iplik Haneh, in Eyub that the guilty was imprisoned. Like all the prisoners, he had to work in the making of ropes. The fanatics who visited the chief of the bigoted faction at his cell returned with their eyes brimful of tears. Their hearts were broken as a result of seeing the holy man, accustomed up to that time only to handling the in-folios of the Talmud, working at that humiliating task, under the watchful eyes of the ferocious prison guards. Accounts of this character inflamed the heart of the medieval Christians, and correspondingly accounts of these fanatics inflamed the Jewish mob and excited it to a high degree.

On the Friday following this event, Sultan Aziz was duty bound to celebrate the ceremony of Selamlik at the mosque of Eyub. When this news spread in the city, all the Jewish population of Constantinople lined up on the shores of Golden Horn. The hills of Haskeüy, up to Sutlidjeh were filled with such a compact crowd of Jews that, from the middle of the Golden Horn, nothing else was discernible, from the bottom to the top of the hills, and especially on the shore of the bay itself, but a vast swarming of Jewish heads. At the moment the imperial boat reached Haskeüy, a formidable monstrous voice formed by the cries of 38 thousand chests was heard; the voices chanted ritual hymns, among others, the famous *Melek Yoshev,* etc. Stupefied, deafened, and frightened at the same time, Sultan Aziz at first thought it was a mutiny. Soon he saw a boat approaching him. Three Jews, standing up, handed to him, after a profound reverence, a petition. The Sultan took notice of its content right away. By this document they asked grace in favor of Rabbi Acrish; they were granted their request. The crowd fell immediately on the gates of the prison, and the innocent victim, as they were wont to say, literally was carried in triumph on the arms of men and given a promenade through the Jewish quarters of Haskeüy. The holy man, now a martyr, almost was on the point of being worshipped by our coreligionists; the more zealous went as far as kissing the hem of Rabbi Acrish's tunic.

With the exception of some pristine domestic traditions, the whole web of Sephardic life was in tatters. Schools were an abomination. Poor equipment, ignorant teachers, pedagogics of the most primitive kind, infested surroundings, vindictive forms of punishment, vituperative language hurled at the students, and other abuses against the sacred humanity of the pupils, prevailed in those surviving establishments where the Law of God was supposed to be taught.

> Los ijos de los gidios vejetan en los *hederim;* ellos salen de estos nidos de iñoranza, sin conocer, ni Biblia, ni hebreo, ni nada.

Against these lamentable conditions, working for the regeneration of the Sephardim were efforts from within and hints and help from abroad. As non-partisans, as distant observers, we must do justice to the Christian missionaries who indirectly were instrumental in bringing cultural benefits. Catholic schools all over Turkey counted among their pupils Jewish boys and girls. If they failed to make converts, they succeeded, on the other hand, in teaching them elementary notions of behavior, hygienic proprieties, and the rudiments of knowledge. The Protestant missionaries, however, brought something unique for the Sephardim. For purposes of propaganda they brought translations of the Holy Scriptures in Judeo-Spanish. Scores of people benefited very much from those cheap books, well printed, in a language that was their own.

> See how things produce at times some results that are unexpected. Even the Spanish language, which is so fine, so poetical, in which so many Jewish writers wrote very precious books, and which we sucked with the milk of our mothers, had decayed in a most shameful manner. Those who called themselves students of the Law, or learned men of the

Law, in talking used three Hebrew words to one Spanish word. Those who were in business made use of a Turkish term, of a Greek term, and of a Spanish term, and at that very clumsily put together. The beautiful language of our ancestors was totally ruined.[6]

There was no hope of extensively circulating the old translations of the Bible; the Oriental Sephardim were unaware of the extraordinary books by the Marrano rabbis, Isaac Cardozo, Immanuel Aboab, Menasseh ben Israel. Only the Protestant translations popularized up to a certain point the living sources of medieval Spanish. The Bible Society of England up to the present has circulated since 1829, in Bibles and Old Testaments, New Testaments, Psalms, Portions, 63,352 items. In view of the fact that books are still a rare luxury in the Orient, this number must be reckoned as a real index of the spread and influence of the unpolluted Spanish of the old versions with modernizations. Saül Mézan has already indicated the value of these Bible Society texts for learning modern languages among the Spanish Jews who were ambitious but who had no opportunity to have any training in a modern school. Saadi Levy, from whose extraordinary memoirs we have been quoting as the indispensable original source for the life of the Sephardim in the Orient, likewise tells us how he came to school himself in his maternal tongue through the Bible Society translations. If we remember that Saadi Levy, who was a self-taught printer, came to be an agent of progress in Salonica and the founder of the great Judeo-Spanish newspaper "La Epoca," then we are obliged to acknowledge the good works of the Protestant missions. They wanted converts, but they unwittingly helped to produce modern men in the Orient.[7]

> The Bible and the prayers, I know almost all of them by heart. To assimilate them with more ease, I put aside the book that Abraham Abinu had given me and read others printed in the Holy Language and in Judeo-Spanish. . . These books I bought from the Protestants and among whom I had many friends, since many of them came to my printing shop. They had brought to our city a large quantity of well-printed books which they sold very cheaply. When I read one of my books which I kept in my closet, I wrote down the words I did not understand. Since I remembered the verse and chapter when I saw the unfamiliar word, I would open the Holy Books, consult the Ladino translation, and learn the meaning and spirit of the words.[8]

Before concluding this discussion on the language situation among the Hispano-Levantine Jews in the nineteenth century just before and after the disintegration of the Ottoman Empire, let us treat briefly of the renewed activities of the Judeo-Spanish presses in the production of books and newspapers. Never before were so many books published in Judeo-Spanish as in the nineteenth century. Works of a religious character as usual appeared under a Hebrew title although the contents were in Balkanized Spanish. Calendars, commentaries on the Bible, summaries of the Zohar, treatises on ethics were some of the works under the category of religious studies. The new genre, the novel, began to spread among the Sephardim. Yiddish literature has produced works of merit and of universal significance. The circumscribed area in which Spanish survived, the political instability, the loss of cultural verve, explain why literature in Judeo-Spanish was unheard of. Only translations, and usually very poor translations, were made from the Hebrew, French, Greek, and German, into Judeo-Spanish. A taste for history was awakened with the presentation of books on universal history, as well as on Turkish, Jewish, and Sephardic history. Poetry had a few cultivators and some of the popular jongleurs made a living by printing the old romances which they sang at festivities. More graphic than anything else is the idea of a polyglotic chaos we obtain through a classification of the newspapers and magazines the Sephardim were asked to read. Newspapers in Judeo-Spanish, transcribed in rashi type, were published in Smyrna, Constantinople, Salonica, Belgrade, Paris, Vienna. *La Puerta del Oriente,* which appeared in 1846 at Smyrna, is probably the oldest. *El Tiempo* and *La Epoca,* the first edited by David Fresco and the latter by Saadi Levy, appeared respectively in Constantinople and Salonica. Turkish was not printed till the eighteenth century. Jews refused to learn the language of the land. Only the followers of Sabbetay Seví and the Karaites of Constantinople made Turkish their mother tongue. The latter half of the nineteenth century saw the appearance of educated Jews participating in the language and institutions of Turkey. An echo of the realization by the Ottomanized Jews that Turkish must become a living tongue for their brethren is seen in the newspaper in Turkish printed in Hebrew characters. *Zéman* and *Djeridié-Terdjumé* are two of the five that were started. Their success was slight. Judeo-Spanish was too deeply rooted to be easily eradicated.

Depuis 1867, a cinq reprises differentes, plusieurs personnes, inspirées por une pensée patriotique, eurent l'excellente idée de répandre la langue turque parmi les Israelites d'Orient au moyen de journaux écrites en caracatères rabbiniques et rédigés en langue turque. Ces entreprises ont échoué, parce que la génèration en âge de lire n'avait pas été exercées des l'enfance a l'étude de cette langue.

The Peninsular Jews were, after all, Jews, and a revival of the Hebrew language before Zionism gripped the Jewish communities of the world began to awaken the Sephardim to their ancestral inheritance. Newspapers in Hebrew accompanied with Judeo-Spanish appeared. *Carmi* and the promising newspaper that Danon founded, *Yossef Daath* or El Progreso, had Hebrew texts and Judeo-Spanish translations of those texts. At its extreme the polyglotic chaos of the time is to be seen in the newspaper *Selanik,* redacted in four languages: Judeo-Spanish, Turkish, Greek, Bulgarian. By the last quarter of the nineteenth century, French had become very popular among the graduates of L'Alliance Israélite Universelle schools and the Catholic mission schools. In many cities French newspapers for Jews were published. At last in Turnu-Severin (Rumania), Elia M. Crespin published, in 1886, the first Judeo-Spanish newspaper in Latin characters: *El Luzero de La Pacencia.* A generation or so before that date, the users of Hakitía in Morocco had been initiated into the Spanish of Spain. And a century before that, a small colony of Peninsular Jews had reached the gates of Spain by coming under British rule in Gibraltar. Had the Alliance realized the importance of teaching Spanish to the Hispano-Levantines, as she did in the case of the Jews of Tangiers and Tetuan, the Spanish language might then have recovered its vitality in the Orient.

To the polyglotic chaos, the well-meaning Jews of France contributed their share. Justice demands a balanced judgement of the great institution of l'Alliance. The French language indeed brought enlightenment to the Sephardim of Tunis, Morocco, the Balkans, and Turkey in Asia. The convulsions of wars would have found the Jews unprepared for emigration. With their European education, the Sephardim of Morocco left for Venezuela; those of Macedonia for France; and those of Turkey for Argentina and the United States. A close examination of the work undertaken and the motives prompting the foundation of schools and shops by the Alliance will throw further light upon the environment of the Sephardic Jews, before the liquidation of so much of their cultural inheritance and the new orientation of their changed lives.

The Alliance Israélite Universelle was, by and large, the most important institution to bring regeneration to the Jews of the Mediterranean countries and the neighboring countries. Most of the factors making for stagnation and stupefaction have already been discussed: economic retrogression, theocratic tyranny, spiritual backwardness, and the surrounding polyglotic chaos. Western Jewry, in the flush of its success, woke to its responsibilities. The French Jews, contemplating the deplorable conditions among their Oriental brethren, were aroused to a feeling of solidarity. These beneficiaries of Emancipation desired to propagate the doctrines and principles of modern tolerance. They were filled with missionary zeal because they were convinced of their being the torchbearers of a higher type of civilization. Consciously or unconsciously, the founders of the Alliance were agents of cultural imperialism of France. Wherever the Alliance opened schools, the medium of teaching was French, "la langue française, destinée a propager au loin le genie du pays qui a le plus fait pour la liberté de conscience...sera preferée dans les ecoles et les maîtres choisis devront ordinairement parler cette langue..." Being philanthropic, the French Jews could win the approval of their fellow citizens in France. They could show by spreading Western culture that the Jewish people were ready to assimilate higher modalities of life. Probing into motivation is not always a benevolent undertaking. Consequently, we wish to avoid any lack of charity and understanding toward the chain of schools of all kinds established in many countries by the Alliance from 1860 onward. From 1860-1870 there were fourteen schools; from 1870-1880, twenty-nine; and by 1910, a hundred and sixteen schools in countries like Morocco, Egypt, Palestine, the Balkans, Turkey, and Tunis.

The first teachers of the Alliance in Turkey, about thirty years ago, had to play almost the role of the Catholic missionaries among the Negroes of Africa. In the eyes of the fanatical population, the establishment of a school was tantamount to the establishment of a proselytizing center for conversion to Catholicism. What cliques, what intrigues, how much distrust towards those unhappy teachers who in the name of civilization and religious brotherhood came to shed a little light in the sordid ghettoes where, as true pariahs of society, we certainly would have vegetated until the present.

The teachers and founders of the Alliance had to win the confidence of the enlightened Jews of many communities. Religious schools had to be abolished or renovated. They built schoolhouses filled with light and cleanliness—something revolutionary in the benighted Orient. Teachers were trained from among the more intelligent Sephardim in Paris. Girls were regarded as educational timber. Besides learning the elementary notions of Western civilization and knowledge as organized in the West, Sephardic boys and girls received a moral training which transformed life in the Orient. Moral self-respect was inculcated through more knowledge, better appearance, better manners, less clannishness. More education raised the standard of living, awakened the desire for better dwelling quarters. Slowly, misunderstanding of and hostility toward members of other religious denominations were weakened. The French schools combatted the defects deeply rooted in the Sephardic character: selfishness, pride, exaggeration of personal sentiments, blind respect for strength or wealth, violence of mean passions.

Inveterate habits of centuries' duration could not in two or three generations be replaced by others of a more pragmatic value. The "inorganic state of Jewish Communities," the lack of unity, the indifference to innovation were the chief obstacles. But through the educational program of the Franco-Jewish schools, some very lasting results were gained. The Sephardic home received some benefits through their children's training. New careers, new professions, new jobs and business undertakings became possible. Large establishments absorbed the graduates of these schools. To a great extent emigration to more prosperous lands is traceable to these schools.

The schools may be criticised on two counts. The strength and the weaknesses of liberal Judaism permeated the spirit animating the schools of the Alliance. The French Jews wished to do away with the differences characterizing the Jews. The need for these differences was not explained. French Judaism should have demanded the same rights for the collectivity as it posited for the individual. The Franco-Jewish schools did not realize the national problem. It was impossible to keep the Jews united with their multiple vernaculars. Naturally the bond of union lay in a rejuvenated Hebrew culture. But the Alliance was most confused in the linguistic solutions it offered. The schools of Tetuan and Tangier included elementary courses in modern Spanish in their programs. The Hispano-Levantines used at home their mother tongue Judeo-Spanish. Instead of aiding them to rejuvenate their Balkanized speech, the schools of the Alliance excluded Spanish from their curriculum. A smattering of French could not impart a living sense of the artificial intruder. The polyglotic chaos was worsened by the French taught at these schools.

> Le Judeo-Castillan était, d'ailleurs, tellement apauvri surtout en termes abstraits et en locutions employées pour designer les acquisitions de la science moderne, que pour s'en servir dans la conversation de gens lettrés, il faillait employer soit des mot français, soit ce qui etait plus commode, des gallicismes a peine deguisés.
>
> Mais l'influence française toute vaste qu'elle a eté ne fut point profonde. Elle n'a entamé que la langue courante et n'a pas touché au folklore: les quelques proverbes de provenance française ne sont repandus que dans certaines villes ou toute la jeunesse a passé par les écoles de l'Alliance."[9]

NOTES

1. David Porter, *Constantinople and its Environs: In a series of letters, exhibiting the actual state of the manners, customs, and habits of the Turks, Armenians, Jews and Greeks, as modified by the policy of Sultan Mohammed. By an American.* New York, 1835, 2 vols., p. 167 *et passim;* Theophile Gautier, *Constantinople,* Translated by Robert H. Gould, New York, 1875, pp. 227-228.

2. After the nationalistic fever subsided, the Sephardic Jews continued speaking and writing their Judeo-Spanish and the Turks have not done anything serious to uproot Spanish from the Hispano-Judaic soil. Only a partial victory has been scored by the Turkey recreated by Mustapha Kemal, namely in the writing of Judeo-Spanish. Judeo-Spanish is now printed in the Turkish Latin alphabet. This is nothing entirely new. I possess Yugo-Slavic newspapers that have *romances* transcribed in the Latin alphabet of Yugo-Slavia.

3. *On the Jews in Turkey during the XIXth Century.* The quotations on the Jews of Constantinople originate in:

A) Moise Franco, *Essai sur l'histoire des Israélites de l'Empire Ottoman, depuis les origines jusqu'a nos jours,* Paris, Librarie A Durlacher, 1897; id, *Les juifs de l'Empire Ottoman au dixneuvième siècle,* in *Revue des Études*

Juives, XXVI, 1893, pp. 111-130; id., *Historie et littérature juives, pays par pays.* Paris, Fernand Nathan, 1905-06.
B) Haím Nahoum, *Jews of Turkey,* A Study included in Eliot G. Mears, *Modern Turkey.* New York, 1924, pp. 86-97.
C) Solomon A. Rosanes, *A history of the Jews of Turkey,* (in Hebrew), Jerusalem, 1931-38, 5 vols.; id., "Judeo-Spanish Literature," in *Otzar Israel* (Treasure of Israel), [an encyclopedia], vol. V, p. 74ff.
D) Several informative articles of Jews of Turkey in *Archives Israélites,* 1840, vol. 1, pp. 198-201; 249-251; vol. 11, pp. 216-222; 270-274, 480-482, 1846, p. 359ff.

4. Almost fifteen years ago Sam Levy, whom we have called with a great deal of respect the "Don Quijote of Modern Sephardism" sent me his copy of his father's memoirs. Most regretfully we report that this invaluable document has not to this day been published. We quoted from Saadi Levy's *Mis Memorias* on the basis of a photostatic copy which is in our possession.

A word or two on Saadi and Sam Levy before we reproduce the racy, colloquial language of the founder and editor of the newspaper *La Epoca. La Epoca* of Saadi Levy and *El Tiempo* of David Fresco were respectively the best Judeo-Spanish newspapers of Salonica and Constantinople. Both were written in a more or less kind of pure Spanish. *El Tiempo* made an extra effort to approximate modern Castilian. Needless to say both were printed in Hebrew characters.

Sam Levy, following in his father's footsteps, has behind him a very long life devoted to the interests of Sephardic culture. In 1949 he stopped the publication of his highly intelligent magazine, *Les Cahiers Séfardis*: Recueil documentaire, historique, retrospectif, d'actualité. From the year after the end of World War II, he defended the entity: *Sephardic Culture within World Judaism.* It was at Neuilly-sur-Seine where he published this fine review. Particularly the entire collection will remain an indispensable source for the history of the Sephardic Communities as they emerged, bloody, almost decimated, but unbowed from the terroristic holocaust they suffered under barbaric Hitler and his Germany.

The original Judeo-Spanish text of the quotation *(Mis memorias,* Book 1, ch. XI):

"Sin ningún apartadijo de rango y de edad, todos los moradores de Salonica, hombres y mujeres, gidiós y no gidios, creían a la existencia de los dañadores (sedim) que eran también llamados *los mijores de mosotros o los de abaxo.* Miles de personas juraban haber *tuvido* a sufrir de las fasfechas y desmodramientos de estos fantasmas, otros afirmaban haber constatado *sus* (sic!) presencia y haber oído *sus* voz; algunos ían (iban) mismo hasta decir haberlos visto y tocado.

Según esta gente flaca de meollo, los dañadores, tomaban mil formas de personarse, de animales o de cosas de casa, como muebles, atuendos de cocina y otras, muchas veces, *los mijores de mosotros* tenían una partida de persona y una partida de animal o de cosa. Dañadores en forma de animal tenían voz de hombre; otros en forma de hombre tenían cabeza de gamello o de vaca. Cantaban como gallo, caminaban con *pieses* (sic!) de pato, remaban en barcas de papel o volaban sin alas. Cántaros bailaban, calderas caminaban, bacinas reían, lámparas abrían la boca, escobas, escrusian dientes, escarabatos lloraban con gemido en fin no venian a imaginarse las *asnedades* que una suma de personas quitaban *seriosamente* de la boca y creían en ellas como en ley de Sinai.

En cuanto a las vestimientas de *los mijores de mosotros* era una verdadera cancarabía cabellos de algodón, sábanas volando, ceñidura de zamarra, botones de velludo, escribanía de hielo, entojos de fuego, bastones de flama, lo todo en una o en mil colores.

Familias enteras que se creían aseladadas de parte de los *de abaxo* abandonaban sus casa y se ían en *cuartieres* leanos sin decir nada a ninguno, espantándose, no lo *embesaran* los sedim y fueran a perseguirlos en *sus* nueva morada. Otros imaginando que el dañador o el *güerco* se les había entrado en el cuerpo ayunaban hasta veinte y un días o tomaban *manesia* para sacar el mal de encima..."

See our bibliography for books on Judeo-Spanish. Anyone interested in the language aspect of this remarkable passage will be helped by Wagner, Luria, Crews, etc. I believe very little attention has been paid to the coining of Spanish words by the Hispano-Levantine Jews on the basis of standard forms. For example, *asnedad* from *asno;* compare with *burro* and *burrada; desmodrarse, desmodramiento* is a happy invention... I italicized many words to call the readers' attention to the peculiarities of Judeo-Spanish as it was used in Salonica.

5. Saadi Levy, *op. cit.* Book 1, chapter XI; *meldar* has at least three meanings; as a verb it means to read; as a noun it means two different things: an elementary school, and the ceremony for celebrating the anniversary of the deceased.

6. In 1846 the English minister at Constantinople in charge of Protestant propaganda asked Antonio Fernández de Córdoba, the Spanish Ambassador for the Ottoman Empire, to give him copies of Amador de los Ríos' articles which had been appearing in *Revista del Español* since 1845 so that he could translate them into the Judeo-Spanish *koiné* and have them printed in Rashi characters for the purpose of informing the Jews of that country of their own illustrious history. Just when the Spanish ambassador was about to leave Constantinople the book in the *koiné* was in press. Was it ever published and dis-

tributed according to plan? See *Al lector* in José Amador de los Ríos, *Estudios históricos, políticos y literarios sobre los judios en España,* Madrid, 1948.

7. Moïse Franco, *Essai sur l'histoire des Israëlites de l'Empire Ottoman,* Paris, 1897, pp. 164-65.

8. See our general Bibliography for S. Levy's *Memorias.*

9. Saül Mézan, *Les Juifs espagnols en Bulgarie* (Editon d'Essai). Sofia, 1925, 150 pages. Saül Mézan has analyzed very effectively the polyglotic chaos of the Hispano-Levantine Communities and the criticism on the Alliance comes from his pen. See in particular, page 41 and following.

VII
The Sephardic Jews in the United States

How strange it seems! These Hebrews in their graves.
Close by the street of this fair seaport town,
Silent beside the never-silent waves,

At rest in all this moving up and down!
The very names recorded here are strange,
Of foreign accent, and of different climes;
Alvares and Rivera interchange
With Abraham and Jacob of old times.
                    Henry Wadsworth Longfellow[1]

In the first decade of this present century, small numbers of Hispano-Levantines entered the United States. At the time much new blood was pouring into this country, prior to the present restrictive immigration rules. The reasons for this late coming of the Hispano-Levantines will be explained in due course, but now it is appropriate to note that upon their arrival they found a large Jewish population already well established, and they also became dimly aware that long before their arrival from the Eastern Mediterranean countries, there had been Sephardic Jews; indeed, Sephardic Jews had been here from the very beginning of European settlements in America. The story of the Sephardic Jews in the New World has manifold phases into which the scope of this book forbids us to enter. We set aside for the moment the natural pride that every Sephardic Jew must feel when he dwells imaginatively upon the achievements of his ancestors. Let us consider this last contingent of the Sephardites into this country, for that is what the latest arrivals of the Hispano-Levantines are.

Marrano Jews helped in the preliminary preparations making Columbus's discoveries possible. Even though Marranos met with difficulties in leaving Spain for the West Indies and Tierra Firma, yet they managed to establish themselves in almost every Hispanic settlement. For centuries the Marranos could not openly lead Jewish lives in America, if they settled in the Hispanic world as subjects of the Portuguese or Spanish sovereigns. On the other hand, once the Marranos departed from Dutch or English ports, they could settle as Jews in the West Indies, in Brazil, or in what came to be the territory of the thirteen English colonies. At first in the commonwealth of Massachusetts as well as in New Amsterdam, prejudices against Jewish settlers were pronouncedly hostile. The Protestant Reformation had sanctioned multiplicity of Christian creeds and logically multiplicity of Christian creeds opened the way to the claim of other religions that they, too, were legitimate approaches to God.

> Although from the very beginning an intolerant theocracy both in Plymouth and in Massachusetts Bay Settlements offered little hospitality to settlers who did not conform to the dominant Christian faith, the Puritan had at all times a very real and intense interest in everything Jewish. Not only the clergymen but many of the leaders were distinguished Hebraists.

The Puritanic predisposition toward the Old Testament and inclination to find inspiration in the Mosaic legislation worked in favor of the Jews desirous of finding a field of economic activity under relatively tolerable conditions. Were we to believe modern scholars as to the origin of capitalism, we would recognize also similar psychological factors in the mentality of Puritan and Jew. Be that as it may, Sephardic Jews came to North America. Opposition to their presence in New Amsterdam was easily overcome because Holland had admitted the Portuguese merchants to her territory. Access to the colonies was inevitable if they were allowed to stay in the mother country. The Reverend Johan Megapolensis, in a letter dated March 18th, 1655, written in New Amsterdam, New Netherlands, complained of the Hispano-Dutch Jews to the ecclesiastical authorities of his country:

> Some Jews came from Holland last summer in order to trade. Later a few Jews came upon the ship De Polheymius; they were healthy but poor. It would have been proper that they be supported by their own people, but they have been at our charge, so that we have had to spend several hundred guilders for their support. They came several times to my house, weeping and bemoaning their misery. If I directed them to the Jewish merchants, they said, that they would not even lend them a few stivers. Some of them have come from Holland this spring. They report

that still more of the same lot would follow, and then they would build here a synagogue. This causes among the Congregation here a great deal of complaint and murmuring. These people have no other god than the unrighteous Mammon, and no other aim than to get possession of Christian property, and to win all other merchants by drawing all trade toward themselves.[2]

Discounting the inevitable antagonism of this Protestant divine, we observe how the less fortunate of the Marrano Jews were seeking a refuge in America. The numbers of Sephardic Jews of the Occidental brand were very limited, and the losses in immigation likewise could not exceed the parental stock in the European countries. Though their numbers were exiguous, yet these Marrano Jews played important rôles in the drama of American national existence. They fought in the Revolutionary War, the War of 1812, and the Civil War.

Up to the middle of the nineteenth century, the Marrano Jews in the United States were on the whole the only Jews who counted in national life. German Jews came in large numbers after the failure of the liberal movements of 1848. More vital in creative energies and more aggressive, the Ashkenazic Jews soon surpassed the Peninsular Jews who were resting on the laurels of their success. Overwhelmed by the large number of their Germanic brethren, the Sephardic Jews became apprehensive of their very existence. The eclipsing of the glory of Sephardism was comprehensive. What the Reverend Bueno de Mesquita said of the London Congregation is equally if not more forcibly applicable to the communities of Sephardic Jews in the United States:

In London, the survival of its early Sephardi settlers as an independent religious unit, based on Spanish characteristics and manners, was fraught with some anxiety. Yet, although they were very few in number, and although they had no legal right to live in England, they did strike root in English soil. But by the middle of the nineteenth century, the Spanish tongue, as well as the Portuguese, had disappeared from their congregational schools, from their Prayer-book translation, from the pulpit and their Mahamad chamber. Further, the growth in numbers and importance of the Ashkenazic Jews was challenging the pre-eminence which, till then, had been enjoyed by the Sephardim. So that one day, a member of the Elders, viewing with alarm this development of the German community, addressed his brother Elders with the words: 'Gentle-

men, I warn you that, unless we take care, we shall find ourselves sub-
merged by the waters of the German ocean.'

The late Judge Cardozo of the Supreme Court of the United States,
in a letter addressed to the author (February 2, 1937), concretizes one of
the points made in the above quotation regarding the survival of Hispanic culture:

> So far as my family is concerned it has no cultural traditions with refer-
> ence to the survival of Spanish or with reference to its Spanish or Portu-
> guese origin. Perhaps the reason is that such origin belongs to a remote
> past.

The absence of Hispanic culture has not been tantamount to an obliteration of identity, notwithstanding all the erosive forces working against
the feeling of self identification. Sephardic Jewry in the West, deprived
of its Peninsular cultural pattern, has endeavored to maintain its being
through the substratum, i.e., the Jewish religion. On the one hand, nationalism and the cultural current flowing from the French Revolution
worked in disfavor of the Peninsular traditions among the Marrano descendants; on the other hand, the heterodox views of science and politics promoted the secularization of life. Nationalism and the inimical
forces of tradition and religion worked together to almost annihilate the
Sephardic communities of the West.

> The secularization of modern life is weakening the hold of religion; the
> disappearance of religious practice from the home is depriving Jewish
> children of that Jewish background to their existence which is of vital im-
> portance to the Jewish future; it becomes increasingly difficult to provide
> for our spiritual needs, to fill positions in the Rabbinical chair, at the
> Tebah and in the pulpit; to staff religious schools adequately, to find
> teachers even for those who desire their services.

The Hispano-Levantines who came to the United States in the first
decade of the current century were fleeing from war-stricken countries,
looking for a better world. Had they begun to come the century before,
the melancholy decline of the occidentalized Sephardic life would not
have occurred. Culturally these Hispano-Levantines were miles away
from their American Sephardic brethren. A long process of acclimatiza-
tion has to take place before there can be any rapprochement. Whether
in time the Mediterranean Sephardim are going to be worthy continua-

tors of the original Jewish settlers of New York, Newport, Philadelphia, is something unpredictable. What is positive and factual is the advent of the Hispano-Levantine.

The chief factor in the emigration of the Hispano-Levantine Jews from their Mediterranean world was the rapid breaking-up of the Turkish Empire, accelerated in the first years of the second· decade of this century. The cupidity, the machinations, and the imperialistic aims of the Great Powers found the Balkan peoples ready for an open revolt against Turkish tutelage. Encouraged by the Pan-Slavic movement and the ambitions of Austria-Hungary, England, France, countries like Greece, Bosnia, Bulgaria, Montenegro and Rumania plotted the dismemberment of the Ottoman Empire. In 1911 Italy was successful against Turkey when she got as her booty the *villayets* of Tripoli and Cyrenaica, and the right to control twelve Aegean islands, the so-called Dodecanese; among these is included the famous island of Rhodes. Following this example, the Balkan peoples formed an alliance (1912-13) with the purpose of liquidating the moribund Turkish Empire which had endured for so many centuries at their expense. As a result of this Balkan crusade, Turkey seemed on the point of making the last bow on the bloody stage of history. If all their ambitions were not satisfied, at least when their wars of *reconquest* were over, practically all of them came out stronger, with new territories annexed to their once tiny domains. When we notice that the "Republic of the Sephardim," Salonica, changes hands and becomes Greek as a result of these wars, we can readily appreciate the convulsive changes experienced by the easy-going Hispano-Levantines. Instantly, by instinct as it were, the Sephardim of the Near East realized that their four-century isolation had come to an end. Their haughty indifference to the national problems of the peoples in whose lands they had been living had to give way to a new attitude. For centuries they had successfully resisted learning the customs and languages of the Greeks and the Slavs, since politically they were of no importance and culturally negligible. Had their indifference stopped in the middle of the nineteenth century, they might have succeeded in establishing closer contacts with their neighbors other than the Turks. Because their communal organizations had stagnated and their economic status had degenerated considerably they were incapable of understanding the nationalistic awakening of Rumanians, Greeks, Bosnians, and Bulgarians. Their loyalty to the Turks also militated against any effort at identification with the future victors. Being persecuted people they could perceive that the machinations of the Great Powers would cause everybody trouble. (The poor Armenians being more gullible and more daring agitated against Turkey to their sorry detriment.) Still another reason for their inability to make an adjustment with the forces that were to win was the misguided educational program of the Alliance.

(Ingratitude is not an ingredient of the Sephardic character. Consequently it is just to say that the Alliance did her best to prepare her wards for the new world in the making. The equipment in Western manners, ideas, and languages with which the Alliance endowed the Sephardic Jews, though meagre, made their emigration less cruel and less hopeless.)

How came it about that the Sephardic Jews heard of the opportunities offered by the United States at the very time that the Turkish Empire was collapsing? Steamship companies doing business with the United States had sent agents to the Near East to solicit trade and passengers. A generation before 1910, hundreds of Greeks and Slavs had preceded the Hispano-Levantine. Some Sephardic merchants, dealers in orientalia, carpets, antiques, and raw materials, had visited the United States at various Expositions. Letters, talks with returning immigrants and the Sephardic merchant, and newspaper accounts of American prosperity exposed the possibility of escape. To the inevitable hardships that come with war, such as losses in life and goods, must be added the military conscription of Sephardic youth in the various Balkan armies as well as in the Turkish fighting forces. It must be remembered that the Sephardic Jews had been spared military experience by the communal nature of their existence under Turkish rule which exempted participation in war in exchange for taxes. By not participating in the army, the Jews were the losers as far as their character formation was concerned. Their virile fiber suffered irreparable change thereby. Unable to understand the compensations that come from having military experience, the Sephardic Jews at first were not willing to submit to conscription or to the excessive money equivalents in lieu of military service. Economic precariousness, war dangers, and military conscription were the evils the Sephardic Jews were determined to avoid.

A few years before the Italo-Turkish War and the Balkan Wars, the Sephardic Jews became aware of the imminent destruction of their secluded life. Major Enver Bey, on July 23, 1908, by a *coup d'état* at Salonica, in the name of the Committee for Union and Progress, restored the Constitution of 1876. The swift end of the bloody tyrant Abdul Hamid started the radical transformations of decadent Turkey. What was started by Enver Bey and Niazi Bey, after terrific territorial losses in a great many wars, the already mentioned ones, the World War I, and the Graeco-Turkish War, was finally accomplished by Kemal Attatürk. Turkey has become a modern nation at last. In the process however, the Sephardic Jews underwent untold suffering and their eroded culture received new fertilizing elements. As in the Balkans, so in Turkey proper, the Jews at first were not prepared to change. The demands made upon the disinherited among the Sephardim were beyond their capacities. Realizing that the new adjustments would entail too much pain, many of the sturdy stock found the means, through borrowing in many cases, to buy steerage tickets for the New Land of Promise.

In the light of years of residence and human significance, the microscopic communities of the Hispano-Levantines in the United States do not warrant an extensive treatment in Jewish or general history. For the purpose we have in view, in this book however, an account must be given of the largest of these communities if the work undertaken in the field of folklore is to be understood in the proper perspective. Significance is not always measured by statistics. In themselves these communities are of no importance. When we project on them the searching beam of history, they retain an exemplary quality not so much derived from their own merit but from remote sources. These humble folk have to their credit their uninterrupted ascension from Peninsular glories. Their ancestors in Spain (and for a century after their banishment) enriched the culture of the Jews and contributed to the general fund of human achievement. Because in the tenement houses of New York City upon their arrival they sang the venerable ballads of chivalric Spain, because they preserved those *romances* and *muwassahas* that were among the most valuable possessions of their exiled forefathers, these Mediterranean Jews cannot be totally devoid of interest and significance for Hispanic letters and Jewish folkways. Little by little as they become cognizant of their lusterless present in relation to their deep historical experiences, they will take the trouble to write up a thoroughly dignified account of their establishment in this country.

When I was a pupil at Woodward High School (1913) in Cincinnati, I remember having been of considerable assistance to Dr. Maurice Hexter of the Jewish Settlement of that city, when he undertook to make a sociological study of three hundred odd Sephardi Jews who had been living in Cincinnati since 1905. Hardly had my historical consciousness been awakened when I dimly understood that my people were a subject for investigation. It was not a very comfortable feeling to have, as the thought dawned upon my boyish mentality, that the small tribe lost in the cheapest section of the sooty city by the muddy Ohio River, was presenting difficulties to the charitable agencies of the Ashkenazic Jews who were by comparison numerous and prosperous. No scruples of a sentimental nature deterred me from helping Dr. Hexter procure data about my fellow Sephardim. We climbed innumerable stairs and always we were ushered into the clean and hospitable homes of waiters, peddlers, factory workers, and petty merchants. Low wages, long hours, periods of idleness, ignorance of the language, unfamiliarity with the customs of Ashkenazic Jews as well as of Gentiles, gave the tiny group an unenviable status. Since I belonged to the second contingent that arrived in 1910, I remember other phases of the social milieu in which the Hispano-Levantines found themselves in Cincinnati. As a mere lad in his early teens I had the advantage of going to the American public schools. A few Sephardic boys and I unwittingly served as connecting links between the Sephardic factory hands and the institutions of the city. Somehow I learned of the existence of public parks. Besides Eden Park and Burnett Woods, I discovered another public place of recreation, with more exciting scenery. In the company of my fellow Sephardim, I explored the discovered land. Our enjoyment was keen when we were surrounded by a beautiful landscape away from the ugliness of the slums of Cincinnati. These slight reminiscences must be coupled with my two or three years of teaching English among my people. While still a high school student, I, with a very imperfect knowledge of the English language, was the only person available to guide the young men and married workers employed during the day at exhausting jobs.[3]

Naturally the histories of the other communities in cities like Rochester, Indianapolis, Los Angeles, Atlanta, Montgomery, Seattle, will have to be written in order for us to get a complete recording of the arrival and the vicissitudes of the Hispano-Levantines in the United States. Mr. Albert Levy, editor of the only surviving Judeo-Spanish weekly in this country, assures me that he was in the midst of writing the chronicle of these communities. Whether Mr. Levy will go beyond the type of history cannot now be known. No matter what type of book he may write, this book will be of great linguistic and sociological import.[4]

Of all the Sephardic Communities, that of Greater New York is by far the most numerous and complicated. New York harbor being the gate to this country, it became the landing place for the latest crop of immigrants. The multi-tentacled metropolis had been insatiable for new raw materials, of the human as well as material kind. The Sephardic Jews were town dwellers in their respective countries, and the anonymity of a large urban center attracted them as it had the millions preceding them. It has been calculated that there are sixty thousand Hispano Levantines in this country now. Over half this number is in New York. As in Cincinnati, the first attempt at sizing up their worth and their problems has come from an expert in the field of Jewish philanthropy. Under the auspices of the Bureau of Jewish Social Research. Dr. Louis Hacker prepared in manuscript form (May, 1926) a rather competent report on *The Communal Life of the Sephardic Jews of New York City.* At the time he wrote his report Mr. Hacker had not yet developed into an authority of national importance on matters economic. Yet this report shows that he was extra-ordinarily well prepared to tackle a new human situation when it was a question of analyzing social phenomena that had interest for the Jews and non-Jews in this country. Mr. Hacker, an outsider, could see the Sephardic Jews with detachment. Since the large Jewish community of New York had a moral obligation to understand its poor relations, for again and again they impinged upon the lives of the Ashkenazic Jews, a sociological survey of the Sephardim of recent date was needed for the proper extension of help.[5]

For centuries Ashkenazic Jews and Sephardic Jews have misunderstood each other. Wherever the Sephardic Jews had been in a majority, Salonica, Constantinople, Amsterdam, London, New York, and in Palestine in the past centuries, they looked down upon the Ashkenazim. Now that the latter form the majority in Jewry and all power and creativity are theirs, the Sephardic Jews have become their wards. Instead of showing hostility and abuse paying the haughty Iberic Jews in their own coin, with disdain and aloofness, the Ashkenazic Jews on the whole, particularly the communal leaders, have shown forbearance and willingness to give a helping hand to their downtrodden brethren. For the masses of Ashkenazic Jews, the Sephardim have always appeared a strange group of Jews.

> Although the Sephardic Jews have in the main settled in those parts of the city inhabited by their Ashkenazic coreligionists, the former find themselves as alien and apart as if they had settled somewhere in China or Sweden. It is quite difficult for the Yiddish and German speaking Jews, who surpass all other Jews in number, to reconcile themselves to the belief that there can be other Jews who do not employ the same means of linguistic utterance; and if for a moment they ignore their linguistic difference and seek a final proof in the ability of the Sephardic Jew to use Hebrew, they are further mystified by the fact that they encounter a Hebrew which is accented and pronounced differently from the one to which they are accustomed. The difference is futher emphasized by the fact that the Sephardic Jews vary somewhat in their ritual and in the chants employed in the synagogue. These differences of languages, rituals, habits, and customs have contributed to the creation of a solidly crystallized Sephardic community whose identity stands out patently.[6]

Professor Luria's succinct characterization, admirable in every way, is ambiguous in its last sentence. If by "a solidly crystallized Sephardic community" we understand the existence of an organized mass of people, then we are not told the truth. On the other hand, the description is correct if the phrase means that however loosely the Sephardic Jews might be organized in an administrative sense, and no matter how many internal differences there may be among them, yet in psychology, ethnology, and culture they form a sociological unity.

Dr. Louis Hacker cannot be accused of prejudice. Notwithstanding his good will and technical equipment, he had a meagre preparation to fathom all the pathetic shortcomings of the Hispano-Levantines and the hidden wells of their moral strength. His report, therefore, though of incalculable value (valuable because it is really the only reliable study so far made of this people) lacks due perspective and inclusiveness. Consequently we shall be cautiously guided by the facts accumulated in this monograph. The diagnosis of this people's psychology in conflict with the new environment receiving them, as given by Hacker, is not only inadequate but also erroneous. Where Hacker sees backwardness as a vestige of Oriental fatalism, and the tendency to localistic fragmentariness as a disposition brought over from the old cities of the Turkish Empire, better informed historians consider these traits as much older than their stay in Turkey and the Balkans.

> The Sephardic Jews, because of religious, linguistic, and psychological differences that set them off from their Ashkenazic coreligionists, were compelled to face their own problems and create their own agencies. They brought with them from their homelands in the Old Turkish Empire a keen sense of localism. The result was the creation here of synagogues and societies based on *Landsmanschaft* lines.

The facts as stated in this quotation from Dr. Hacker are indisputable. The tendency of the Sephardim to set themselves apart from other Spanish Jews other than their fellow townsmen was indeed at the bottom of the creation of organizations of an exclusivistic nature. From their arrival to the present, all efforts at federating the minute mutual-aid societies have failed, despite the progressive intra-communal assimilation of their members. When it comes to observational data, Dr. Hacker is on solid ground. Only when he tries to allocate causes and origins does he fail. The localism of these people, which he attributes to their Oriental homelands, goes back to their Peninsular formation and perhaps the latter started with the desert and Palestinian beginnings of the Jews. Our guess is that Semitic tribalism combined with Iberic temperament worked together to give rise to an accentuated separatistic psychology among the Sephardic Jews.

> This characteristic of ethnic psychology manifests itself wherever chance and historical vicissitudes have thrown the homes of the Sephardim. No matter where he established his residence, the Spanish Jew hastens to reconstitute the streets of his native city, transferring thereto his language, his customs, his culinary habits, his worries and quarrels. Each regional group forms a small world unto itself on the side of other little worlds and particularly far from the non-Jewish world. One almost could say that he carries in his luggage his little fatherland, his synagogue. This phenomenon of isolation in relation to the totality of the Jews and that one of regrouping oneself around a temple, almost as a part of one's household, is noticed very clearly, even in our days, in the colonies that the Salonicans have established recently in New York, in Paris, or in Tel-Aviv.[7]

Right at the start of their residence in New York City, the Hispano-Levantines established on the East Side the typical Mediterranean coffee-house as a place of recreation. Since many of the immigrants were unmarried, their culinary likes and dislikes had to be attended to. Consequently the coffee-house offered restaurant service.

> The typical Oriental café or coffee-house flourished among the Sephardim for yet another reason. It is familiar enough that the Mohammedan lands from which the Sephardim come are man-dominated. The women are social nullities. The result is that here too, in the West, the home is not the scene of social intercourse but rather the café that fills that place. It must be remembered that in the Levant the café has played the combined rôles of eating house, club, business exchange and gaming room. The Oriental café in New York partakes of similar functions.[8]

This characterization is on the whole correct. The aspersion that Sephardic women do not count is due to a lack of perspective on the part of Mr. Hacker. If the Sephardic home is humble and insignificant, then the women are humble and insignificant. Importance and nullity are in their case a question of social position. The nullity or importance of the wife is in direct proportion to the social position of her husband.

More than once have coffee-houses been raided by the police on real and on imaginary charges. When the municipal judges were intelligent, the victims of misunderstanding were released at once. Their card playing and billiard shooting even when money was interchanged by the players, rarely assumed destructive proportions. Here is an account given by a Sephardic worker of an unjustified raid on a café which he witnessed relaxing at the café from fatigue after working hours:

> Asentado en un cantón reposándome de la canseria del laboro del día, en un café sefardí, arrodeado de unos cuantos amigos, tratando de las cuestiones del día, el resultado del cual non era más que satisfacer nuestros instinctos de crítica—súbito uno de mis compañeros grita: 'Amigo, estás arrestado.' '¿Por quién?', le demando yo. Y antes mismo de escapar de responderme me veo entornado de tres detectivos, ordenándome de asentarme y non hacer ningún movimiento.

In this case, as we are told by one of the victims, the secret police in their great zeal for law and order committed an unjust act in arresting persons who had done no wrong. On a previous occasion, for having gone to the café, the victims were sent to jail for 380 days!

In the absence of appropriate institutions in their new environment, the Sephardic Jews had to have recourse to the coffee-house. Within the last ten years, however, with the distribution of the 30,000 odd Sephardim in the Bronx, Brooklyn, and other sections of New York City, the grip of the café has been attenuated if not completely broken. Of all sorts exclusively Sephardic clubs have sprung up. And many of the more prosperous and enlightened have joined organizations of a more inclusive nature, Ashkenazic or Gentile. Clearly, the accusation of fatalism and lack of curiosity levelled at them is far from true.

> The Sephardim consider themselves a people apart. They are 'Spanish Jews,' with a distinct historical consciousness and a pride and dignity that strengthens their unlikeness. True, the generality of them is not so prosperous or so well adjusted to the American life as are their Ashkenazic kinsmen, but aloofness is due not to a pathetic attempt at the maintenance of self-respect but to a feeling of superiority.

To the above well-thought-out words of Dr. Hacker, who often miscalculated in matters concerning the character of the Hispano-Levantines, must be added the following observation made by Dr. de Sola Pool, the spiritual head of the oldest Sephardic congregation in the United States.

> ...the tradition of a noble past and the possession of an honored family name have never allowed poverty and oppression to degrade the Levantine Jews and rob them of their self-respect. We would be wrong were we to regard an Aboulafia, an Aboab, a Kamhi, etc., as members of the lower classes, even though they may be peddlers or shoe polishers. They do not so regard themselves.[9]

Students of Spanish literature are familiar with the psychology of the impoverished hidalgo, the classical example being the *escudero* in *Lazarillo de Tormes*. Pride of self in poverty is a luxury ill afforded by those who have to live in a utilitarian world. This Spanish sense of superiority even in the absence of positive goods to justify it contributed to the delayed rapprochement of Sephardim to the more prosperous and more successful Ashkenazic Jews. There have been many intelligent Hispano-Levantines who have deplored this unwarranted conceit.

> Nosotros sefardim que nos glorificamos tanto de nuestros abuelos españoles por sus contribuciones a su pueblo y al mundo, nos creemos superiores en carácter a nuestros hermanos Esquenazim y percuramos a

non asociarnos con ellos; nosotros sefardim que nos sentimos transpor-
tados encima de Olimpos (montaña onde los dioses de los viejos griegos
vivían) cuando un hablador nombra los nombres ilustres de Ishac (sic),
Halevi, Rambam, Ben Gabirol, y de otros sabios, no queremos ver que
malgrado que nuestros padres eran ricos nosotros nos morimos a la ham-
bre. Los bienes del pasado no pueden hartar nuestro estómago. La buena
fama de ayer no puede conservar la pureza y la nobleza de nuestro nombre de hoy.[10]

As in the sixteenth century, so in the twentieth the Sephardic sense of
belonging to a world of tradition and achievement worthy of conservation goes hand in hand with an almost innate incapacity, so it seems, to
overlook slight and feigned differences in the name of the very unity to
which they owe allegiance.

This characteristic pride and clannishness that so set off the Sephardic
Jews...really make an internal disharmony. Before the stranger there is
a solid front; among themselves there is a plethora of petty bickering,
misunderstanding, and obscure rivalry.

Pressure from various sources has been at work to iron out the differentiating factors. All attempts thus far at creating a centralized agency
for the administration of Sephardic communal life have failed, despite
the fact that linguistically their dialects have finally formed a recogniz-
able Koiné, and despite the daily contacts among members of the distinct nuclei hailing from different cities and countries.[11] English is now
becoming the medium of their intercourse; yet the Judeo-Spanish common dialect evolved in New York is written and spoken by all. Another
version of the language situation prevailing now is the following given
by the American philologist who studied the Monastir dialect, starting
his investigation among the Hispano-Levantines who have formed their
hermetic groupings in New York City.

The foreign-born Sephardic Jews still cling to the patois which they acquired in the place of their birth, although their language is picturesquely
punctuated by what passes for English or by English words Hispanized.
Literary inclinations are on the whole satisfied by the reading of Judeo-
Spanish newspapers. The American-born generation or those who came
to this country when quite young are drifting away from the language
and customs of their fathers. An attempt is made to overcome this ten-

dency in the Talmud Torah. There the language of the class is Judeo-Spanish, commonly called Ladino. Hebrew exercises and passages from the Bible are translated into Judeo-Spanish. But this method will not prevail long, and Judeo-Spanish will disappear as surely as did Spanish and Portuguese among the descendants of the first Spanish and Portuguese Jews in New York.[12]

Judeo-Spanish is still considered the vital nexus between the Hispano-Levantine and God. The alarming deliquescence of the medieval mores in the all-absorbing American environment has begun to frighten the few men in the New York colony who have any historical consciousness at all. Albert Matarasso, who has received rabbinical training here and abroad though not engaged in the ministerial profession, associates the loss of interest in religious matters with the ignorance of the men who officiate at the synagogue during the three High Holy Days. He demands services in Judeo-Spanish:

> Deseamos andar a la casa del Dio por lo menos tres dias del año, pero es intolerable; todos los andamos e reptando (sic) lo mismo y en lengua que no la entendemos...Nuestras oraciones para nosotros debrían ser hechas en la más grande parte en la lengua que entendemos que es en el judeo-español. Nuestros hazanim debrían saber trasladarlas y esto hasta que nosotros vivimos...

From the unexpected quarters we have rejuvenation of the over-bastardization of the Spanish language as spoken by our people. A considerable number of boys and girls have rediscovered the significance of the jargon spoken at home through the high school courses in the Castilian language. By far the more significant factor in this modernization of the Spanish dialects of medieval origin is to be found in the daily contacts between the Hispano-Levantines and the Spaniards and Hispano-Americans who live by the thousands in the city of New York. The doctor, the lawyer, the accountant, the insurance agent, the dentist, the druggist, the merchant, the waiter, and the factory worker, are inevitably thrown into the company of Spanish-speaking peoples with the consequence that the outlandish excrescences are filed away or dropped off when confronted with the genuine samples of the Spanish language in its modern vigor. School and shop, street and subway, radio programs and newspaper articles, moving pictures and restaurants, are some of the agencies contributing to this strange phenomenon of an artificial rehispanization of the Hispano-Levantines. So long as New York remains a meeting place for so many thousands of Hispanic folk, the chances for the complete obliteration of the Hispano-Jewish dialects are considerably diminished.

Not only have the processes of unification and purification of their dialects grown apace, but in every other aspect of social and business relationship we observe the breaking down of provincial differentiations. Sons and daughters of families who belong to societies that bear stamps heralding their distinct origins have been interchanged in marriage. Friendships, business partnerships, coffee-house associations, attendance at parties and synagogue services, membership in common societies, the patronizing of dramatic representations—in all the mentioned contacts, the Hispano-Levantines have gradually been amalgamating with their American environment. Survivals of the early days in the form of prejudice and exclusiveness concretized in societies formed on the sole basis of place of origin, continue to prevent the conscious recognition of the new situation making for an organization of a new type.[13]

In 1936 Albert Amateau summarized this experience as a Sephardic leader who with many other public-minded men failed in unifying the regional societies of the brethren:

In those days (1915-1925) with expert eyes many of us saw the wrong road taken by our colony with its multiple societies, with its separate burial plots, its synagogues and Talmud Torah, and its separate bank accounts. We worked on behalf of unity, so that worthy works might be produced to satisfy the needs of our colony in due time. We foresaw the social and communal chaos in which our colony finds itself today. But we were not listened to or understood...

The personal ambition of some leaders who wished at any price to keep their influence as guides of their respective groups, the intrigues of the iš-biterigís, who never consented to an efficient community among our people, and the politics of intrigue of a group of rich men—Sephardim of the older generations, helped by a newspaperman who fortunately has kept away for the good of our colony—, and the ignorance of our brethren; these are the factors that combined to keep our colony in a disorganized state, leaving it without leadership and protection. With the exception of a few individuals who have been successful in business or at their professions, our people are today more backward and more disunited than ever. We lack everything; agencies for social, cultural, industrial and religious help. Our mutual aid societies, with one or two exceptions, must be considered in moral bankruptcy, since, they do nothing but collect money without doing anything for their members, and by the mere fact that they exist, they prevent the formation of a true unity, the true community that all men of good will wish for and are looking for.

Discounting for the time being the bitterness that interlineates the above summary, coming as it does from a man who meant well but failed to achieve unity, the exactitude of the indictment is unquestionable. This Hispano-Semitic dispersiveness is a factor to be weighed most seriously whenever we wish to appraise the character of the Spanish Jews.

The men of Castoría, in their synagogues, employed a slightly different cantilation that was unpleasing to the men of the island of Chios. Incidentally, it is in the Oriental temperament to be suspicious even of the slightly unfamiliar, with the result that because of a localism that was the development of centuries men from towns only thirty miles apart were prone to regard one another with distrust.

Where Mr. Hacker says Oriental, substitute the word Spanish, and the characterization is most apt.

Among the first immigrant generation local feeling is still as real as it was when they first stepped on the American shore. Add to this their natural conservatism, a suspicion easily aroused and a fondness for casuistry that sees profound differences where none exist, and the reason for the independent existence of small, inefficient, poorly managed societies is quickly to be found.

Dr. Hacker in 1926 was able to account for thirty-six societies among the Hispano-Levantines living in New York. Most of them bore and still bear Hebrew appellatons. Here are some of the names (in English) of these organizations that have managed to survive, even if they, as in the majority of cases, do not go beyond offering sick and death benefits: Union and Peace; Love of Peace; Love and Truth; Rod of Life; Bond of Brothers; Fountain of Life; Life and Love; Tree of Life. Under these ambitious, supremely ethical values, men and women from Monastir, Castoría, Adrianople, Constantinople, Dardanelles, Gallipoli, Smyrna, the islands of Chios, Rhodes, etc., have kept to a certain extent their love for the peculiarities and idiosyncracies of the old world milieus.[14]

Many are the forces threatening to extinguish these minute group-ings. For one thing, two irresistible moulding agencies are at work to dissolve the now objectionable clannishness. The American ethos has them like all the other ethnic sections of the country in its grip. If the larger social mass always absorbs the smaller groups, it is inevitable that concomitant with Americanization, the Sephardic Jews will sooner or later be assimilated within the Ashkenazic cauldron. Slowly but fatally the Sephardic Jews through intermarriage are entering the North Euro-pean traditions of Jewry. The future always has surprises. ¿Quién sabe?

NOTES

1. Morris A. Gutstein, *The Story of the Jews of Newport, Two and a Half Centuries of Judaism,* New York, 1936, 1658-1908, pp. 251-254. The poem by Longfellow, "The Jewish Cemetery at Newport," was composed in 1858; also see the poem of Emma Lazarus, "In the Jewish Synagogue in Newport" (1867) in above work, pp. 254-255.

2. For the complete letter of Johann Megapolensis, see *Early American Jews* by Lee M. Friedman, Cambridge, Mass., Harvard University Press, 1934, pp. 51-52.

3. Maurice B. Hexter, "The Dawn of a Problem," in *Jewish Charities,* December, 1913, Vol. 3, pp. 2-5.

4. This chronicle has not been published and the weekly *La Vara* has stopped publication since the redaction of this chapter.

5. Louis Hacker, *The Communal Life of the Sephardic Jews of New York City.* The complete report is preserved at the Bureau of Jewish Social Re-search. A resumé of this report was published by Louis Hacker in *The Jewish Social Service Quarterly,* December, 1926, Vol. 3, No. 2, pp. 32-40.

6. Max A. Luria, "Judeo-Spanish Dialects in New York City," in *Todd Memorial Volumes,* Philological Studies, 1930-1931. (Edited by John Fitz-Gerald and Pauline Taylor.) See on the status of the Judeo-Spanish dialects, page 9, and on the relation of the Sephardic Jews to the Ashkenazic Jews, page 8. For a further discussion on the theme Sephardic and Ashkenazic, see *Addenda* to Notes on the last chapter of this book.

7. Joseph Nehama, *Histoire des Israélites de Salonique,* Salonique, Librairie Molho, 1936, Vol. III, p. 66.

8. See Note 5.

9. David de Sola Pool, "On Spanish Jews of Levantine Origin in the United States," in *Jewish Charities,* March, 1913. (An address by Dr. de Sola

Pool on the same question delivered before the Conference of the National Association of Jewish Social Workers meeting in Memphis, Tennessee, May 1914.)

10. This is a quotation from one of the numerous articles by Albert Matarasso, an indefatigable community and intellectual leader among the Salonician Jews, which were published in the now defunct weekly *La Vara*. A translation into French of his synthetic account of the early history of the Hispano-Levantine Communities appeared in two installments in Samy Levy's magazine *Les Cahiers Sefardis* under the title of "Historique du Sefardisme aux U.S.A." (Recueil Documentaire-Histoire Rétrospectif-D'Actualité [Published in Neuilly-sur-Seine], June 20, 1947, pp. 240-244; September 30, 1947, pp. 347-351.

11. From 1940 to 1950 there has been considerable progressive activity in the laying of the foundations for the establishment of an all-embracing Society of the Sephardic Jews. In part, the ideal is being realized now. Here are some of the new factors that contributed to the creation of the new spirit:

a. The older generations have been disappearing and the new generations born and educated in the United States are now taking an active interest in their communal affairs.

b. Some very important rabbis came to New York fleeing from the Nazis and their allies: the late Rabbi Ovadia from Paris, Rabbi Isaac Alcalay from Yugoslavia, Dr. Moses Ventura, chief rabbi from Alexandria. (Dr. Ventura received his *doctarat de l'État* from the Sorbonne and is a student of Hebraic-Arabic philosophy.) Rabbi Cardozo, belonging to the Marrano tradition, is shepherding in the Bronx a congregation of Hispano-Levantine Jews. These rabbis and scholars intellectually are of a higher category than the laymen who at the beginning acted as spiritual leaders.

c. Wealth and well-being of these Sephardim and the American philanthropic tradition influencing them, have also had their share in this movement toward unity.

12. Max A. Luria, "A Study of the Monastir Dialect," in *Revue Hispanique*, 1930.

13. *The Sephardi* published by The Central Sephardic Jewish Community of America, Inc. (225 W. 34 St., New York), attests to the existence of the realized dream of unity and cooperation among the Sephardic Jews. The Sephardic Jewish Center of the Bronx with its Synagogue and Religious School is to this day the greatest achievement of the Hispano-Levantine Jews. Everything indicates that The Sephardic Home for the Aged is going to become a concrete reality. As of the month of September 1950, we know that the campaign to raise an additional $150,000 is going to end in success.

14. Atomism and disintegration are still realities of the Sephardim of New

York City. We reproduce the list of the Sephardic synagogues that functioned for the Jewish high holy days in the Fall of 1950. The names of the societies and their places of prayer tell an interesting cryptic story of Sephardic Israel.

High Holy Day Services

Congregation	*Will be held at*
	Brooklyn
Ahavath Shalom Monastir	699 Williams Avenue
Ahi Ezer Damessek (Syrian)	6322 21st Avenue
Hadassah Congregation	2109 67th Street
Hessed ve Emet Kastorialis	69 Malta Street
Hessed ve Emet Kastorialis	Savoy Mansion, 6322 20th Avenue
Kehila Sephardith (Greek)	2022 66th Street
Kehila Kedosha Janina	Washington Palace, 157 South 9th Street
Magen David Congregation (Syrian)	2022 66th Street
Middle Group	Jewish Community House of Bensonsonhurst 78th St. and Bay Parkway
Sephardic Congregation of C.I.	2911 West 16th Street
Sephardic Cong. Keter Zion	621 Hinsdale Street
Torat Israel, Sephardic Organization of Brighton Beach (Sheepshead Bay)	Brighton Community Center 3200 Coney Island Avenue
Agudath Ahim (Syrian)	Btesh Synagogue, 64th Street and 20th Avenue
Congregation Shaare Zion (Syrian)	1760 Ocean Parkway
Youth Service	699 Williams Avenue
	Bronx
Ahavath Shalom Monastir	457 East 172 Street
Congregation Shearith Israel of Janina (Greek)	1) Eames Center, 120 Eames Place 2) 926 Simpson Street
Sephardic Jewish Center of Bronx	122 East 169th Street (two services)
Sephardic Service	Hebrew Convalescent Home 3573 Bruckner Blvd.
Sha-are Rahamim	Day Nursery, 1697 Washington Avenue
Zehout Arabim	1272 Bronx River Avenue
Youth Service	Filo Center Club Gerard Avenue and 169th Street

Manhattan

Ahavath Shalom Monastir	163 Eldridge Street
Congregation Kehila Kedosha Janina (Greek)	280 Broome Street
Congregation of the Rhodes League	Bernstein's Kosher Caterers, 135 Essex Street
Kal Kadosh Beth El of Sephardic Jewish Brotherhood	1) 133 Eldridge Street 2) 162 Allen Street
Spanish and Portuguese Synagogue	Central Park West and 70th Street (two services)
United Sephardim of New York	136 Allen Street

Long Island

Sephardic Congregation of Long Beach	Elon Caterers 462 Park Place

VIII
Spain and the Sephardic Jews

And on the seventh of the Month of Ab in the self same year, the exiles of Jerusalem which were in Spain went forth dismayed and banished by the King's command. May they come back with joy, bearing their sheaves. From a description of the Hebrew Bible written for R. Jacob b. Samuel Aboab by A. Abraham Caliph and finished in Toledo, Spain in Nisan, 1492, three months before the expulsion; in *Jewish Life in Oriental Countries,* New York, New York Public Library, 1927, pp. 11-12.

For two centuries there have been scholarly, political and belle-lettristic efforts in Spain to re-establish a contact with the history and culture of the Sephardic Jews not only in terms of the past but also in connection with the contemporary colonies of Hispanic Jews in North Africa and in the Levant with a vague feeling for a future reabsorption of them. Voluminous works could be written on the subject: *Spanish Revival of Interest in the Sephardic Jews.*

Here we can only allude to the topic in summary fashion. The interest in the Sephardic Jews has cut across political ideologies. Dr. Angel Pulido under the Monarchy, Fernando de los Rios under the Second Republic and finally Francisco Franco the *Caudillo* have taken steps to translate into acts the intense interest felt by Spaniards towards their fellow Spaniards of Jewish faith. The Spanish government of Franco like the short-lived Republic of the Thirties has extended Spanish citizenship to any Sephardic Jews who would desire to acquire it. For the

last decrees see *Sefarad* for 1949. Nothing short of complete admiration
for Sephardic culture was the benevolent attitude of Menéndez y
Pelayo. His extraordinary critical works are full of references to Jewish culture: poets, dramatists, philosophers, beliefs and scientific
achievements of the Sephardim received from him just appraisal and
appreciation.[1]

Spain's greatest novelist after Cervantes, Benito Pérez Galdós, in
Gloria and *Misericordia* presented most sympathetic pictures of fictional Jews. If we are not wrong in our inferences, Galdós seems to say in
Misericordia: not until there is a cordial reconciliation between Iberia
and Israel can there ever be a recuperation of the Spanish spirit. Emilio
Castelar, Menéndez y Pelayo, and Benito Pérez Galdós, epitomize
Spain's enthusiastic benevolence towards the Sephardim. Like great
sectors of modern Spain, they wished for a return of the Spanish-speaking Jew to his own Sefarad.

Only Spaniards have expressed in modern times an unabashed kin-
ship with the Jews. Rather than feeling a sense of repulsion toward the
Jews many have discomfitingly claimed Jewish ancestry for themselves.
This partially true and considerably mythic identification with the Jew
makes the modern Spaniard a strange Christian in the anti-semitic
hostility of the world.

Contemporaneously Dr. Angel Pulido and the Marqués de Hoyos,
D. Isidoro de Hoyos y de la Torre, were travelling in the Near East to
gather data and information on the Sephardic Jews. Don Isidoro de
Hoyos saw how advantageous it would have been for the Sephardim
were they to modernize their Spanish. Expressing ideas that Miguel de
Unamuno would have approved he maintained:

> ...No soy, ciertamente, de los que condenan irremisiblemente el
> ladino o *spanyol* como lenguaje incapaz de todo adelanto e impropio
> para toda obra de alguna importancia, ni de los que le motejan de mera
> jerga o jerigonza como muchos, y entre ellos no pocos illustrados
> israelitas, lo califican. Entiendo que descartando de él las voces
> puramente hebreas y turcas y otras marcadamente extranjeras, y cor-
> rigiendo ciertos giros también en un todo extraños a la índole de nuestra
> lengua, y pulido y fijado ese dialecto por personas de gusto y de in-
> teligencia empapados en la lectura de nuestros clásicos, podría llegar a
> ser un lenguaje agradable y expresivo, susceptible de la mayor dulzura y

•

elegancia. Es más, creo que una vez perfeccionado de esta suerte y exten-
dido por medio de algunas obras y publicaciones notables, podría ejercer
un beneficioso influjo sobre nuestro propio idioma Castellano, en que,
con notoria sinrazón, han quedado anticuadús y fuera de uso tantas
palabras y frases útiles, elegantes y significativas. En Buckarest, en Bel-
grado en Constantinopla y en una porción de ciudades en donde yo creía
que había de encontrar grandes dificultades para ser comprendido, aún
llevando con nosotros medios de expresión en francés y en alemán, estos
idiomas eran en cierto punto innecesarios, porque allí se practica el
idioma castellano con grandísima abundancia. No es conocido el número
de individuos que en esos pueblos hablan el idioma castellano, porque no
sé que haya estadística que nos pueda dar a conocer el número de judíos
españoles.[2]

Dr. Angel Pulido as a Senator and author of several works on the
repatriation of the Sephardim was one of the romantic champions of
this very much needed rapprochement between Sephardim and
Spaniards. In the session of the Spanish Senate of November 13, 1903,[3]
Don Angel defended most warmly the case he was presenting before the
public opinion of his country. Among many things relevant to his topic
he said:

> Concretando más, diré, que en muchos pueblos de Oriente he visto que
> utilizan dicho idioma [el idioma español] para las relaciones íntimas y
> aun para las relaciones comerciales, pero lo que sí puedo asegurar a S.S.
> es que el castellano es para ellos considerado, con muchísima razón,
> como el idioma propio, como el idioma natural, y que, en algunos sitios,
> se tiene un grandísimo interés en su conservación. . .

Then Dr. Pulido told the Senators of Enrique Bejarano's campaign
in Bucharest to revive interest in the Spanish language. At a certain celebration, held in a school, Bejarano recited a poem which Pulido
thought worthy of reading to his fellow Senators.

> Se me ha dicho que se leyó una composición original del director de
> aquel establecimiento (que es Don Enrique Bejarano, un sabio políglota
> que posee muchos idiomas, y es sumamente apreciado en el Oriente):
> composición que me voy a permitir leer aquí, por ser breve, espresiva del
> estilo que usa el *castellano oriental,* muy parecido a nuestro castellano
> antiguo, y notable, porque en ella se manifiesta un amor grande a

nuestra Patria y a nuestra lengua, que creo estamos en el caso de apreciar convenientemente.

:Dice así esta composición:

La Lengua española

A ti lengua santa,	Con tí nos hablamos
A tí te adoro,	Al Dios de la altura
Más que a toda plata	Patrón del Universo
Más que a todo oro	Y de la Natura.
Tú sos la más linda	Si mi pueblo santo
De todo lenguaje,	El fué captivado
A tí dan las ciencias	Con tí mi querida
Todo el ventaje.	El fué consolado...

El segundo hecho que he podido apreciar es que nosotros, por sucesos conocidísimos de nuestra historia, tenemos más de medio millón de individuos desparramados por todos los pueblos de Oriente que practican nuestro idioma, que le tienen grandísimo cariño, y a los cuales miramos, sin embargo, con completo desden y hállanse tan estendidos, que ni nos damos cuenta de las publicaciones españolas que ellos tienen.

Once over the exposition of his theme, Senator Pulido began to ask questions as to what the Spanish government could do to establish concrete relations, commercial and cultural, with the Hispanic Levantines:

Pues creo que la Academia de la Lengua debe poner en este asunto un interés muy grande, debe mirarlo con algún cariño, *y debiera procurar*... primero, que se conservase el idioma español en aquellos sitios y segundo, *que el idioma aquél se diferenciase lo menos posible del nuestro,* es decir, que no fueran por las fatalidades de los tiempos separándose cada vez más estos idiomas... hasta llegar a diferenciarse por completo, en un porvenir más o menos remoto.

Crear algunas relaciones, fomentarlas, y en lo posible, hacer que *se establezcan comunicaciones literarias para que aprecien allí el cariño con que nosotros vemos que usan nuestro idioma.*[4]

Dr. Angel Pulido's cultural propaganda on behalf of the Sephardim had a magnetic effect on the educated Spanish Jews of the Orient and a few intellectuals in the Peninsula became enthusiastic followers of Dr. Pulido. Rafael Cansinos-Assens, an able writer and messianic dreamer, through cabbalistic calculations came to the unshakable conclusion that he was a descendant of the Marranos. On the strength of this belief he began to take an absorbing interest in the Sephardic question. He backed up Pulido's thesis in his journalistic articles: before long Dr. A. S. Yahuda was invited to occupy the chair of Hebrew and Rabbinical

Literature at the University of Madrid and young Rafael, hailing from romantic Seville, became the Sephardic professor's friend and joined the small group of Moroccan and European Sephardim who happened to be living in Madrid. Numerous pamphlets, essays, short stories, poems and novels, dealing with the Sephardim came from Cansinos-Assens' pen.[5]

From *Las Luminarias de Hanukah* (Un episodio de la Historia de Israel en España. Novela, Madrid, 1924) we shall quote two passages. In the first one we get an echo of Pulido's influence on ebullient Rafael and in the second we perceive the hallucinations and mystical day-dreaming of a Spaniard believing himself a modern Marrano.

> El señor Farsi y el joven Rafael laboran incansables, por el ideal de una reparación para los desterrados bajo la égida del señor Florido,[6] que presta a la campaña sus auspicios políticos. El israelita auténtico y el que lleva en sus venas sangre del venero proscrito y generoso, procuran inspirar su entusiasmo a sus amigos, periodistas y literatos. Están en communicación con los sefardíes de Oriente que les envían números de sus periódicos que se publican en Turquía, en lengua española y en caracteres hebraicos, rotulados con títulos tan expresivos, dolientes y esperanzados, como estos que se llaman *El Alba y el Lucero de la Paciencia*. En estos periódicos asume el verbo más amplio un escritor sefardí, Sam Levy,[7] que habla en nombre de todos los desterrados. Las palabras de Sam Levy son leídas por los amigos del Señor Farsi con atención profunda y conmovida. Tienen un estilo plañente y vigoroso que impresiona los corazones. Clama, con el acento de una indigencia moral, patética, implorando el amor y la piedad de España para la lengua española, que como un suntuoso manto apolillado llevado de España al destierro por los proscritos, deshácese ya entre las manos de la nueva juventud.

Rafael Cansinos-Assens constructed for himself a myth around his enthusiasm and identification with the Jews of Spain. His sister with whom he has lived all his life has never shared his fantastic lucubrations:

> España se le hacía querida en las evocaciones de aquellos desterrados que, sin haberla visto, cantaban sus bellezas tradicionales, según los recuerdos conservados en su familia. Pero él sentía más vivamente que ellos la afrenta hecha a su estirpe *y anhelaba una reparación solemne,* una restitución de la tierra y de los tesoros usurpados; pensaba que si su familia, gracias a una abjuración, había permanecido en España, hízolo tan sólo en previsión de tiempos mejores, para entregar un día las llaves de este suelo sagrado a los descendientes de los proscritos, cuando retornasen. *El quería ver a su estirpe establecida nuevamente en la Península*

con todos los honores, en posesión de los antiguos templos, que aún se conservaban intactos, aunque transformados en iglesias, en posesión de sus blasones y tesoros usurpados; ayudar a la realización de ese ensueño sería la misión de su vida, que así adquiriría un sentido providencial, justificando la apostasía de sus ascendientes. Considerábase él mismo como uno de aquellos templos encalados que se habían salvado de la destrucción, aceptando en su ámbito al Cristo, pero que un día serían restituídos al primitivo culto.[8]

Less apocalyptical than Cansinos-Assens but not less visionary, Ernesto Giménez Caballero, went even further than the Sevillan writer; he made a visit to the Balkan communities. Influenced in his style by Azorín and the new writers of the Generation of 1898, he forged for himself a language full of startlingly interesting modes of expression. Here is his impressionistic portrait of a Sephardic school teacher of Uskub:[9]

El Maestro Vitrán

Estando papeleteando estos datos llegó el maestro judío de la escuela: Vitrán. Desde el primer momento me impresionó este Vitrán. Era un tipo flaco, sombrío y encendido, con un raro reparto de distinción y de amargura en toda su esencia. Hablaba vehemente y silenciosamente. Tipo del intelectual fracasado, descontento, agónico, rebelde, que se debate en une lucha de anarquía interior, de dura disciplina interna, que está menospreciado por la masa burguesa del pueblo y siente una fría superioridad indecible. Me bastó cambiar unas palabras con él para decidir que el sería mi norte y guía de Uskub que él podría ser el elemento utilizable en el caso de ordenar alguna investigación o misión local.

Nos quedamos en la escuela. Nos sentamos junto a una ventana que daba al Vardar, y a las lejanas montañas de nieve.

Tímida y suspicazmente comenzó a narrarme su vida.

Era un aristócrata, un hidalgo de la mejor estirpe sefardí.

Su familia tenía origen en Madrid: Vitrán era un madrileño. Por deformación de la palabra Madrid, se llamó a su familia "del Madero." Toda ella había sido de casta rabínica sacerdotal, fina. Todavía sus abuelos prestaron altos servicios a la comunidad de Salónica. Y él y su hermano desempeñaron selectas funciones en la *Selanik* de antes de la guerra. Poseía una casa abundante y una rica biblioteca. Pero el fuego criminal y atroz de 1917 le arrasó todo su haber y hogar

Se vió forzado a la emigración. Llegó a Monastir y no pudo organizar su vida. Entonces pasó a Skoplje, con su mujer y sus dos hijos. Y en Skoplje vivía desesperado, en una gran miseria, inquieto, con un fuego bíblico consumidor de su destino.

Me llevó a su casa. Su casa era una alcoba y una cocina. Tenía otras dos estancias, pero las alquilaba a huéspedes. La mujer de Vitrán me acogió llena de gracia y de alegría; me quiso ofrecer confitura y pan. Yo sólo le acepté una taza de café con leche. Los dos hijos de Vitrán se me aceraron me saludaron distinguidamente. Y viendo mi Zeiss-Ikon, me pidieron un retrato. En un instante los cuatro Vitrán se pusieron endomingados y les filmé unos metros. Me anocheció en su casa. Hacía frío. No tenían apenas luz. Estuve apurando este hogar judío hasta lo último, escuchando sus miserias y sus angustias. *Me creían enormemente influyente en el judaísmo. Me creían un judío de alta marca.* No les quise disuadir. Cuando el día siguiente alguien dijo a Vitrán que yo no era hebreo, noté que palidecía y que al poco se alejaba de mi extrañamente.

Vitrán era un romántico, un fanático, un desinteresado, un alma firme, y quizá creyera que yo le había impurificado su hogar y su conciencia con mis palabras y mis modestos dones.[10]

Adolfo de Castro, Father Fidel Fita, Amador de los Ríos, Fernández y González, were some of the scholars who laid the foundations for the interest and enthusiasm which members of the Institución Libre de Enseñanza,[11] shared fully. Don Francisco Giner de los Ríos and his devotees read and assimilated the findings of this great school of scholars. Pérez Galdós, Blasco Ibáñez, Concha Espina, Cansinos-Assens are the fiction writers who transferred to their compositions the spirit of this awakened revival in Hispano-Judaic culture. Dr. Angel Pulido and the Marqués de Hoyos were the natural products of this reorientation to a glorious past. Abroad scholars of Ashkenazic background were, like Meyer Kayserling and Isidore Loeb, incited by the Peninsular awareness with their discoveries in the field of history and literature. Simultaneously the magazines of the Academies of Literature and Language and History of Spain along with the first-rate *Revue des Études Juives* of French Jewry, not to mention the other Journals published in Germany, for decades, published incessantly studies and articles on Hispano-Judaic culture. Little by little educated Ashkenazic Jews drifted into Spain and by instinct as it were identified themselves with the Sephardic tradition making it their own. José Máximo Kahn under the pseudonym of Medina Azara joined the circle of intellectuals in Madrid. And now after the Civil War, (he was for a short time the Spanish Consul at Salonica) is living in Buenos Aires, where he continues his youthful love for everything Sephardic.[12]

We have coined the expression neo-Sephardim for the new Jews who although, in the great majority of cases are of Germanic and Slavonic origin, yet because they are being thoroughly hispanized in Latin America, cannot avoid becoming the new branch of Spanish-speaking Jews. Theirs is the glorious destiny to emulate the Jews of Spain and in the course of the centuries to come, create a culture as great if not greater than the preceding one. Naturally the Ashkenazic Jew is proud as anyone else. For this reason there is a hostility on the part of some of them to be called neo-Sephardim.

The final phase up to 1950 is the intensive work carried on by a new group of Hebraic scholars in Spain who have started the very fine magazine *Sefarad: Revista de la Escuela de Estudios Hebraicos* (1940) that commands at present universal prestige. Jewish scholars from many countries have already contributed to it valuable studies. These men are publishing a great number of books. In particular we must mention here Millás-Vallicrosa's *La Poesía Sagrada Hebraico—española,* Madrid, 1940 and the second edition of 1949.

This exciting activity in Spain has not passed unnoticed among the Sephardic Jews of the Orient, Western Europe and North Africa. A visit or journey through Spain has never failed to produce an unforgettable impression on the Spanish Jews who returned to the home of their ancestors. In 1900 a *Sefardi,* born in Brusa, the former capital of Turkey in Asia Minor, went to visit Spain. Sr. M. J. Bensasson says:

> Si me encuentro en esta hermosa tierra, lo es por las ventajas que ofrecen los artículos 2 y 11 de la Constitución de la Monarquía Española, ni tampoco a los efectos del plausible Decreto Real del 15 de Junio de 1881, pues si a aspirar fuera pretendería con todo derecho el segundo párrafo del artículo primero de la citada Constitución (porque soy de origen puramente español y no ruso); pero este no es mi ánimo.
>
> Me encuentro aquí por invitación verbal de uno de mis hermanos de España: D. José Prats y García Olalla, actualmente ingeniero en el Ministerio de Fomento de Madrid, quien en su viaje a Constantinopla en 1895 me honró con su amistad, *y con el que por casualidad entablé relaciones a bordo de un vapor en el que viajábamos por el Mediterráneo a cuyo señor había tomado por equivocación por uno de mis correligionarios al oirle hablar castellano.*

Bensasson's mistake in taking a Spaniard for a *Sefardi* has again and again been repeated in the case of many others. But the emotional impact on setting foot on Spanish soil, as expressed by Bensasson could also be duplicated in the author's experience as well as in the experiences of Estrugo, whom we shall quote soon:

> Nunca olvidaré lo fantástico que se me representaba un viaje por España, a pesar de reconocerme, aunque muy superficialmente, oriundo de este hermoso país y jamás se secarán las lágrimas que a mis ojos asomaron al influjo de la inexplicable emoción que me dominaba al pisar por primera vez, a fines del año 1900, la amada patria de nuestros mayores y cuando atravesando la frontera, los funcionarios de la aduana de Port-Bou, me hablaban en el idioma de mis padres.
>
> Desde entonces, nunca me consideré extraño en la península ibérica, y mi entusiasmo en los primeros momentos fué tan grande, que al llegar al hotel, siendo pasada ya la media noche, llevado de dicho entusiasmo y sin darme cuenta de lo que hacía, abracé lleno de alegría a la anciana camarera del establecimiento, a la cual causaron tanta risa como asombro aquellos mis transportes de júbilo.[13]

The great Biblical and Arabic scholar, Dr. Abraham S. Yahuda and Ariel Bension, both born in Palestine, went beyond ecstatic effusion in their love and understanding of old and modern Spain. We have already dealt with Bension's fervid appreciation of the *Zohar*. As for Dr. Yahuda suffice it to say, he left behind him in Madrid, a group of students who have brought fame to themselves and to their great teacher. The phase of revival of interest in Sephardic Culture which we are analyzing meant a great deal to a privileged group of Levantine and Moroccan Jews who ventured to come to the Iberic Peninsula. Matters of the heart mean more in the long run, than matters dealing with economics and dry as dust erudition. We feel no embarrassment nor shame in emphasizing the cordial emotion that ran through the nerve system of these Sephardim and warmed up the cockles of their hearts when they saw Spain for the first time. José Estrugo discovered his Spanish culture inheritance in the United States. His name, in a small way, will be associated with the political activities of the thirties.

Estrugo tells us how no one in Spain took him for a Jew or a foreigner.

> Hace algunos meses, en una tertulia de Madrid, estábamos entre un grupo de españoles tres sefardíes. Un español amigo que nos conocía,

quiso hacer un experimento e invitó a los contertulios a que designaran quiénes eran los tres hebreos que había en el grupo, antes de presentarnos. Los tres hebreos que todos escogieron eran españoles, quizá cristianos viejos. La verdad es que no existen entre los sefardíes los conocidos tipos clásicos semitas y estos abundan más en España que en los centros sefarditas. Estos tipos son muy raros y constituyen la excepción...

As in the case of Bensasson, Estrugo experienced great and deep emotion on his arrival in Spain:

En octubre de 1922 llegué por primera vez a España, en un barco que traía al puerto de Vigo muchos españoles repatriados de Nueva York. La alegría de estos emigrantes era inmensa, pero la mía lo era mucho más. Ellos volvían a sus hogares, pero yo me reintegraba a una patria milenaria, de la cual habían arrojado a mis mayores... Me parecía que iba a encontrar intactas las hermosas moradas que según contaban los viejos, habían vendido por una burra, o un pedazo de lienzo... moradas cuyas llaves oxidadas había visto algunas veces en las juderías como reliquias de Toledoth (Toledo), la Jerusalén sefardita.

Por primera vez en mi vida me sentía verdaderamente aborigen, nativo ¡Aquí no era, no podía ser un intruso. Por primera vez me sentía en mi casa, mucho más que en la judería donde había nacido! No me avergüenzo de confesar que me incliné, en un arranque de emoción indescriptible, y besé la tierra que pisaba por primera vez. Un siglo casi después de terminada la Inquisición.[14]

Franco's Spain saved from annihilation several hundred Sefardíes from Hitler's madmen. This is an illustration of how Spain has shown her benevolence. From causes arising out of other situations, almost one hundred thousand Sephardim are scattered throughout Iberic-America. If nowhere else, it will be in this newest of Spain where the medieval Sephardic Jew, through a rejuvenation of his language, will be equipped with a civilized medium of expression and through it heed the whisperings and voice of the Spirit.[15]

NOTES

1. From the eighteenth century on, especially under the reign of Charles IV, sporadic efforts were made to rescind the Decree of expulsion of 1492. Don Pedro Varela prepared on March 22, 1797 a document for the King asking that

the law against the admission of Jews into Spain be abolished. See Alcubilla *Diccionario de la Administración,* Vol. VI, Article *Judios.*

Earlier in that century Feyjóo who was always on the alert about all that concerned Spain did not neglect to study the Jew's claims to return to the Peninsula: See Carta octava: *Reconvenciones caritativas a los profesores de la Ley de Moisés en respuesta a un judío de Bayona de Francia,* in *Cartas Eruditas y curiosas* en que por la mayor parte se continúa el designio del *Theatro Crítico Universal* Escrito por el Señor don Fray Benito Gerónymo Feyjóo y Montenegro, Tomo tercero, cuarta impresión. Con privilegio, Madrid, En la Imprenta del Supremo Consejo de la Inquisición, 1759, pp. 93-128.

Jews on their initiative were also anxious to see that belated justice was done to them on the question of the Decree. Dr. Philipson, editor of *Allgemeine Zeitung des Judenthums* in 1854, in the name of the Jewish communities of Marseilles, Bordeaux and Bayonne addressed a request to the Cortes on the same subject.

In 1865 Jews of French nationality living in Spain asked the Spanish government for the privilege of having their own cemetery. cf. *Archives Israélites,* 1867. p. 1076.

Sir Moses Montefiore and H. Guedalla and the Consistories of Bordeaux and Bayonne asked the government of General Prim for the suppression of all discriminatory legislation against the Jews. Don Romero Ortiz, Minister of Justice and Marshal J. Serrano answered them on December 1st, 1866:

"Notre glorieuse Révolution ayant proclamé avec les autres conquêtes des droits de l'homme, la liberté religieuse, l'édit du XVème siècle est abrogé de fait. Par conséquent, vous êtes libres d'entrer dans notre pays et d'y exercer librement votre culte."

Of course the victory-flushed general and his secretary did not duly appreciate what it meant to grant entry and religious tolerance to the Jews.

Sr. Emililio Castelar spoke on behalf of the Jews at the Cortes, on April 12, 1869...

In 1871 nine Jews were naturalized by the King of Spain cf. *Allgem. Ztg. des Judenthums,* 1869 p. 476; 1871 pp. 781-824; 1875, p. 730; 1876, p. 224; 1876, p. 339.

There were officially in 1887, 406 Jews in Spain according to the Census of the country.

To these factual jottings must be added the very benevolent attitude of King Alfonso XIII toward the Jews.

An extremely well informed article on the Spanish interest in the Jews containing facts not very well known is Juan Pérez de Guzmán's "Los israelitas de origen español en el Oriente de Europa," in *La España Moderna* July 1904, number 187, pp. 5-28.

2. Isidoro de Hoyos y de la Torre: *Los judíos españoles en el Imperio Austríaco y en los Balkanes.* Estudio Histórico. Madrid, Establecimiento Tipográfico de Fortanet, 1904, p.53 (This work is useful for its list of *Proverbios judaicos* and for a tabulation of Periódicos judeo-españoles pp. 89-92.)

3. For the numerous works by Angel Pulido on Sephardic Jews see our *General Bibliography.*

4. Reproduced in M.J. Bensasson, *Los israelitas españoles: España y sus hijos de Oriente,* Alicante, Sirvent y Sanchez, 1905 (Under the author's name we read: Caballero de la Real Orden Española de I. L. C.) pp. 121-136.

5. On Cansinos-Assens see M. J. Benardete's short account in *Columbia Dictionary of Modern European Literature,* General Editor Horatio Smith, New York, Columbia University Press, 1947, p. 137.

6. *Florido* is a thinly disguised name for Pulido.

7. Sam Levy is the son of Saadi Levy from whose memoirs we quoted above.

8. Rafael Cansinos-Assens, *Las Luminarias de Hanukah.* (Un episodio de la Historia de Israel en España) Novela, Madrid, Editorial Internacional, 1924, pp. 113-114, p. 76.

9. "Skoplje es el nombre serbio de la antigua Uskub (Pero llamémosla en medieval tradición hispana: Escopia)"

10. E. Giménez Caballero, *Monograma sobre los judíos de Escopia* in *Revista de Occidente,* Madrid, March 1930, pp. 365-366.

11. L'Abbé Pierre Jobit *Les Educateurs de l'Espagne Contemporaine,* Paris, E. De Boccard, 1936, 2 vols.

12. (a) Like all the major themes referred to in this work the "Sephardic and Ashkenazic historical and cultural contacts" could be the subject of a book in itself. These contacts go back to medieval times and then continue in Italy, Holland, Turkey, Safed, the Americas and finally in modern *Israel.*

(b) Ashkenazic rabbis, such as Rabbi Asher ben Yehiel, came to Spain. Rabbi Asher, a German by birth, who was also familiar with conditions in France, as he visited that country on his way to Toledo (early part of XIVᵉ century), wrote: "When I first arrived here, I asked in amazement by what legal right Jews could to-day legally convict anyone to death without a Sanhedrin. In none of the countries that I know of, except here in Spain do the Jewish courts try cases of capital punishment") Cf. Abraham Newman, *The Jews in Spain* Vol. 1, pp. 138-139.

(c) Rabbis of Ashkenazic origin who were called to head synagogues of Italy and Amsterdam.

(d) The acceptance of Sephardic poetry for books of prayers and the universal approval bestowed on the *Zohar* and the final sanctioning of Caro's *Shulhan Aruh* by Eastern Jewry.

(e) The comingling of the two in mystic Safed where we see the Ashkenazic Isaac ben Solomon Luria exercising tremendous influence among the Sephardim (Cf. S. W. Baron, *The Jewish Community,* Vol. II p. 142 where he speaks of the uniformity of Jewish worship: "The uniformity was, indeed, so great that the hasidic group, arising in, and for many generations exclusively recruited from the Ashkenazic communities in Poland, could speedily abandon the traditional Ashkenazic and adopt the Sephardic ritual, because the latter was now more deeply imbued with the mystic connotations of the great Palestinian cabalist, Isaac Luria, himself an Ashkenazic.")

(f) The rôles both branches of Judaism played in the tragic-comic drama of Zevian messianism.

(g) Moses ben Mordecai Zacuto, author of a drama in Hebrew, *Yesod Olam,* 1642 (The Eternal Foundation) perfected his knowledge of Talmud in Poland; David Franco Mendes contributed articles to Mendelsohn-Wessely's Hebrew periodical *Ha-Meassef.*

(h) Aversion, misunderstanding, clannishness of Sephardic Jews in the Levantine countries toward their fellow-Jews. (In Bulgaria two types of Ashkenazic Jews: the older group hispanized but faithful to their rites. Their synagogue was known as *El Kal de los locos,* and the recently arrived immigrants disinclined to learn Judeo-Spanish. Cf. Säul Mézan: *Les Juifs Espagnols en Bulgarie,* Sofia, Edition d'Essai, 1925, p. 15.

(i) The Sephardic Congregations in the U. S. originally entirely Sephardic or of Iberian ancestry in membership have gradually changed composition so that now a great many of these congregations have followers that are either mixed or entirely Ashkenazic.

(j) Intermarriage on a large scale between the members of the two divisions.

(k) Hispanization of Ashkenazic Jews in Latin America and the emergence of the new Sephardic Jew.

(l) Mutual respect and hearty cooperation of the two branches in *Israel,* although the leadership in great part is in the hands of the Ashkenazim.

(m) In several places throughout this volume we have had occasion to mention the remarkable response of the better educated young men in Turkey, Rumania, Yugo-Slavia, Greece and Morocco to Spain's manifest interest in the Sephardic Communities. Two distinguished rabbis and savants, Abraham Danon 1857-1925. (Cf. *Sa vie et ses oeuvres,* Paris. Imprimerie H. Elias, 1925) and Bejarano, contributed to learned journals many studies on the history and culture of their people. Kalmi Baruch from Yugo-Slavia studied under Menéndez Pidal in Madrid and like Dr. A. S. Yahuda has some of his philological studies published in the world-known *Revista de Filología Española.*

Enthusiasm for Spain and her marvellous Castilian tongue expressed itself in Vienna with the establishment of the first *Casa sefardita.*

Mosco Galimir, born of a distinguished Sephardic family in Rumania, once living in the Austrian capital, succeeded in creating a center for the propagation of Sephardic culture on the basis of the Spanish language. Cf. *Le Quatuor Galimir* in *Les Cahiers Sefardis,* September, 1947, pp. 337-338:

"Mosco Galimir avait le culte du séfardisme et du parler Castellan de nos pères. Il disait, avec juste raison, que sans la conservation du judéo-espagnol, le séfardisme finirait par disparaître. Il parvint à faire partager cette vérité primordiale à un groupe de jeune coreligionnaires enthousiastes avec le concours desquels il acheta à Vienne une propriété situeé: II Weintraubengaese, 9, qui devint la *Casa sefardita,* la premiere du genre. Son succés fut considerable. Elle groupa, jusqu'à quatorze cent cinquante membres..."

13. M. J. Bensasson, op. cit. p. 15 and p. 8.

14. José M. Estrugo, *El Retorno a Sefarad.* Un siglo despés de la Inquisición, prólogo de Gabriel Alomar. Madrid, 1922, pp. 30, 36-37.

15. We choose to leave out of this volume any discussion of the Jews in Latin-America. There are not as yet any reliable works on the sefardies of the different countries in Brazil and the Spanish-speaking countries. Far be it from us to supply here any representative bibliography on the Jews in the Hispanic world in America. Only as a sample we refer to *Judaica:* publicación mensual. 51-53, número dedicado a los judios de la América Latina. 1937.

Also see:

1) *Medio siglo de vida judía en la Argentina. Judaica.* No. 89, November 1940, pp. 203-216.

2) *Los judios en Cuba* por Eduardo Weinfeld, *Judaica.* No. 26, October 1939, pp. 104-110.

3) *Les sefardis du Mexique* I: *Les Juifs indiens, in Les Cahiers Sefardis,* September 1947; (C'est a un pur hazard, nous dit M. Behar, que je dois d'avoir appris qu'il existait des *Juifs-Indiens,* plus exactement des Sefardis autochtones, cent pour cent mexicans.)

Without documentary evidence, at least for the present, let us most briefly remind the reader of outstanding cultural events achieved by *Sefardies* in many Latin American countries. Rabbi Isaac Algazi in Montevideo, Uruguay, published an ambitious work on the essence of Judaism, *El Judaismo. Religion de amor;* in Mexico City, Benito Alazraki, born there, offered to the public his first book of poems *La Voluntad de la Tierra* (1944). (León Felipe in the prologue to this book said: "Para mi, y creo que para la l'España de viejas tradiciones liberales, para todos los españoles del Éxodo, del Llanto, su voz nacida en el destierro sefardita, mucho más largo y acaso más doloroso también que el nuestro nos suena como el lamento, como el grito angustioso de un niño extraviado, de un hermano perdido..."")

Chilolo Zarco, born in Istanbul, lives in Guatemala City. Although he earns his living as a small manufacturer of ladies lingerie, nonetheless, as his avocation, he devotes his leisure to writing. *Esto no lo aprendí en la escuela*, his first book, savours of the delicious wit and didactic wisdom of Sem Tob de Carrion. Still another detail about him points to the mysterious chemistry of Hispanic soil and ethos: He is married to a young woman from El Salvador, whose parents belonged to the select few of her country.

The blind man from Salonica, Sr. Florentín, is the founder of the first asylum for blind children in Caracas; Dr. Benchetrit from Spanish Morocco, did more than anyone else to attend and cure the lepers of Venezuela and Columbia.

Perhaps among the very few books published by the Sephardim on Jewish ethics is this work: *Fundamentos de la Moral Hebrea* por Ezra Behar, Habana, 1931.

Appendices

1.   SEPHARDIC SALONICA

Sephardic Salonica is no more. The Republic of Sephardism has been destroyed by the criminal barbarism under Hitler and his gang. What a historical irony! The Spanish Jews who survived Iberic totalitarianism finally fell under the merciless ax of extermination wielded by a people that reached the heights of modern civilization. God of Israel, save us from those people whose learning is rootless, and whose literacy makes them an easy prey to prevarications and perversions!

Salonica ominously was getting ready for the holocaust that put an end to its beauty and original design for living. Its raison d'être, its mode of being was irrevocably destroyed when the Ottoman Empire was torn into shreds through Sultanic incompetence and European lust for power. The rabbis of Iberia gathered their flocks on the fair lands of Salonica. Iberic atomism married to Semitic tribalism begot in the Sephardim a recalcitrant individualism that took centuries to iron out. The *rabbinocracy* of Salonica excluded the deleterious cultural ingredients derived from a whole century of Marranism. Practically no book composed in Latin characters came out of the Levantine Judeo-Spanish presses. Whatever was published in Salonica, Constantinople and Smyrna appeared in Hebrew characters. The Peninsular people formed nuclei around their synagogues and homes of studies bearing the name of their original homes in Spain. Through a curious philological law the Spanish dialects, Catalonian, Gallegan, Andalusian, Portuguese, were suppressed or assimilated by Castilian. Surviving traits of intonation, vocabulary, presence of certain sounds, indicated through the centuries the possible homeland of these Jews who forgot their local tongues. Recently an article appeared in the Hebrew *Edoth,* devoted to Jewish folklore and ethnology, pointing out how the Judeo-Spanish of Palestine contaminated the Yiddish of the early settlers of Jerusalem. If a stagnant dialect could impregnate a foreign tongue like Yiddish, what wonder that an imperial language like Castilian should have triumphed over transplanted dialects and even over the Greek of the Byzantine

Jews of Constantinople! There is a rare copy of the Pentateuch in the library of the Jewish Theological Seminary published in Constantinople during the XVIth Century. Of the three columns on each page, all in Hebrew characters, the language of one is in Greek. The Greek-speaking Jews submitted to the chivalric tongue of the Spaniards.

In Salonica communal differences took a long time to disappear, but they did disappear. All historians argue that the controversy that played havoc upon Salonician Jewry was the quixotic messianism of Sabbetai Seví. Dissensions, wrangling, defections, conversions to Islam, threw that city into convulsions that almost smothered her. Then a pall of ignorance and superstition fell upon Salonica. Not until the middle of the nineteenth century was an attempt made to revive the religion and cultural life of Salonica. The Alliance Israélite Universelle founded by French Jews to help their Levantine brethren began its arduous work. Its intentions were praiseworthy. French chauvinism misread the text at hand. Instead of saving those Jews through their centuries-old vernacular, the French coreligionists discouraged the study of Spanish. Their policy over-Balkanized a super-Balkanized community. Omitting these mistakes we can graciously admit that the Alliance deserves gratitude. It did bring the West to the Middle East. The relief, however, was temporary.

Austria-Hungary, the Greeks, Bulgarians, the Great Powers were getting ready for the final immolation of the Turkish Empire. Salonician Jewry was one of its victims. Economic life became precarious. Political safety was at a premium. Wars, revolutions, invasions, all conspired to make life in Salonica a hell on earth. The scattering of the Jews of Macedonia began before the World War of 1914-18. Communities of those Jews were established in Italian, Spanish, French cities. New York, Mexico, and Argentina also became magnets of attraction. Hitler gave the unpardonable coup de grâce.

When a whole historical cycle comes to an end, the time is at hand to throw a nostalgic glance at its significance. Levantine Jewry that lost its creativity stirred before the inevitable catastrophe. Fortunately there were at hand two Salonician Jews so well prepared by education, culture and talent, as to undertake an evaluation of what Salonica meant to the Sephardim.

Joseph Nehama, a brilliant teacher and a successful banker, began before this last war an ambitious history of Salonica. Six volumes of this work have already appeared. Nehama wrote in French. Through the help of his compatriot Michael Molho, for a short time the chief rabbi of the horribly decimated Jewish community of their city, who supplied Nehama with rabbinical documentation. Nehama belongs to the historical school of Michelet. Fiction imagination, recreations and facts commingle in a super style in Nehama. This history is a masterpiece, it is worthy of an English translation. If Nehama used his imagination, Rabbi I. S. Emmanuel, up to recently the rabbi of Curaçao and for a brief period of Panama, utilizing the techniques of the scholar, wrote a solid History of Salonica, also in French. Like Rabbi Newman of Dropsie College and others in the field he worked with the Responsa and he submitted these Responsa of Salonica to an acute analysis. Marvellous discoveries were Emmanuel's compensation. For example, he reconstructed the guild organization of the Salonician workers. For that contribution alone Emmanuel's work (only the first volume has seen the light of day) deserves the thanks of all students of Jewish history.

Nehama's fictional gift and Emmanuel's scholarly techniques did not touch the depths of the individual Salonician's soul. The Salonician Diaspora had gifted men who profited from their struggles in their new environments. It was the turn of the English language to evoke in a Salonician of New York the memories of yester-year. Leon Sciaky's *Farewell to Salonica* (Current Books, New York) is a most delightful book written in an English worthy of a great master of that language. Sciaky came to the United States. Slowly he was won over by our country. His idealism and zest for life threw him into the Progressive Education movement. The Middle Ages, the Orient, Spain, echoes of French culture, Turkey and Macedonia were imbedded in his multitudinous psyche. Teaching youngsters of the better classes awoke in him memories of his rich past. Fragments of the Balkanic world were served to his pupils as illustrative materials. Fascination, exotic spells and adumbrated truths overpowered Sciaky's classes. Avidly they asked for more. Out of that demand came the composition of *Farewell to Salonica*.

What kind of a world does Sciaky present us?

He is at his best when he reconstructs the splinters of the image of his childhood and early adolescence. Street scenes, popular types, folk ways, family relations are by him imbued with the poetic tinge. With

Sciaky we enter the realm of essences. His grandfather is his endearing mentor. When he speaks of his grandmother and her sense of the revolutionary changes that were destroying their millenial culture, Sciaky transmits a pathos that clutches at the heart.

> Life had changed enough about her. Had not the Jewish women discarded the veil, to go about with their faces uncovered? Had not Western fashions come to the city, to change the appearance of her younger generation? New schools had been opened and were now teaching in foreign tongues. The young people were forgetting the traditions of their fathers and made little of age-old customs. God preserve us! She did not want to live to see the day when Spanish, the language of our ancestors, would be forgotten.

Sciaky's curiosity as a boy enabled him to see a great deal of the city. The fact that now he lives in the Catskills, shunning the city, is a revelation of his love for nature. America sharpened his sensibility. With the help of this disciplined sensibility he reconstructs the seascapes and landscapes around Salonica. The Sciakys were wholesale grain merchants. Of most importance were the contacts of the family with the countryside for the growing boy. Often he was taken by his beloved grandfather to the villages. Virgilian bucolic emotion without the enervating quality we find in classical pastoral literature suffuses Sciaky's descriptions of the villages he lived in or visited during vacation time. Recalling his stay at Kilkish, a Bulgarian village, not far from his city, he relishes his love for those simple folks.

> They were part and parcel of the soil they tilled, those sowers and reapers of grain, as earthy as the pungent, freshly turned furrows curling over plows in the spring. Shearers of sheep and spinners of wool and weavers of cloth were they, driving their cattle to pasture and tending the herds on the grassy slopes. Hewers of wood and makers of sun-dried bricks to build their homes, laboring long and hard to produce the life-sustaining wealth: food, shelter and clothing. And great would have been their contentment if they could have had the full measure of that bread their sweat had grown. If it had not been for the despoiler!

Besides childhood reminiscences of things seen and heard and of his bucolic evocations, Sciaky does give a vivid idea of how national and world politics insidiously were destroying a pluralistic society. Austria-

Hungary's suicidal policies to control Serbia and reach for the possession of that Macedonian prize, the Turkish Revolutionary Movement incubating there among young peoples of all the Levantine nationalities, Italian imperialistic meddlings in Africa and in the Aegean Sea, Tzaristic Pan-Slavism among the mountain peoples of Montenegro, Serbia and Bulgaria, the rivalries between England and Germany—all these struggles, plots and wars shook to the ground the foundation of Salonica. Balkanic rivalries and World Wars put an end to Salonician Jewry. "Of forty thousand Spanish Jews who were in Salonica at the beginning of the war but a pitiful two hundred or so remain..." These figures given by Sciaky must be corrected by the following authentic facts:

> At the eve of the war, the Jewish population of Greece amounted to 75,000 souls. The war annihilated this portion of the Jewish family which, in its immense majority, belonged to the Sephardic category. There survive in all Greece 10,700 Jews, 5,000 at Athens, 2,000 at Salonica and 3,500 are scattered in all the other localities. (See *Situation Actuelle du Judaisme en Grèce,* by Jos. Nehama, in *Les Cahiers Sefardis,* November, 1946.)

Leon Sciaky's first book is an extraordinary achievement. A few more books lie germinating in the soil of his soul. For one thing we must remind him of two or three remarks. His lyricism always virile encases a germ of dissolution. Not that it is saccharine. Essences unless implemented with realistic resistances beget fireflies which light up but do not illuminate the dark corners of existence with the steadiness demanded by earthy life. A recovery of his Spanish inheritance, an acquaintance with La Celestina and Don Quijote, might enable Sciaky to give substances and body to his Proustian memories. An irresistible conviction gets hold of the conscious Sephardic Jew when he lays down the book after enjoying it to the full, that Sciaky has distorted his own image. Sciaky is not the son of a wealthy Balkanic Bey. Deeper in his self is found his Iberic ancestry. He must descend into it to salvage the Spanish Jew in him. Authenticity in literature is reached only by faithfulness to what one is inescapably.

IN MEMORIAM: NESSIM BEHAR (1848-1931)

Like Saül Mézan I have shown myself both appreciative and critical of the educational program of the Alliance Israélite Universelle (founded by six men in 1860). My family and I owe a great deal to this remarkable institution. My maternal uncle, Abraham Habib, was one of the first Sephardic young men, born in the town of Dardanelles (Chanak Kalessí) who was sent to Paris to study at the expense of the Alliance at its school for teachers located at Auteuil. He died before finishing his studies and is buried in Paris. My brothers and sisters and I received our first elementary schooling in the schools of the Alliance. Through unsuspected by-paths the Alliance affected my life again when between 1918 and 1919 I came to know in New York, Nessim Behar, the extraordinary Sephardic educator, who at that time was close to seventy years of age. Nessim Behar was one of the many teachers the Alliance had trained in Paris who, like missionaries, started and directed schools in Mesopotamia and Jerusalem. When I met him he was still very vigorous. He was the apostle incarnate, gentle, persuasive and indefatigable in everything he undertook. The courage and stamina he had shown in Jerusalem when fanatic Ashkenazic and Sephardic Jews, in 1882, threatened his plan and life, he displayed in the slums of New York when he started his campaign to Americanize the Hispano-Levantine Jews who had in recent years come to the United States.

The mettle of his character was tested in the Holy City.

Behar se trouva pourtant un jour dans une position assez critique. En passant par une ruelle étroite de l'interieur il rencontre trois gaillards qui lui crient: Ah! le voilà l'homme qui vient déruire la religion dans la sainte cité, tuons-le! Avec ce sang-froid dont il ne s'est jamais departi, Behar leur dit tranquillement: Vous pouvez me tuer, mais vous n'ignorez pas que le *pacha* (gouverneur) est mon ami et je puis vous annoncer qu'il vous fera pendre.*

In Jerusalem he had to rescue the children of the Sephardim from the streets and the inefficient religious schools. It had not taken him long before his school began to attract pupils. He reported to Paris his experiences.

Il en vient de tous côtés et si miserables. L'espoir d'être accueills par nous soutient ces malheureux et leur donne la force de resister aux tentations des missionnaires qui leur offrent un abri confortable, des vêtements une nourriture abondante. Quelques-uns succombent à ces solicitations, la masse résiste malgré sa misère sans nom. C'est presque un miracle. A nous de lui ofrir les mêmes avantages.*

When I met Nessim Behar in the cafés of the East Side, located for the most part on Rivington Street, between the Bowery and Second Avenue and on Allen Street, he was preaching in his halting Judeo-Spanish—learned in his childhood in Jerusalem where he was born—the need and urgency of learning English. He knew it was of no use to dissuade the new immigrant of the evil of petty gambling. I became attracted to him because I saw in Nessim Behar a man who was trying to elevate my coreligionists. Before I had met him I was doing in my own way some cultural propaganda. At my own expense I sold at a penny a piece my Judeo-Spanish translations of poems by Longfellow. Why did I choose the one that begins:

> Tell me not in mournful numbers
> Life is but an empty dream.
> For the soul is dead that slumbers
> And things are not what they seem!

Was it because I sensed that my people's souls were somnolent and slumbering! In my high-school days (Woodward High School, in Cincinnati, Ohio 1913-16) I contributed to the school magazine a translation from the Judeo-Spanish on a Stoic-ethical theme. Nessim Behar, then, found in me a most willing collaborator. I joined him in his visits to the tenements where the Sephardic Jews were living.

We went up and down the malodorous tenements, knocking at the doors of those humble, temporary homes of the new arrivals at the very hour when the men were having their supper after working long hours at very unhealthy and unremunerative jobs. Nessim Behar, the apostle, expected these bodies, whose energies had been squeezed out of them, to have enough physical stamina to respond to the appeal of the spirit. Some, overcome by shame, others, out of respect for the venerable, diminutive old man, made a big sacrifice in the name of culture and the future; heeding the call, they attended the special classes organized exclusively for them at the school of their neighborhood.

Nessim Behar, the Palestinian, the ex-director of the Alliance schools in the Orient, in his very old age showed his younger compatriots what it meant to be in a new land that offered opportunities and showed the means of achieving material goods and the fruits of the spirit. This old teacher, this new patriarch, affected the lives of many. On February 21, 1928, under the auspices of the former Ambassador to Turkey, Mr. Abraham Elkus, a banquet attended by Ashkenazim and Sephardim was offered in honor of Nessim Behar.

I see in him not only a fine example of a human being but also a Sephardic symbol. The Alliance made him, France and Israel spoke through him, the Sephardic tradition was still powerful enough to impose its Judeo-Spanish on Nessim Behar. In the slums of New York the polished French of the *Alliance* was of no use to him. Nessim Behar could only communicate the new gospel to my people through our Spanish dialect. Spirit may be expressed in any language but it is meaningful to us only when it is transmitted through the language we have suckled, as it were, with our mothers' milk.

---

*Jacques Bigart, *A la mémoire de Nessim Behar,* (1848-1931), Paris, Alliance Israélite Universelle, 1931, pp. 10-11.

Bibliography

I. HISTORY

José Amador de los Ríos, *Historia social, política y religiosa de los judíos de España y Portugal,* Madrid, Imprenta de T. Fortanet, 1876, 3 vols.

José Amador de los Ríos, *Estudios históricos, políticos y literarios sobre los judíos en España,* Madrid, 1848.

Fritz Baer, *Die Juden in christlichen Spanien,* Berlin, 1929-1935.

Fritz Baer, *Toledot ha yehudim bi Sefarad ha nosrit,* (History of the Jews in Christian Spain), Vol. I. From the origins to the eve of the destruction of the Jewish aljamas in 1391; Vol. II. From the destruction of the Jewish aljamas in 1391 to the expulsion, 1492, Tel-Aviv, Edition Am Obed, 5705 (1945). (Reviewed by J. M. Millás Vallicrosa, in *Sefarad,* V, 1945, pp. 417-440, and VI, 1946, pp. 163-188.)

Salo W. Baron, *A Social and Religious History of the Jews,* New York, Columbia University Press, 1937, 3 vols. (Vol 3—notes and an extensive bibliography).

Salo W. Baron, *The Jewish Community. Its History and Structure to the American Revolution,* Philadelphia, The Jewish Publication Society of America, 1942-5702. (Authoritative bibliography.)

Adolfo de Castro, *Historia de los judíos en España* (desde los tiempos de su establecimento hasta principios del presente siglo), con apéndice, Cadiz, 1847, (English transl. by Edward D.G.M. Kirwan, Cambridge, John Deighton, 1851).

Américo Castro, *España en su historia: cristianos, moros y judíos,* Buenos Aires, Editorial Losada, 1948.

Julio Cejador y Frauca, *"Bibliografía del semitismo español,"* in *Historia de la lengua y literatura castellana,* Madrid, 1922, Vol. XIV, pp. 371-374.

I.S. Emmanuel, *Histoire des Israélites de Salonique,* Paris, 1936, Vol I, (The only volume published).

Francisco Fernández y González, *Instituciones jurídicas del pueblo de Israel en los diferentes Estados de la Peninsula ibérica,* Madrid, 1881.

James Finn, *Sephardim, or the History of the Jews in Spain and Portugal,* London, 1841.

Fidel Fita, *La España hebrea,* Madrid, 1889-1898.

Forum Judicum, (The Visigothic Code), transl. by S. P. Scott, Boston, 1910.

Moïse Franco, *Essai sur l'histoire des Israélites de l'Empire Ottoman depuis les origines jusqu'à nos jours,* Paris 1897.

Abraham Galante, *Documents officiels turcs concernant les Juifs de Turquie. Recueil des 114 lois, reglements, firmans, berats, ordres et decisions de tribunaux,* Istambul, 1938.

Abraham Galante, *Histoire des Juifs d'Anatolie. Les Juifs d'Ismir* (Smyrne), Vol. I, Istanbul, Imprimerie M. Babok, 1937. (Author lists chronologically all his publications up to this date.)

Abraham Galante, *Histoire des Juifs d'Istanbul,* Constantinople, 1942.

Abraham Galante, *Turkler Ve Yahudiler. Tarihi Siyasi Tetkik* (Turks and Jews) (In Turkish, in the modern Latin Alphabet), Istanbul, Tan Matbassi, 1947.

H. Graetz, *History of the Jews,* (English transl.), New York, 1927, 6 vols.

H. Graetz, *Les Juifs d'Espagne* (945-1205), Transl. from the German, Paris, Michel Lévy, Editeurs, 1872.

E. H. Lindo, *The History of the Jews of Spain and Portugal,* London, 1848.

Valeriu Marcu, *The Expulsion of the Jews from Spain,* New York, 1936.

Jacob R. Marcus, *The Jews in the Medieval World.* A Source Book, Cincinnati, The Union of American Hebrew Congregations, 1938.

Michael S. Molho, *Contribución a la historia de Salónica,* (In Judeo-Spanish, printed in Rashi characters), Salonica 5692-1932.

Joseph Nehama, *Histoire des Israélites de Salonique:* Vol. I, La Communauté Romaniote, les Sefardis et leur Dispersion; Vol. II, La Communauté Sefaradite. Periode d'Installation, (1492-1536); Vol. III, L'age d'or du sefaradisme Salonicien (1536-1593) (two parts); Each volume is called a *tome* and each part *fascicule;* hence Vol. III has two fascicules. Paris, Librairie Durlacher, (or) Salonica, Librairie Molho, 1936.

Abraham A. Neuman, *The Jews in Spain,* Their Social, Political and Cultural Life during the Middle Ages, Philadelphia, The Jewish Publication Society of America, 1942-5702, 2 vols.

William H. Prescott, *The History of Ferdinand and Isabella, The Catholic* (Edited by John Foster Kirk), Philadelphia, 1872, 3 vols.

Solomon Rosanes, *A History of the Jews in Turkey,* (In Hebrew), Jerusalem, 1931-38, 5 vols.

Cecil Roth, *A History of the Marranos,* Philadelphia, The Jewish Publication Society of America, 1932. (Spanish transl. by Aaron Spivak, Buenos Aires, 1941-5701.)

II. MUWASSAHAS AND ZEJELES

(N.B.: Rather than organize the items appearing under this heading in alphabetical order, we give them in the order of their importance. They are interconnected.)

A. R. Nykl, *El Cancionero de Aben Guzman,* (Ibn Quzmán), Madrid, Imprenta de Estanislao Maestre, 1933. (This work was published by the Escuelas de Estudios Arabes de Madrid y Granada).

A. R. Nykl, *Hispano-Arabic Poetry and its Relations with the Old Provençal Troubadours,* Baltimore, (Printed... by J. H. Furst Company), 1946.

Ramón Menéndez Pidal, *Poesía Arabe y Poesía Europea* (con otros estudios de literatura medieval), Buenos Aires, Espasa-Calpe, Argentina, S. A., 3rd edition, 1946. (This article, in substance, was a lecture read by its author on February 28, 1937, in Havana, Cuba.)

José Millás Vallicrosa, *La poesía sagrada hebraico-española,* Madrid, 1940, (2nd edition, 1949).

S. M. Stern, "Les vers finaux en espagnol dans les muwassahas hispano-hebraiques; Une contribution à l'histoire du muwassah et à l'étude du vieux dialect espagnol mozarabe", in *Al-Andalus,* XII, 1948, pp. 299-346. (N. B.: F. Cantera's, D. Alonso's and Emilio García Gómez' studies are comments on Stern's fundamental discovery.)

Francisco Cantera, "Versos españoles en las muwassahas hispano-hebreas," in *Sefarad,* IX, 1949, pp. 197-234.

Dámaso Alonso, "Cancioncillas 'de Amigo' mozárabes," in *Revista de Filología Española,* XXXIII, 1949, pp. 297-349.

Emilio García Gómez, "Nuevas observaciones sobre las harjas romances en muwassahas hebreas," in *Al-Andalus,* XV, 1950, pp. 157-177.

III. JUDEO-SPANISH LITERATURE

Grace Aguilar, *The vale of cedars: or, The Martyr. A story of Spain in the XVth century.* 2nd ed. London, Groombridge and Sons, 1851.

Isaac S. Algazi, *El Judaismo:* religión de amor. Buenos Aires, Editorial Judaica, 1945.

Moses ben Baruch Almosnino, *Regimiento de la Vida.* (aljamiado) published from the press of Joseph Gaabez. Salonica 1564. (Other editions, Salonica 1564, Venice 1604). Edited in Latin characters by Samuel Méndes de Sola and associates in Amsterdam, 1729. Dedicated to Aaron David Pinto.

Moses ben Baruch Almosnino, *Extremos y grandezas de Constantinopla* (in Spanish with Hebrew characters). Translated and republished by Jacob Cansino, Madrid, 1638. (Translated here means transliterated).

M. J. Benardete, "R. Cansinos-Assens" in *Columbia Dictionary of Modern European Literature,* General Editor Horatio Smith. Columbia University Press. 1947, p. 137.

Blanche Bendahan, *Mazaltob* (Novel based on Hispano-Moroccan customs of Tetuan and Gibraltar), Paris. Editions du Tambaurin, 1930.

H. V. Besso, "Dramatic literature of the Spanish and Portuguese Jews of Amsterdam in the XVII and XVIII centuries", in *Bulletin Hispanique.* *59* (1939) pp. 215-238. (Published separately by the Hispanic Institute in the United States in 1947).

H. V. Besso, "A further contribution to the Refranero judèo-español", in *Bulletin Hispanique,* vol. 37 (1935) pp. 209-219.

R. Cansinoṣ-Assens, "El sacrificio de Miriam, narración de tiempos antiguos", in *Judaica,* (Buenos Aires) Sept. 1938, pp. 63-75.

R. Cansinos-Assens, *España y los judíos españoles: el retorno del éxodo.* Tortosa, 1919.

R. Cansinos-Assens, *Los judíos en la literatura española.* Buenos Aires, 1937.

R. Cansinos-Assens, *Las luminarias de Hanukah* (un episodio de la historia de Israel en España.) Madrid. Editorial Internacional. 1924.

Cynthia Crews, "Judeo-Spanish Folk-Tales in Macedonia," in *Folklore,* June 1932, pp. 193-225.

A. Danon, "Proverbes judéo-espagnols de Turquie", in *Zeitschrift für Romanische Philologie,* 1902, IX, pp. 440-454.

J. M. Estrugo, *El retorno a Sefarad cien años después de la Inquisición.* Prólogo de Gabriel Alomar. Madrid. Imprenta Europea, 1933. (Songs, proverbs, customs of the Sefardies).

R. Foulché-Delbosc, "Proverbes judéo-espagnols", in *Revue Hispanique,* 1895. II, pp. 312-352.

Abraham Galante, "Historie de Sabbetai Sevi. Traces de la famille Sevi", in *Histoire des Juifs d'Anatolie.* Les Juifs d'Izmir (Smyrna) Istanbul (Imprimerie M. Babok) vol. I, Chapter XXXI, 1937.

Abraham Galante, *La presse judéo-espagnole mondiale.* Istanbul, 1935 (16p.)

M. D. Gaon, "Israel Najera, poète du judaisme oriental", in *Mizrah ou Maarav,* IV, 1930.

Carl Gebhardt, "León Hebreo: su vida y su obra", in *Revista de Occidente,* XLIV, No. 132. p. 233 ff.; XLV, p. 133 ff.; XLV, 134. p. 113 ff.

R. Gil, *Romancero judío-español,* Madrid, 1911.

Ignacio González Llubera, *Coplas de Josef: A Medieval Spanish Poem in Hebrew Characters,* Cambridge University Press (England) 1935.

Ignacio González Llubera, *Three Jewish Spanish ballads* (in M. S. British Museum. Add. 26967), Oxford 1938.

M. Grünbaum, *Jüdisch-Spanische Christomathie.* Frankfurt am Main, Verlag Von J. Kauffmann, 1898.

A. Hemsi, *Coplas sefardíes* (Chansons judeo-espagnoles), Alejandria, Edition Orientale de Musique, 1934-1937; cf. P. de Montoliu, *Hispanic Review,* VI, 1938 pp. 166-8.

A. Hemsi, "La musique populaire des Sephardim", in *Mizrah ou Maarav* III, No. 6. 5689.

N. B. Jopson, "Los sefardíes de Salonica", *Tierra Firme,* numero 4, in *Occident and Orient,* 1936.

Judaica (Buenos Aires, 73-75, July-September 1939) (Special number on the life and culture of the Sephardic Jews. Contents: A. S. Yahuda, *Carta a Judaica;* Salomon Resnick, *El judío-español;* Leo Spitzer, *El judeo-español de Turquía;* R. Cansinos-Assens, *Un entierro en sefarad;* N. B. Jopson, *El estilo literario en el judeo-español;* Salomon Birnbaum, *Descendientes de marranos;* E. Giménez Caballero, *Judíos españoles de Sarajevo;* Sabetay J. Djaen, *Sobre algunos escritores en ladino;* Maximo José Kahn. *El proletariado sefardí de Salonica;* José Opatoschu, *La máquina;* A. Tcherikover, *Una cofradía de cabalistas sefardíes;* Paul Groussac, *Pascua sangrienta;* Salo W. Baron, *Un iluminista sefardí de la época napoleónica;* A. R. Malaji, *El porvenir del ladino;* A. R. Malaji, *Páginas de literatura judeo-española.*

Mayer Kayserling, *Sephardim: Romanische Poesien des Juden in Spanien.* Leipzig. 1859.

Mayer Kayserling, *Geschichte des Juden in Spanien und Portugal.* Berlin, 1861.

Mayer Kayserling, *Die Jüdische Frauen in der Geschichte, Literatur und Kunst.* Leipzig, 1879.

Mayer Kayserling, *Biblioteca Española-Portuguesa-Judaica.* Strasbourg, 1890. *(Dictionnaire Bibliographique)* [Des auteurs juifs, de leurs ouvrages espagnols et portugais et des oeuvres sur et contre les juifs et le judaisme. Avec un aperçu sur la littérature des juifs-espagnols. Et une collection des proverbes espagnols.]

Mayer Kayserling, "Quelques Proverbes judéo-espagnols", in *Revue Hispanique.* 1897, IV. p. 82. (Refranes o proverbios españoles de los judíos españoles, ordenados y anotados...) Budapest, Imprenta de Sr. C. I. Posner y hijo, (a costa del autor) 1889, 24.

Leone Ebreo, *The Philosophy of Love.* London, The Soncino Press. 1937.

J. N. Lincoln, "Aljamiado Prophecies", in *Publications of the Modern Language Assoc. of America.* Baltimore, LII, (1937) pp. 631-644.

Max A. Luria, "Judeo-Spanish Proverbs of the Monastir Dialect", in *Revue Hispanique,* 1933, LXXXI, pp. 256-273.

R. Menéndez Pidal, "Catálogo del Romancero judío-español", in *Cultura Española,* pp. 1050-55.

Michael S. Molho, "Matrimonios Sefardies de Ayer", in *Revista bimestre Cubana,* Vol. XLVI, No. 3, Nov.-Dec. 1940, pp. 414-439. (Partial translation by Henry V. Besso in *American Hebrew,* Aug. 7, 1936. pp. 156ff.)

Michael S. Molho, *Le Meam-Loez, Encyclopédie populaire du Sephardisme levantin.* Thessalonique, 1945, 29 pages.

Michael S. Molho, *Usos y Costumbres de los Sefardíes de Salónica.* Madrid, Barcelona, Instituto Arias Montano, 1950. (Vol. III in series Biblioteca hebraico-española).

A. Moscuna, "Spanolische Sprichwörter" (aus Tatar Bazardzyk in Ost Rumelien) en *Der Urquell. Ein Monatschrift für Volkskunde.* Vienna, 1897, I, pp. 84-86 and 204-205.

A. H. Navon, *Joseph Pérez* (Juif de ghetto), roman. 7th edition. Paris, Colmann-Lévy, éditeurs. 1925.

A. H. Navon, *Tu ne tueras pas.* Roman de moeurs judéo-espagnoles. Paris, Aus. Editions L. J. S., 1937.

Joseph Passy, "Twenty-five proverbs of Philippopoli, Bulgaria", in *Der Urquell. Ein Monatschrift für Volkskunde.* Vienna. I, pp. 205-206.

Antonio Portnoy, *Los judios en la literatura* española medieval, Buenos Aires, 1942.

J. A. van Praag, "El Diálogo dos Montes de Rehuel Jessurum", in *Melanges Salverda de Grove* (1933), p. 242-55. [Auto del judío portugués Pablo da Pina, único representado en una sinagoga de Amsterdam].

Santob de Carrion, *Proverbios morales.* Edited with an Introduction by Ignacio González Llubera, Cambridge. At the University Press. 1947.

Leon Sciaky, *Farewell to Salonica, Portrait of an Era.* New York, Current Books, 1946.

Seymour Resnick, *The Jew as portrayed in Spanish Medieval Literature* (Doctoral dissertation, unpublished, presented at New York University, 1950).

Salomon Resnick, *Los judíos a través de la literatura europea,* in *Cinco ensayos sobre temas judíos.* Buenos Aires. 1950.

A. Yaari, *Catálogo de libros en ladino.* Jewish National University Library of Jerusalem. Jerusalem, 1934. 866 books—265 published before 1888. 42 additions made by J. de Silva Rosa en K.S. XIII (1936), 131-7.

Y. Yehuda, "Mishlé Israeleth Yeudith," in *Siyyon,* Jerusalem. 5687-1927 II pp. 80-97.

IV. JUDEO-SPANISH LANGUAGE

Kalmi Baruch, "El Judeo-español de Bosnia", in *Revista de Filología Española,* XVII (1930), pp. 113-154.

José Benoliel, "Dialecto judeo-hispano marroquí o hakitia", in *Boletin de la Academia Española,* 1926, vol. III, pp. 209-233; 342-363; 507-538; XIV (1927), 137-168; 196-234; 357-373; 366-580. XV (1928), pp. 47-6l, 188-223.

Salomón Birnbaum, "Dzudesme la langue des Juifs sephardis" in *Jiwobleter,* 1937.

D. S. Blondheim, *Les parlers judéo-romans et la vetus latina,* Paris 1925.

A. Danon, "Essai sur les vocables turcs dans le judéo-espagnol" in *Keleti Szemle.* IV (1903), pp. 215-227; V (1904), pp. 111-126.

Abraham Galante, "La langue espagnole en Orient et ses déformations", in *Bulletin de'Institut Egyptien.* I (1907), pp. 15-23.

R. Gil, "La lengua española entre los judíos," in *España Moderna,* junio 10, 1909, pp. 30-43.

L. Lamouche, "Quelques mots sur le dialecte espagnol parlé par les israélites de Salonique", in *Romanische Forschungen,* XXIII (1907), pp. 969-991.

Max A. Luria, "A study of the Monastir dialect of Judeo-Spanish based on oral material collected in Monastir, Yugoslavia", in *Revue Hispanique, LXXXIX* (1930), pp. 323-583. [Published separately by Hispanic Institute, Columbia University, New York City.]

Max A. Luria, "Judeo-Spanish Dialects in New York City", in *Todd Memorial Volumes, Philological Studies* (Edited by John Fitz-Gerald and Pauline Taylor).

J. A. van Praag, "Restos de los idiomas hispanolusitanos entre los sefardíes de Amsterdam", in *Boletín de la Academia Española,* 1931, pp. 177-201.

J. Subak, "Zum Judenspanischen" in *Zeitschrift für Romanische Philologie.* XXX, (1906), pp. 129-185.

M. L. Wagner, "Algunas observaciones generales sobre el judeo-español", in *Revista de Filología Española,* vol. X, 1923, pp. 225-244.

M. L. Wagner, "Caracteres generales del judeo-español de Oriente", in *Revista de Filología Española,* Anejo XII (1930).

M. L. Wagner, "Espigueo judeo-español," in *Revista de Filología Española,* XXXIV, 1950, pp. 9-106.

A. S. Yahuda, "Contribución al estudio del judio-español", in *Revista de Filología Española,* II, 1915, p. 199.

V. OTHER WORKS CONSULTED

E. N. Adler, *Auto de Fé and Jew,* London, 1908.

E. N. Adler, *Jews in many lands,* London, 1905, pp. 146-147.

Moses B. Amzalak, *A tipografia hebraico em Portugal no século XV,* Coimbra, Imprensa da Universidade, 1922.

Moses B. Amzalak, *Shabbetai Zevi: Una carta em portugués do século XVII en que se testemunham factos relativos a su vida,* Lisbon, 1928.

Argentina: 50 años de vida en el país (XX aniversario de Die Presse). Buenos Aires, 1938.

P. Baudin, "Les Isráelites de Constantinople", in *La Turquie et les Ottomans,* Paris, 1896.

P. Baudin, *Abdul Hamid II, le progrès de la Turquie, son avenir et la science dans l'islamisme,* Paris, 1894.

M. Behar, "Les sefardis du Mexique: les juifs indiens", in *Les Cahiers Sefardis,* September 1947.

Pierre Belon de Mars, *Les observations de plusieurs singularitez et choses memorables, trouvées en Grèce, Asie, Judée, Egypte, Arabie et autres pays estranges, redigées en trois livres.,* Paris, 1553. (Visited gold and silver mines near Salonica: Livre I, p. 45 ff.; Livre III p. 181 ff; Chapter XIV on Jews in Turkey).

G. Belzoni, *Travels* (1815-19), London, 1821, 2 vols.

Benjamin of Tudela, *The Itinerary of Rabbi Benjamin of Tudela.* Translated and edited by A. Asher, London and Berlin, 1840-41, 2 vols. (Spanish translation: *Viajes de Benjamin de Tudela* (1160-1173). Traducción de Ignacio González Llubera, Madrid, V. H. Sanz Calleja, 1918).

M. J. Bensassón, *Los israelitas españoles: España y sus hijos de Oriente.* Alicante, Servent y Sánchez, 1905.

Ariel Bension, *The Zohar in Moslem and Christian Spain.* London, 1932. *(El Zohar en la España musulmana y cristiana* Biblia del misticismo judaico y del ambiente español en que ha sido revelado. Prólogo de Miguel de Unamuno), Madrid, 1934.

Victor Bérard, *La Turquie et l'Héllenisme Contemporain,* Paris, 1893.

A. Rustem Bey, "Turkey taking her place among modern nations", in *Current History,* February 1927, XXV, 670 ff.

E. R. Bevan, and Charles Singer, ed., *The Legacy of Israel,* Oxford, At the Clarendon Press, 1927.

Biblia de la casa del Duque de Alba. Traducida del hebreo al castellano por Rabí Mosé Arragel de Guadalfajara (1422-1433?), Madrid, Imprenta Artística, 1920-22, 2 vols.

Biblia de Ferrara, Biblia en lengua española, traduzida palabra por palabra de la verdad hebraica por muy excelentes letrados, vista e examinada por el officio de la Inquisición con privilegio illustríssimo Señor Duque de Ferrara, Ferrara, 1553.

Jacques Bigart, *A la mémoire de Nissim Behar* (1848-1931). Paris, Alliance Israélite Universelle, 1931.

David S. Blondheim, "Notes on a Portuguese work on manuscript illumination", in *Jewish Quarterly Review,* XIX (1928-29)', pp. 97-137; XX, (1929-30), pp. 89-90; 283-284.

Book of Prayer, According to the custom of the Spanish and Portuguese Jews. Edited and translated by David de Sola Pool, New York, 5696-1936.

La Boz de Turkiye (March 1, 1948) "La España protectrisa de las razas perseguidas." (Excerpt of this article reproduced under title of "Reconocimiento a la politica magnanima de España para con los judíos perseguidos" in *Sefarad,* VIII (1948), p. 239.

B. Braunstein, *The chuetas of Majorca: Conversos and the Inquisition of Majorca.* Scottsdale (Pa.), 1936.

Corneille Le Bruyn, *A voyage to the Levant; or travels in the principal parts of Asia Minor, the Islands of Scio, Rhodes and Cyprus etc. With an account of the most considerable cities of Egypt, Syria, and the Holy Land* ...Done into English by W. F., London, 1702.

Bueno de Mezquita, "On the meaning of Sephardism." in *Le Judaísme Sepharadi* (Organe mensuel de l'Union Universelle des Communautés Sephardites), July-August-September, 1935.

Jacob Canaani, "The economic situation of Safed and the surrounding country in the 16th and half of the 17th century," in *Siyyon* (In Hebrew) VI, 1933-34, pp. 172-217.

Cancionero de Baena, ed. Eugenio de Ochoa and P. J. Pidal, Madrid, 1851.

The Carvajal family in Mexico, *Procesos de Luis Carvajal (El Mozo).* Publicaciones del Archivo General de la Nación. XXVIII, México, Talleres Graficos de la Nación, 1935.

Alfonso Toro, *La familia Carvajal.* Estudio histórico sobre los judíos y la Inquisición de la Nueva España en el siglo XVI basado en documentos originales y en su mayor parte inéditos que se conservan en el Archivo general de la ciudad de México, México, Editorial Patria, S. A., 1944, 2 vols.

Américo Castro, *Aspectos del vivir hispánicos: espiritualismo, mesianismo, actitud personal en los siglos XIV y el XV.* Santiago de Chile, Editorial Cruz del Sur, 1949.

G. Cirot, "Recherches sur les juifs espagnols et portugais à Bordeau," in *Bulletin Hispanique,* IX, 1907.

G. Cirot, "Les juifs de Bordeaux, leur situation morale et sociale de 1500 à la Revolution" in *Revue Historique de Bordeaux,* II-XXXII (1909-39) (14 installments).

Hermann Cohen, *Moeurs des juifs et des arabes de Tetuan,* Avec une lettre de S. Munk, 2nd edition, Paris, 1927.

Israel Cohen, *Letters from Abroad: "Salonica: Where glory is departed",* in *Menorah Journal,* XII No. 5. October, November 1926, pp. 522-27.

Vital Cuinet, *La Turquie d' Asie, geographie administrative, statistique, descriptive et raisonnée de chaque province de l'Asie Mineur,* Paris, 1890-1900, 4 vols.

Abraham Danon, Sa vie et ses oeuvres. Paris, Imprimerie H. Elias, 1925 (Contains the biography and bibliography of A.D.)

Abraham Danon, "Influencia de Sabatai Cevi," in *El Progreso* (A magazine redacted in Hebrew, Judeo-Spanish and Turkish), Adrianople, 1888-89, pp. 269, 300, 315, 331.

Abraham Danon, "Documents et traditions sur Sabatai Cevi et sa secte," in *Revue des Études Juives,* XXXVII (1898), p. 103 ff.

Abraham Danon, "Amulettes Sabatiennes," in *Journal Asiatique* 10ᵉ serie, XV (1910), p. 331 ff.

Abraham Danon, *Études Sabatiennes,* Paris, Durlacher, 1910.

Abraham Danon, "La Communauté juive de Salonique au XVIᵉ siecle," in *Revue des Études Juives* XL (1899), p. 206 ff: XLI (1900), p. 98, 250.

Abraham Danon, in *Allg. Zeit. des Jud,* 1887, p. 538 ff.; *Rev. des Études Juives,* xxx, 264 ff.; *Actes du Onzième Congrès des Orientalistes,* sect. iii, p. 57, Paris, 1899; *Sefer ha Shanah I* (1900), 154 ff.

Francisco Delicado, *La Lozana andaluza.* Ed. Fuensanta del Valle, Vol. I of *Libros españoles varos y curiosos* (1528), Madrid, 1871 (See M. Menéndez y Pelayo, *Origenes de la novela,* pp. clxxxviii-ccii).

Martin William Leakes, *Travels in Northern Greece,* London. 1835, Vol. III. pp. 235-257.

I. S. Emmanuel, *Histoire de l'industrie des tissues des Israélites de Salonique,* Paris, 1935.

I. S. Emmanuel, *Histoire des Israélites de Salonique* (140 av. J.C. a 1640). Historie Sociale, Economique et Litteraire de la Ville. *Mère en Israel* illustrée par 19 clichés. (Contains the above work of 1935) avec une Lettre à l'auteur de S. E. Ben-Sion M. Ouziel, Grand Rabbin de Jaffa et Tel-Aviv. Thonou, 1936 (Librairie Lipschutz, Paris).

Isidore Epstein, *The Responsa of R. Solomon ben Adreth of Barcelona (1235-1310) as a source of the History of Spain.* London, 1925.

Isidore Epstein, *The Responsa of R. Simón b. Zemah Durán, as a source of the History of the Jews in North Africa.* London, 1930.

José M. Estrugo, *El retorno a Sefarad un siglo después de la Inquisición.* Prologo de Gabriel Alomar, Madrid, 1933.

Arturo Farinelli, *Marrano: Storia di un vituperio,* Genoa, L. S. Oschki, 1925.

Michel Febre, "Théâtre de la Turquie" (Middle of the XVIIth century), in *Revue des Études Juives,* XX.

Francisco Fernández y González, "Ordenamiento formado por los procuradores de las aljamas hebreas pertenecientes al Territorio de los Estados de Castilla en la asamblea celebrada en Valladolid," in *Boletín de la Real Academia de la Historia.* 1885, pp. 145-189 ff.

Francisco Fernández y González, "El mesianismo israelita en la península ibérica durante la primera mitad del siglo XVI," in *Revista de Europa,* XVIII, No. 406.

M. Fishberg, *The Jews,* New York, 1911, pp. 152-153; *Jewish Encyclopedia.* Article *Dönmehs.*

Maurice Fishberg. *The Jews: A Study of Race and Environment,* London 1911 (On Sephardim and Ashkenazim, p. 106 ff.)

Alice Fernand-Halphen, "Une grande dame juive de la Renaissance: Gracia-Mendesia-Nasi," in *Revue de Paris,* September 1st, 1929.

Fidel Fita, "Fragmentos de un ritual hispano-hebreo del siglo XV," in *Boletín de la Real Academia de la Historia,* XXXVI, 1900.

Benito Gerónimo Feyjóo y Montenegro, "Reconvenciones caritativas a los profesores de la Ley de Moisés en respuesta a un judío de Bayona de Francia," in *Cartas eruditas y curiosas,* Madrid, Imprenta del Supremo Consejo de la Inquisición, III (1759), pp. 93-128.

Waldo Frank, *Virgin Spain,* New York, 1926.

Lee M. Friedman, *Rabbi Hayim Isaac Carigal, his Newport Sermon and his Yale Portrait,* Boston (Privately printed), 1940.

Abraham Galante, *Don Joseph Nassi, Duc de Naxos d'après de nouveaux documents.* (Conference faite a la Societé Beni-Berith le samedi 15 febrier 1913.) Constantinople, Etablissements J. & A. Fratelli Haim, 1913 (Documents given in the text).

Abraham Galante, *Esther Kyra d'après de nouveaux documents. Contribution a l'histoire des Juifs de Turquie,* Constantinople, Soc. Anon. de Papeterie (Haim), 1926.

Abraham Galante, "Un nouveau document historique sur le prétendu meurtre rituel de Damas et de Rhodes," in *Mizrah ou Maarav,* IV, 1930.

Abraham Galante, "Juifs portugais en Orient," in *Mizrah ou Maarav,* III, No. 6, 5689.

Abraham Galante, *Abdul Hamid II et le Sionisme.* Istanbul, 1933 (Documents sur l'audience de Th. Herzl).

Abraham Galante, *Medecins juifs au service de la Turquie,* Istanbul, 1938.

Abraham Galante, *Nouveaux documents sur Sabbetai Sevi: organization et us et coutumes de ses adeptes,* Istanbul, n.d.

R. Galdós, *La Biblia de la Casa de Alba. Excerpta, el Libro de Rut.* Introducción, observaciones y notas. Guipúzcoa, Nueva Editorial. S.A., 1928.

Théophile Gautier, *Constantinople.* Translated by Robert H. Gould, New York, 1875.

E. Giménez Caballero, "Monograma sobre los judios de Escopia," in *Revista de Occidente,* March 1930, p. 365 ff.

Gonzalo de Illescas, *Historia pontifical,* Madrid, 1609 (Book VI, chapter XX, pp. 234-235).

Henri Gross, "La famille juive des Hamon" (Contribution a l'histoire des juifs de Turquie) in *Revue des Études Juives.* LVI-LVII (1908), pp. 1-26, 55-78.

Paul Greenbaum, "Les juifs d'Orient d'apres les geographes," in *Revue des Études Juives.* XXVII (1893), pp. 121-135.

Morris A. Gutstein, *The Story of the Jews of Newport: Two and a half centuries of Judaism* (1658-1908), New York, 1936.

Abraham Hallevi, "Les sefardim de Roumania," in *Mizrah ou Maarav,* LI (1928), p. 257 ff., III, no. 6.

Joseph Ha Cohen, *La vallée des pleurs* (Les chroniquers juives, I). Chroniques des souffrances d'Israel depuis sa dispersion jusqu'a nos jours par maitre Joseph Ha Cohen, médecin d'Avignon, 1575. Publié pour la première fois en français par Julien See. Paris. 1881. (The Hebrew original *Emek ha bakah* edited by S. D. Luzatto and M. Letteris. Cracow, 1895.)

A. Hebraeus, "Die Spaniolische Juden," in *Ost und West,* X, pp. 351-367.

Louis Hacker, "The Communal life of the Sephardic Jews of New York City." Resumé of this report in *The Jewish Social Service Quarterly,* December, 1926, pp. 32-40.

Maurice B. Hexter, "The dawn of a problem," in *Jewish Charities,* III, December, 1913, p. 2 ff.

Isidoro de Hoyos y de la Torre, *Los judios españoles en el Imperio Austriaco y en los Balkanes.* Estudio histórico. Madrid, Establecimiento Tipográfico de Fortanet, 1904.

Eleazar Huerta, "El humor en el engaño de las arcas," in *Poética del Mio Cid.* Santiago de Chile, Ediciones Nuevo Extremo, 1948, pp. 112-118.

James A. Huie, *The history of the Jews from the taking of Jerusalem by Titus to the present time.* Boston, 1884.

A. Z. Idelsohn, *Gesänge der Orientalischen Sephardim.* Jerusalem-Berlin-Wien, 1923.

A. Lionel Isaacs, *The Jews of Majorca,* London, Methuen and Co., 1936.

Joseph Jacobs, *An inquiry into the sources of the history of the Jews in Spain,* London, 1894.

Samuel Haig Jameson, "Social mutation in Turkey," in *Social Forces,* XIV, May, 1936, no. 4, pp. 482-496.

L'abbé Pierre Jobit, *Les educateurs de l'Espagne contemporaine.* Vol. I, Les Krausistes; Vol. II, Lettres inédites, de D. Julián Sanz del Río. (Traduction française et d'une introduction historique et d'une biographie de Sanz del Rio). Paris, E. de Boccard, Editeur, 1936.

Judaica (Buenos Aires), Números 51-53, dedicados a los judíos de la América Latina, 1937.

Maximo José Kahn, "El judaísmo sefardita" y "el cante jondo," in *Apocalipsis hispánico,* México, Editorial América, pp. 135-181, 183-215.

Maximo José Kahn, Articles on Sephardic Topics in *Revista de Occidente,* 1923-1936: El patriarca judío XXIX, No. 85, p. 103 ff.; "Cante jondo" y cantores sinagogales, XXX, No. 88, p. 53 ff.; La vida poética de un judío toledano del siglo XII, XXXIV, No. 102, 339 ff.; La cuna ibérica de los hebreos, XL, No. 119, p. 182 ff.

David Kaufmann, "Don Joseph Nassi, Founder of Colonies in the Holy Land and the Community of Cori in the Campagne," in *Jewish Quarterly Review,* O.S. II (1889-90), pp. 291-97, 305-310.

David Kaufmann, "L'incendie de Salonique du 4 AB 1545," in *Revue des Études Juives,* XXI, p. 293 ff.

David Kaufmann, "David Carcassoni et le rachat par la communauté de Constantinople des Juifs faits prisonniers durant la persecution de Chmielnicky," in *Revue des Études Juives,* XXV, 202 ff.

M. Kayserling. *Christopher Columbus and the participation of the Jews in the Spanish and Portuguese discoveries.* Translated by Charles Gross. New York, 1894.

Solomon Katz. *The Jews in the Visigothic and Frankish Kingdoms of Spain and Gaul.* Cambridge, Mass., The Medieval Academy of America, 1937.

[Andrés Laguna], *Viaje de Turquía,* Edición y prólogo de Antonio de G. Solalinde (Colección Universal). Madrid, 1919, 2 vols. (Hitherto ascribed to Cristóbal de Villalón. For the real author see Marcel Bataillon, *Erasme en Espagne.* Recherches sur l'histoire spirituelle du XVIᵉ siecle, Paris. Librairie, E. Droz, 1937, pp. 712-735).

Abraham I. Laredo, "Ashkenazim y Sefardim," in *Bulletin de l'Association Charles Natter: Noar, 1947.* (October-November) No. 13. (See Sefarad, VIII (1948), Fasc. I, p. 230).

A. I. Laredo and David Gonzalo Maeso, "El nombre de 'Sefarad'" and "Sobre la etimología de la Voz 'Sefarad'" in *Sefarad* IV (1944), pp. 349-363.

N. Leven, *Cinquante ans d'histoire: L'Alliance israélite universelle.* Paris, 1911-20, 2 vols.

N. Leven, *Les origines et le programme de L'Alliance israélite.* Paris, 1923.

Israel Levi, "Les juifs d'orient d'après des geographes," in *Revue des Études Juives.* XX (1890), pp. 88-107.

Saadi Levy, *Mis memorias* (A photostatic copy is in the possession of M. J. Benardete.)

M. Levy, *Die Sephardim in Bosnien,* Sarajevo, 1911.

Isidore Loeb, "Le nombre de juifs de Castille et d'Espagne au moyen âge," in *Revue des Études Juives.* XIV (1887), pp. 161-183.

Isidore Loeb, "Les controverses religieuses entre les chretiens et les juifs au moyen âge en France et en Espagne," in *Revue de l'Histoire des Religions,* XVII (1888), pp. 311-337; XVIII, pp. 133-156.

Isidore Loeb, "Polemistes chretiens et juifs en France et en Espagne," in *Revue des Études Juives.* XVIII (1889), pp. 43-70; 219-242.

Isidore Loeb, "La correspondence des juifs d'Espagne aves ceux de Constantinople," in *Revue des Études Juives,* XV, pp. 262 ff.

Jean Le Madden, *Le voyageur francais, ou la connaissance de l'ancien et du nouveau monde;* mis au jour par M. L'abbe Delaporte, Quatrième édition. Paris, 1772. 2 vols.

Jacob R. Marcus, *The Jew in the Medieval World.* A source book. Cincinnati; The Union of American Hebrew Congregations, 1938.

Albert Matarasso, "Historique du Sefardisme aux U.S.A.," in *Les Cahiers Sefardis,* June 20, 1947, pp. 240-244; September 30, 1947, pp. 347-351.

J. E. Budgett Meakin, "The Jews of Morocco," in *The Jewish-Quarterly Review IV* (1891-92), pp. 369-396.

Sidney Mendelssohn, *The Jews of Asia. Especially in the sixteenth and seventeenth centuries.* London, 1920 (Turkey, pp. 1-51).

Sidney Mendelssohn, *The Jews of Africa. Especially in the sixteenth and seventeenth centuries.* London, 1920.

Ramón Menéndez Pidal, "Poema de Yuçuf," Materiales para su estudio en *Revista de Archivos., Bibliotecas y Museos.* VI (1902), pp. 91-129; 276-309; 347-369.

Ramón Menéndez Pidal, *Poema de Mio Cid* (Clásicos Castellanos, No. 24). Madrid, 1913, pp. 33-37.

Marcelino Menéndez y Pelayo, *Origenes de la Novela.* Madrid Casa Editorial Bailly-Bailliere, 1910. 4 vols. (In particular III, p. XXXIX on Amatus Lusitanus; Garcilaso de la Vega, el Inca's translation of Leon Hebreo's *Dialogos de amor* included in the work.)

Marcelino Menéndez y Pelayo, *Historia de los heterodoxos espanoles.* Madrid, 1880-1882, 3 vols.

Marcelino Menéndez y Pelayo, "De las ideas estéticas entre los arabes y judíos in *Historia de las ideas estéticas en España,* Madrid, 1883, vol. I, pp. 281-321.

Marcelino Menéndez y Pelayo, "De las influencias semíticas en la literatura española," in *Estudios de critica literaria.* Vol. 2, 1912, pp. 363-412.

R. R. Merriman, *Suleiman the Magnificent.* Cambridge, Mass., 1944.

Menasseh ben Israel, *Origen de los americanos: Esto es de Esperanza de Israel.* Prologo de Ignacio Bauer, Madrid, Compañia Ibero-Americana de Publicaciones, Madrid, n.d.

Saül Mézan, *Les juifs espagnols en Bulgarie,* Sofia, Editions d'Essai, 1925.

Saül Mézan, *De Gabirol à Abravanel: Juifs espagnols, promoteurs de la Renaissance,* Paris, 1936.

Jacob S. Minkin, *Abarbanel, and the expulsion of the Jews from Spain.* New York, 1938 (Bibliography).

Michael Molho, *Histoire des Israélites de Castoria.* (Avec la collaboration de Abraham Mevorah). Thessaloniki, 1938.

Michael Molho, *In Memoriam* (Hommage aux victimes juives des Nazis en Grèce). Publié sous la direction de M. M. Rabbin de la Communauté juive de Salonique. Salonique, 1948. Vol. I. (The continuation will be printed in Buenos Aires where M. M. is chief rabbi of the *Sefardiés* of Argentina.)

Peter Mundy, *The Travels of Peter Mundy in Europe and Asia.* 1608-1667. Edited by Lt. Col. Sir Richard Canac Temple; Vol. II *Travels in Asia* 1628-1634. London, 1914.

Lady Mary Wortley Montague, ·*Letters of* ———— *written during her travels into Europe, Asia and Africa,* London, 1727.

Lady Mary Wortley Montague, *The Letters and Works of Lady W. Montague.* Edited by her great grandson, Lord Wharncliffe, London, 1837, 3 vols.

M. G. Montefiore, "Un recueil de consultations rabbiniques du XVIᵉ siècle," in *Revue des Études Juives.* X, p. 183 ff.

Alfred Morel-Fatio, "Les lettres des juifs d'Arles et de Constantinople," in *Revue des Études Juives.* I, p. 301 ff.

Jerónimo Münzer, *Viaje por España y Portugal en los años* 1494-1495. Versión del latín y notas por Julio Puvol. Madrid, 1924. (For the Latin text of this book see *Revue Hispanique* for the year 1920.)

Haim Nahoum, *Jews* (Being the section on the Jews of the chapter, "Leading minorities, their achievements and aspirations,") of *Modern Turkey:* a politico-economic interpretation, 1908-1923, inclusive, with selected chapters by representative authorities. Edited by Eliot Grinnell Mears, New York. pp. 86-97.

Nicolas de Nicolay (Sieur d'Arfeuille), *Les navigations, pérégrinations et voyages faits en la Turquie* etc. Anvers, Par Guillaume Silvais, imprimeur du roy, 1576. (Many editions, at least four in French, 1568, 1576, 1577, 1586; two in Italian, 1577, 1580. English translation by T. Washington the Younger, London, Imprinted by T. Dawson, 1585.)

Roger North, *The Lives of the Right Hon. Francis North... of the Hon. and Rev. John North,* 1826, 2 vols.

Manuel L. Ortega, *Los hebreos en Marruecos.* Prólogo de Pedro Sainz Rodríguez. Tercera edición, Madrid, Compañia Ibero-Americana de Publicaciones. S. A. 1929.

S. S. Pariente, "Le baisement des mains à Smyrne" in *Revue des Études Juives.* p. 133 ff. and XXII p. 137 ff.

Juan Pérez de Guzmán, "Los israelitas de origen español en el oriente de Europa" in *La España Moderna.* July 1904, No. 187, pp. 5-28.

David de Sola Pool, "On Spanish Jews of Levantine origin in the United States," in *Jewish Charities,* March, 1913.

David de Sola Pool, "Early relations between Palestine and American Jewry" in *Brandeis Avukah Annual of 1932.* Edited by Joseph Shubow, Boston, 1932, pp. 536-548.

David Porter, *Constantinople and its Environs.* In a series of letters exhibiting the actual state of the manners, customs, and habits of the Turks, Armenians, Jews and Greeks, as modified by the policy of Sultan Mohammed. By an American, New York, 1835, 2 vols.

Angel Pulido Martin, *El doctor Angel Pulido y su época.* Prólogo de D. Jacinto Benavente, Madrid, 1945.

Manuel L. Ortega, *El doctor Pulido.* Madrid, Editorial Ibero-Africano-Americana, 1922. [See chapter IX Pulido, apóstol; X Apóstol sefardi; XIII El doctor Pulido y el movimiento hispano-hebreo. La casa universal de los sefardies; XIV Los sefardíes y el doctor Pulido.]

Angel Pulido y Fernández, *Los israelitas españoles.* 1904.

Angel Pulido y Fernández, *Españoles sin patria y la raza sefardi.* 1905.

Angel Pulido y Fernández, *Reincorporacion de las colonias sefardies a la vida de España.* 1913.

Angel Pulido y Fernández, *Relaciones comerciales hispano-hebreas* (Memoria del Congreso Geográfico mercantil de 1913).

Angel Pulido y Fernández, *Mica* (Homenaje a la mujer hebrea). 1923.

Angel Pulido y Fernández, "El sefardismo en España" (Speech delivered before the Sephardic Jews of Paris, 1919.)

Angel Pulido y Fernández, *El pueblo hispano-hebreo, primera base mundial de España.* 1920.

Angel Pulido y Fernández, *La reconciliacion hispano-hebrea.* 1920.

Angel Pulido y Fernández, *Esplendor, desarrollo y soberanía mundial de la lengua española.* 1921. (See *Sefarad* VI, 1946, pp. 212 ff.)

Solomon Reinach, "Les écoles juives de Salonique," in *Republique Française,* 1st of April, 1882.

Solomon Reinach, "Les juifs d'orient d'après les géographes et les voyageurs," in *Revue des Études Juives,* XVIII, 1889, pp. 101-107; XX, 1890, pp. 88-96.

Journal d'Antoine Gallant pendant son séjour à Constantinople. [1672-1673], publié et annoté par Charles Schefer, Paris, 1881 (makes reference to *Sabbatai Zevi.)*

Jacob Resnick (J. Ha-Rosin), *Le Duc Joseph de Naxos,* Contribution a l'histoire juive du XVI⁰ siècle, Paris, Librairie Lipschutz, 1936.

Seymour Resnick, *The Jew as portrayed in early Spanish Literature,* (A doctoral dissertation presented and accepted at the University of New York, 1950. Not published as yet.)

Claudio Sánchez Albornoz, *Estampas de la vida en Leon durante el siglo X.* Con uno prólogo sobre el habla de la época por Ramón Menéndez Pidal. Tercera edición, Madrid, Espasa Calpe, S. A., 1934.

Cecil Roth, *A life of Menasseh ben Israel; Rabbi, printer and diplomat,* Philadelphia. The Jewish Publication Society of America, 1935 (Bibliography).

Cecil Roth, *The House of Nasi: Doña Gracia.* Philadelphia, The Jewish Publication Society of America, 5708-1947 (Bibliography).

Paul Rycaut, *The history of the Turkish empire from the year 1623 to the year 1677* London, 1687, pp. 174-184. ("This source...is probably the most accurate contemporary account of Shabbethai Zebi." Remark by J. Marcus, op. cit.. p 269.

S. Mitrani Samarian, "Un typograph juif en Espagne avant 1482," in *Revue des Études Juives.* LIV, 1907, pp. 246-252.

J. Saracheck, *The doctrine of the Messiah in medieval Jewish literature* New York, 1922.

J. Saracheck, *Faith and reason: the conflict over the rationalism of Maimonides,* Williamsport (Pa.), 1935.

J. Saracheck, *Don Isaac Abravanel,* New York, 1938.

Solomon Schechter, "Safed in the sixteenth century: a city of legists and mystics," in *Studies in Judaism* 2 (second series), Philadelphia, 1908, pp. 202-285.

Gershom Scholem, *Major trends in Jewish mysticism,* New York, 1941.

M. Schwab, *Les incunables orientaux et les impressions orientales au commencement du XVI⁰ siècle.* Paris, 1885.

S. Schwartz, *Os christaos-novos em Portugal no seculo XX,* with a preface, Pro Israel, by R. Jorge. Lisbon, 1925.

S. Schwartz, "The Crypto-Jews of Portugal," in *The Menorah Journal,* XII, 1926, pp. 138-149; 283-297.

Werner Sombart, *The Jews and modern Capitalism* (English translation from the German with notes by M. Epstein) London, 1913.

(Ezra Stiles), *The literary diary of Ezra Stiles,* Edited by Franklin B. Dexter, New York, 1901.

C. L. Stoltz, "Life in the communities along the Bosphorus," in *Journal of Geography,* May 1932.

Bensión Taragan, *Les communautés israélites d'Alexandrie: aperçu historique depuis les temps des Ptolemées jusqu'à nos jours.* Alexandrie, Les Editions Juives, 1932.

B. Toledano, "Contribution à l'Histoire de la ville de Safed," in *Mizrah ou Maarav,* V, 1932, No. 6.

Owen Tweedy, "Turkey in step with twentieth century civilization," in *Current History Magazine,* XXXIX, November 1928.

Universal Jewish Encyclopedia, New York, 1948 (History, Philosophy and Literature of the Jews, with particular reference to Spain).

Samuel Usque, *Consolaçam ás tribulaçoens de Israel,* ed. Mendes dos Remedios, Coimbra, 1906.

Pietro della Valla, *The travels of Sig. Pietro della Valla. . . into East-Indies and Arabia Deserta* London, 1665. (Visited Aleppo in 1625.)

Salomón ben Varga, *Chebet Jehuda* (La Vara de Jehudá). Traducción española con un estudio preliminar por Francisco Cantera Burgos, Granada, Liberia López-Guevara, 1925.

H. Vrooman, "Turkey: a social laboratory," in *American Scholar,* March 1933.

A. Wadler, "Die Juden in Serbien," in *Zeitschrift Demog. Stat. I. Juden,* 1906, pp. 145-148; 168-173.

S. Weisenberg, "Die Spaniolen," in *Mitteil. Anthropol. Ges.,* Vienna, X, 1907, pp. 225-239.

A. Yaari, "Further Salonica publications," (Hebrew), in *Kirjath Sepher,* Jerusalem, XI, 1930.

UPDATED SELECTED BIBLIOGRAPHY

The following works have appeared since 1952, and shed light on topics discussed by Professor Benardete in this book.

Angel, Marc, *The Jews of Rhodes: The History of a Sephardic* Community, New York, 1978.

_____ "The Sephardim of the United States: An Exploratory Study," *American Jewish Year Book,* Philadelphia, 1973, pp. 77-138.

_____, ed., *Studies In Sephardic Culture,* New York, 1980.

Argenti, Philip, *The Religious Minorities of Chios,* Cambridge, 1970.

Armistead, S. and Silverman, J., *The Judeo-Spanish Chapbooks of Yacob Abraham Yona,* Berkeley, 1971.

_____, *Romances judeo*-españoles de Tánger, Madrid, 1977.

Ashtor, Eliyahu, *The Jews of Moslem Spain,* Philadelphia, 1973, 1979.

Baer, Yitzhak, *A History of the Jews in Christian Spain,* Philadelphia, 1961, 1971.

Barnett, Richard, ed., *The Sephardi Heritage,* New York, 1971.

Cohen, Martin, *The Martyr,* Philadelphia, 1973.

Emmanuel, Isaac and Suzanne, *History of the Jews of the Netherlands Antilles,* Cincinnati, 1970.

Goldman, Israel, *The Life and Times of Radbaz,* New York, 1970.

Hassan, Jacob, Rubiato, T., and Romero, E., eds., *Actas del primer simposio de estudios sefardies,* Madrid, 1970.

Kaplan, Aryeh, Trans., *The Torah Anthology-Me'am Lo'ez,* New York, 1977...

Levy, Isaac, J., *Refranero Sefardi,* New York, 1969.

Lewis, Bernard, *The Emergence of Modern Turkey,* London, 1961.

Maeso, D.G. and Recuero, P.P., *Me'am Lo'ez,* Madrid, 1964...

Molho, Michael, *Literatura Sefardita de Oriente,* Madrid, 1960.

Netanyahu, Benzion, *Abravanel,* Philadelphia, 1968.

Pool, David and Tamar de Sola, *An Old Faith in the New World,* New York, 1955.

Pool, David de Sola, *Portraits Etched In Stone,* New York, 1952

Saporta y Beja, Enrique, *Refranes de los Judios Sefardies,* Barcelona, 1978.

Scholem, Gershom, *Sabbatai Sevi,* Princeton, 1973.

Stillman, Norman, *The Jews of Arab Lands,* Philadelphia, 1979.

Sutton, Joseph, *Magic Carpet: Aleppo-in-Flatbush,* New York, 1979.

Tamir, Vicki, *Bulgaria and Her Jews,* New York, 1979.

Usque, Samuel, *Consolation for the Tribulations of Israel,* Philadelphia, 1965 (Trans. Martin Cohen).
Werblowsky, R.J., *Joseph Karo: Lawyer and Mystic,* London, 1962.
Yerushalmi, Yosef H., *From Spanish Court to Italian Ghetto,* New York, 1971.
Zimmels, H.J., *Ashkenazim and Sephardim,* London, 1958.

Two other books, scheduled for publication in 1982, are also of importance:
Angel, Marc D., *La America: The Sephardic Experience in the United States,* Philadelphia, The Jewish Publication Society of America.
Armistead, S. and Silverman, J., *Judeo-Spanish Ballads from New York,* The University of California Press. (This work is based on Professor Benardete's Master's thesis at Columbia University.)

We must also note that Professor Benardete's book was published in Spanish translation under the title "Hispanismo de los Sefardies levantinos," Madrid, 1963. (Translator: Manuel Aguilar)

INDEX

Index

A

Aboab, Immanuel 38, 85
Aboab, Yaacob 119
Abrabanel, Bienvenida 68, 74, 88
Abrabanel, Isaac 67, 91
Abrabanel, Judah (Leon Hebreo) 67, 74, 98-9
Abrabanel, Samuel 67, 88
Acrish, Izhak 145f
Adereth, Salomon ben 77
Adrianople 2, 17, 54, 63, 87, 126, 130, 139, 172
Alcabez, Solomon Halevi 82, 106
Aleppo 13, 86, 89, 109, 122
Algiers 26, 54
Aljama 27, 28, 55, 58, 76
Alliance Israélite Universelle 140, 149f, 161, 193, 197f
Almosnino, Moses 56, 71, 74, 97, 119, 134
Alonso, Dámaso 9, 10, 11, 12
Amateau, Albert 171f
Amatus Lusitanus 70, 100, 101
Amsterdam 14, 66, 85, 116, 122, 134, 135, 164
Arabic 8, 9, 10, 13, 21, 54, 57, 59, 65, 76, 78, 82, 95, 117, 134
Aragel, Moses 23, 30, 58
Argueti, Isaac 130
Ashkenazic (explanation of term) 91
Ashkenazim 14, 15, 16, 41, 42, 43, 62, 63, 64, 65f, 77, 82, 84, 88, 90, 112, 117, 132, 158, 163f, 168, 183, 184, 188f, 197
Ataturk, Kemal 138, 139, 152, 162

B

Balkans 15, 35, 64, 139, 149, 150, 160, 162, 166, 182
Behar, Nessim 197f
Bejarano, Enrique 179f, 189
Belon, Pierre 68, 69, 70, 71, 84
Benjamin of Tudela 26
Benoliel, José 3
Bensasson, M.J., 184f
Bronx 4, 168
Brooklyn 4, 168
Brussa 17, 87, 184
Bulgaria 112, 139, 160

C

Caballero, Enrique Giménez 4, 182
Camondo, Count 145
Cansinos-Assens, Rafael 4, 180f, 183
Cantera, Francisco 8, 9, 11
Cardoso, Isaac 38
Cardozo, Benjamin N. 159
Carigal, Isaac H. 86
Carmona, Behar 140
Caro, Joseph 74, 77, 78, 83, 85, 105
Carrión, Sem Tob de 57
Castelar, Emilo 4, 178
Castile 22, 23, 34, 53, 57, 58, 59, 61, 64, 65f, 87
Castoria 2, 172
Chuetas 36, 46f
Cincinnati 163
Constantinople 2, 13, 17, 35, 38, 54, 61, 62, 68, 69, 70, 74, 75, 82, 84,